Marcelo's Secret

This carefully guarded secret
— if exposed —
meant torture and death

George Vergara

To Auden,

Love.

Nana and
Grandpa Ken

July 2020

ISBN-13: 978-1490432915
ISBN-10: 1490432914

Contents

Prologue

Once there was a secret that, for centuries, was carefully guarded by many families. If exposed, this secret meant torture and death. Now, almost forgotten, this secret surfaced when those holding it are no longer in danger of being persecuted or killed.

This historic and romantic saga is the story of Marcelo Espinosa— raised a Catholic, son of Secret Jews— who fled the clutches of the Spanish Inquisition in Madrid, Spain during 1587. It sheds light upon all those Sephardic Jews who fled the Spanish Inquisition and came to live in the Spanish New World.

But, the story really began some three hundred years earlier when medieval Spain had the world's single largest Jewish community. Some hundred thousand Jews lived and worked with Christians and Moors in an almost peaceful though generally segregated coexistence. It became known as the "Golden Age" of both Jewish and secular achievements.

However, anti-Jewish attitudes were on the rise throughout Europe. In 1290, King Edward I of England signed the Edict of Expulsion for its Jews; France followed suit in 1306. In Spain, the anti-Jewish sentiment exploded in the summer of 1391 with angry anti-Jewish riots. These riots led to a massive forced conversion of Jews to Christianity. Jewish converts were known as *conversos* or newly baptized Christians.

Years later, it was a mixture of racial and religious prejudice against the *conversos* that would give birth to the Spanish Inquisition. The established Christian society saw these *converso* families as opportunists who secretly maintained their Jewish faith. They became known as crypto or secret Jews.

The Edict of Expulsion from the Tribunal of the Holy Office of the Inquisition was established in 1478 in Granada, Spain. This Edict was made law by Spain's King Ferdinand II of Aragon and Queen Isabella I of Castile. Their marriage had united Christian Spain; war and the Treaty of Granada ended the Muslim Caliphate's eight hundred year rule within the Iberian Peninsula.

The Edict of Expulsion's purpose was to rid the Spanish Empire of non-Christians: Muslims, Jews, and heretics— those who would not accept the Christian faith by embracing the Catholic Church. Pope Sixtus IV had instructed the Spanish to ensure due process, allow legal counsel and appeal to Rome. However, King Ferdinand defiantly rejected Papal control. Thereafter, the Inquisition was a tool of the monarchy not just the church.

On March 30, 1492 the Crown issued the expulsion decree, the order taking effect just four months later, the last day of July. Thousands of Jews fled Spain, liquidating their homes and businesses at great loss. They became known as "Sephardim" coming from Sefarad, the Hebrew name for Spain.

Sultan Bayezid II welcomed Sephardim who traveled to the Ottoman Empire with open arms. He remarked that the bigoted King Ferdinand had "impoverished his own country and enriched mine." Jews were permitted to settle in lands from Bosnia to Syria and from Greece to Israel.

Throughout those four difficult months, Dominican priests encouraged countless numbers to convert to Christianity. Many Jews made the conversion and were baptized into the Catholic Church. Some accepted Christianity and relinquished all vestiges of Judaism.

But, many others safely kept their Jewish way of life hidden as crypto or secret Jews. Some decided against changing both culture and language by choosing the dangers of the Spanish New World. They traveled illegally with forged documents. Frequently their documents, hiding all traces of their past, gave them new Spanish surnames, many taken from tombstones.

The Inquisition awaited those refusing conversion. If discovered to be "pretenders" of the Christian faith, they were summoned before the Tribunal of the Inquisition for investigation and judgment. Many were sentenced to burn at the stake, the fires of Hell.

In 1497, the Spanish Inquisition made its way to Portugal. Thousands of Jews had moved there assuming they would be safe but were displaced a second time. Many fled to the far reaches of the Spanish New World. Once there, some felt safe enough to continue practicing their Jewish faith and traditions.

Then, as the Inquisition marched triumphantly into the Spanish New World, it became obvious, for their own survival, they had to convert to Christianity. Eventually, the Spanish Inquisition in the New World became relentless in its pursuit of all but true believers. "Secret Jews" were now targets as were all non-Catholics: Protestants,

Muslims, heretics, pirates, blasphemers, bigamists, even liberal thinkers.

When Queen Isabel II abolished the Inquisition in 1834, more than thirty-four thousand Sephardic Jews, in Spain and the New World, had been tortured and killed. Therefore, almost all visible vestiges of Judaism in the Spanish New World were hidden. Only in recent times has the truth gradually emerged from the depths of repression.

This book is dedicated to my mother Maria Casias Vergara with love— and to all her family and ancestors who descended from Marcelo Espinosa, a Secret Jew. It's my hope that his story will encourage descendants of those early Spanish settlers to make an effort to capture the truth of their own past.

George Vergara, July 2011

Chapter 1
The Escape

Madrid, Spain, 1587 — Marcelo's 19 year-old legs felt leaden as he forced himself forward over wet cobblestones as he climbed the hill that towered above his home. Rain stung his face and blurred the light from the lantern his father held to guide their way through the shadows. Marcelo glanced over his shoulder to make sure his mother was following close behind.

Reaching the top of the hill, they could barely make out the forbidding shape of the monastery looming above them. Stumbling to the front gate, Marcelo's father frantically yanked the bell rope to sound their arrival. Soaked to the skin, they waited. There was little hope of being heard. Thunder had muffled the bell's ring, and the priests inside surely wouldn't be listening for visitors in this tempest.

But suddenly the heavy gate swung open. Abbot Valdez's harsh whisper reached them through the rain. "Hurry! The entrance isn't far! Get inside quickly before someone sees you!"

As the gate began to close behind them, they rushed in. Abbot Valdez led them through a long corridor into his small office. As he closed the door noiselessly, he motioned for them to sit on a set of beautifully carved chairs facing his desk. They removed their heavy, wet capes and laid them near the fire burning in the hearth.

Thunder and the pounding of the rain were the only sounds as they sat rigidly before their old friend, exhausted and dripping wet from the journey. They stared silently at the water that had dripped from their clothes onto the floor, not knowing what to say.

"How can this dreadful tragedy be happening to you, Antonio?" Abbot Valdez said quietly. "You haven't harmed anybody."

Earlier that day, Antonio had come to tell him his family had received a summons from the Inquisition. Antonio knew they could lose everything—their work, their home, even their lives. His main concern was to save his son's life.

The abbot turned a compassionate but resolute expression on Marcelo and then looked back to his parents.

"My dear Antonio, Josefina, you're entrusting your son's life to me. I'll do all in my power to keep him safe," he said firmly, his dark eyes piercing the firelight. "I'm so sorry things have turned out this way. I've carefully devised a plan that should succeed, but it is dangerous for each of us. We could lose our lives. So, we must be very careful, firm in our purpose. Two horses are ready; Marcelo and I will leave immediately. The thunderstorm and darkness will conceal us as we leave."

Abbot Valdez explained that he would take Marcelo to a secluded Trappist Monastery a day's ride away. "The abbot there is a dear friend and will understand our situation." He turned to Marcelo. "You'll be cloistered there as a novice monk. To avoid any suspicion, you'll have to convince everyone you're sincere in your chosen vocation. Antonio, Josefina, tell everybody your son has run away in fear of the Inquisition. You don't know where he's gone." His tone softened. "Now is the time to say goodbye. Pray you'll be reunited once you're acquitted at your trial."

Tears running down her cheeks, Josefina pulled her son's face to her and kissed his forehead. Marcelo felt her slip something over his head and around his neck. He looked down to see a small hand carved crucifix made of wood and silver hanging from a leather strap.

When he began to protest, she put her fingers to his lips. "Don't question me now. Later you'll examine this and understand. Keep this with you always. Know it's a symbol of my love for you."

Tears spilled from Marcelo's eyes. "Oh, Madre," he whispered, "Madre, Madre!" But then he remembered his father and Abbot Valdez and regained control of himself.

His father looked grief-stricken, his eyes wide and unblinking. He pulled Marcelo to him and broke into tears himself. "I'm sorry, Marcelo, so sorry!" he whispered as he held him. "One day we will all be together when this tragedy is resolved."

Antonio turned to Abbot Valdez and handed him a large leather pouch containing gold coins to be used for Marcelo's expenses during their journey.

• • • •

Abbot Valdez and Marcelo rode all night and most of the next day. They stopped only long enough to hurriedly eat a few pieces of bread and cheese, washing them down with red wine. They rested themselves and their horses for a few hours, sitting in a large hollow tree that sheltered them from the rain.

At sunset, from the forest's shadows, they saw the Trappist monastery. Exhausted and afraid, Marcelo longed to be within those walls. They tied their horses to a railing next to the gate and unloaded Marcelo's bag. A monk, dressed in a brown robe belted with a knotted rope, silently appeared beside them.

"I'm Abbot Valdez from Madrid. I've come to see my friend Abbot Martinez."

The monk didn't speak but motioned for them to follow him inside. The monastery's stone floor was so smooth that Marcelo wondered how many footsteps had worn the stones to such a fine finish.

Abbot Martinez greeted them inside a small kitchen. A monk handed Marcelo a mug of broth and led him to a wooden table where food had been placed out. The two abbots went to an adjoining room and closed the door. They embraced and sat across from each other at a large table.

"It is so good to see you're still alive and well. What brings you to our monastery?"

"My dear friend," Abbot Valdez replied, "I've brought you this young boy, Marcelo. His parents have been summoned by the Inquisition, accused of being insincere Catholics who are secret Jews. Their future doesn't look good." He knew there was substantial evidence that could prove that this was the case. "The boy's father, Antonio, is one of my best friends. I met him soon after you left for the seminary. I promised Antonio and his wife I'd do my best to keep their son alive. My only solution was to bring him here. You could accept him as a novice monk. He would be hidden until we know whether his parents live or die."

"You're asking something very dangerous," said Abbot Martinez. "But I could never say no to you, my dear old friend!" He smiled warmly. "Let's speak no more until we bless our plan with a cup of our best wine!"

They hurried to the kitchen where Abbot Martinez poured wine into two goblets. Encircling each other's arm, they raised their cups, nodded, smiled, and drank.

These two abbots were schoolmates many years ago. Each chose to hide from the Inquisition by withdrawing from the outside world. They decided their Jewish God and the Catholic God was, indeed, one and the same. They would serve Him, creating as many good works as possible from within a harsh and repressive church.

Both abbots recognized the danger they had accepted and had closely guarded each other's secret. They were really two Jews wrapped in monastic robes who had deviously and repeatedly outwitted the Inquisition. If discovered, their lives would be brutally destroyed.

"Yes, I'll take on your young friend, Marcelo," confirmed Abbot Martinez, "but his life will not be easy! There is little conversation here, just plain food and hard work. Marcelo will not be allowed to venture farther than our gardens. And, he must master our Trappist lessons."

Martinez explained, "If Marcelo is questioned, he will have to repeat, without hesitation, all the answers to our Catholic dogma, practices, and rituals. Marcelo will only be safe if he responds as a true novice, even to the most skeptical examiner.

Abbott Martinez paused to refill his cup. "Another boy named Arif, a Moor, came to our monastery two months ago. He is the same age as Marcelo. Relatives brought the boy to hide him from the Inquisition. They don't like Moors any better than us Jews." Martinez later learned the Inquisition had killed Arif's parents but put off telling the boy until he was more stable.

Both abbots agreed that Marcelo and Arif must leave Spain as soon possible. Neither would know the other's story— it would be safer that way. But, until they leave, they would be good company, one for the other.

Valdez explained his plan. "Marcelo's uncle, Tobias, lives in Mexico City. He went there after the Inquisition gave him a serious fright. Jewish at heart, he lives the life of a highly respected Catholic. I'm sure he will take Marcelo into his home if we can just get him to Mexico. If Marcelo's parents are put to death, Tobias will be Marcelo's only living relative."

"Thank you for accepting Marcelo. I'll find a way to repay your loyalty and friendship." Abbot Valdez stood, "I must say farewell to Marcelo."

Abbot Valdez opened the door to the room where Marcelo was left alone. He was sound asleep slumped over the table. As both abbots gently shook him, Marcelo wakened stared blindly into the corner of the austere room. Then, he slowly raised his head, grasped the crucifix he was wearing around his neck.

"What do you have there?" Abbot Martinez asked. Marcelo reluctantly held out his hand to show the crucifix. "You won't be able to wear that in our monastery. It's against the rules."

"Ah," said Abbot Valdez, taking the crucifix from Marcelo's hand. "Let me show you how the top of this vertical section opens." Valdez found a hidden latch with his thumbnail and opened a hidden cylinder; a tiny rolled parchment paper was inside.

"Marcelo this may look like a crucifix, but it's also a mezuzah." Valdez explained that the mezuzah is traditionally fixed to the doorpost of its owner's home. It holds the most precious prayer of the Jews, the Shema. When entering their home, Jews kiss their fingers and touch the mezuzah. "It's a ritual so ingrained and hard to give up, your mother had it placed in the crucifix so she could keep the Shema close to her heart."

Abbot Valdez closed the compartment and reached over to place the leather strap and crucifix over Marcelo's head. Glancing at Abbott Martinez, "Marcelo's mother asked him to always wear the crucifix. It was the last thing she gave him when she bade him farewell."

Abbott Martinez hesitated, "It is our custom not to wear any crucifix other than the rosary we keep in the pocket of our habit. I'll make an exception for Marcelo, but keep it hidden from the others."

Abbot Valdez placed his hand on Marcelo's shoulder. He spoke gently but with firmness, "This monastery is your home until the Inquisition decides your parents' fate. You'll be safe here but you must follow the rules without exception."

"Marcelo, you are now a novice embarking upon an austere path to become a monk. It's the same path I chose for exactly the same reasons. I will try to get word to your mother and father so they know you are safe."

Marcelo rose, Abbot Valdez placed his hand on the boy's head and prayed, "May the Lord bless you and keep you. May the Lord make His face to shine upon you and grant you peace."

Abbot Martinez guided Marcelo to the hallway. "There's an empty cell at the end of the hall, the door is open. Hurry along, get to bed and sleep." Marcelo grabbed his few belongings and stumbled off to find his room. He was asleep— with his clothes on— seconds after he threw himself onto the bed.

Abbot Martinez led Valdez to a small room with a straw mat. He was familiar with the exhaustion shown on his old friend's face. He knew the fear Valdez would endure seeking to save this innocent boy's life. Valdez fell asleep as soon as his head touched the hard straw pillow.

Early next morning Abbott Valdez rode off, back to Madrid. Could he find a way to work his plan for Marcelo's escape?

Chapter 2
The Trappist Monastery

Rising, Marcelo relieved himself using the bucket in the corner of his room. Then, quickly washed his face and dressed. He joined the shadowy figure and followed him down the frigid corridor, stumbling, still half-asleep. They entered a candle-lit chapel. Hooded monks, heads bowed, knelt in rows facing a massive wooden cross. Marcelo was pushed down to his knees beside three others in the last row.

The chanting began. Its sounds were almost hypnotic, soothing but strangely comforting. Between prayers, silence was for meditation.

Marcelo closed his eyes; saw his father working in his bakery. His uncombed black curly hair, an unruly, bushy beard. His white shirt, black pants covered with flour.

His father's day always started well before dawn, baking had to be finished before breakfast. A serious, stern man, he spoke little, kept his feelings to himself. During spare time, he went to the cellar to read his beloved books. He never missed the evening meal, no matter how exhausted. Looking back, surely much of his father's reading was from the holy book, the Talmud.

During the quiet of meditation, Marcelo built up angry feelings in his heart. He hated the Catholic rituals! They held no meaning— life no longer had meaning. Rage was stuffed below layers of sorrow. He was terrified by what the Inquisition could do to his parents. He loved them more than anything.

Marcelo wanted to stand; both knees were throbbing. He tried to concentrate on the sounds of the monk's chant; echoes resounded throughout the stone chamber. Now, his pain was so severe he couldn't endure kneeling one minute more. The chanting stopped. The monks rose as if one, walked, single file, out the far door. They entered a large room filled with long, narrow wooden tables.

Mesmerized, he watched the monks as they drew their hoods back to rest on their shoulders; their heads bowed in prayer, waiting for their morning meal to be served. The rising sun beamed through a single high window. Now seated, they all ate in silence. Marcelo soon learned that very little was ever spoken.

After the meal, Abbot Martinez rose, rapped for attention. Introducing Marcelo as a new novice, he asked for each one to help with his journey. Brother Juan was designated as responsible for Marcelo's religious training and adaptation to the monastery. Marcelo would receive instruction along with four other novices and be given his work assignments.

Later, Brother Juan walked over to introduce himself. "Marcello, the first thing we must do is go to the Sewing Room. We will get you a robe, you'll wear it always, even for sleep."

The robe was made of a coarse brown cloth that would be hot, heavy, and scratchy. His sandals were large and uncomfortable. A rosary made of rope was cinched around his waist. Marcelo began to look like a monk.

Taking Marcelo's arm, Brother Juan said, "Now I'll show you around the monastery." He seemed to enjoy his task because it gave him a chance to break silence. Marcelo learned his own routine, where to be and when. By day's end, Marcelo had met all eighteen monks and the four other novices.

Marcelo felt overwhelmed. He hated this disruption to his life. His hatred and anger for the Inquisition grew stronger. But, he knew he could never reveal these emotions.

• • • •

Brother Juan found Marcelo the next day after Matins. Since Marcelo had experience with horses he was assigned to work in the stables. "Come, I'll introduce you to our animals, your new friends. Arif will be glad to see you," said Brother Juan. "I'm sure he's tired of working alone, feeding and grooming the horses, milking the goats and cows and then gathering the eggs."

They walked to the stables tucked behind the monastery. The enclosure seemed small and crowded for six horses, two cows, four goats, and a brood of clucking chickens pecking at the ground.

Arif, a bronzed-skin young man, had dark brown eyes, thick black hair and heavy eyebrows. His shoulders were muscular and rounded. He seemed shy, had few words to say. The two novices looked at each other, neither one knowing what to think or say. They shook hands as Brother Juan walked away. Marcelo couldn't help but notice the contrast of his pale hands with Arif whose hands were strong and calloused. Looking back Brother Juan reminded them that vespers would be starting soon; they had to be there.

As they worked together taking care of the animals, Marcelo and Arif gradually became friends. Initially, they exchanged brief conversations. Simple questions asked and answered. Each was suspicious of the other. Neither knew if it was safe to talk about their personal situation. Both knew they could only talk freely when alone in the stables, without Brother Juan hovering nearby.

One day, while both were collecting eggs, Arif looked up and asked, "Marcelo, if becoming a novice monk makes you so sad, why are you here? I'm being hidden from the Inquisition... are you?"

Arif didn't wait for an answer. "I'm not supposed to talk about my family. I think they got into trouble with the Inquisition. I don't know what they did. I wasn't home when they were taken away. When my father's best friend found out what happened he brought me here to wait until my parents are released."

With unusual candor, Arif trusted Marcelo enough to reveal his story.

"I was raised in Granada. I have no brothers or sisters. We had a beautiful farm where my father bred and raised horses to sell all over Europe. We were Muslims pretending to be Catholics, but it just wasn't in our hearts. My parents were betrayed and summoned by the Inquisition. They hid me here because they were afraid I would be tortured and forced to tell the names of our Muslim friends. Now I'm here living in terror waiting to learn my parent's fate."

As he heard Arif's story, Marcelo broke down in tears.

"Arif, our stories are so similar. I'm sad because I also carry a secret that eats away at my heart. The Inquisition had summoned my parents for practicing Jewish traditions, pretending to be good Catholics. My parents took me to a Franciscan monastery in Madrid before I was brought here. They had to hide me in case they were found guilty. They'd do anything to keep me from being tortured."

"Thanks for sharing your secret. Now, I know I'm not alone! We've got to trust each other while waiting to learn our family's fate." Hearing Brother Juan approach, Arif broke off their conversation.

• • • •

Several days later, they were alone in the stables, feeding the animals. Marcelo whispered to Arif, "I miss being able to talk to my friends and family. It makes me even more depressed."

Marcelo paused for a moment, listened, and then continued. "For me the monks' rule of silence is bizarre. There's no consolation. Even God is no comfort. I keep asking for His help but there's no answer. I get angry and only feel worse. I hate this place! It smells stuffy and these robes are scratchy. My cot is hard and lumpy— the food is awful. Arif, you're the only good thing I've found here. If it weren't for your friendship, I don't know how I'd tolerate staying here, or even go on living."

Even though Arif shared many of these emotions, he was careful not to judge Marcelo. He was happy to have him as a friend. Monotony was difficult for both boys.

The monastic routine never changes. Monks wake before dawn, hastily wash and dress in order to gather in the chapel for prayers, meditation and hymns. Then, eat breakfast in silence; meditate silently for an hour before doing morning chores. Some garden; others made cheese and wine. Several clean the monastery. At noon, gather in silence for lunch followed by the rosary. Then, do more chores until dinner. After dinner: vespers, prayer, hymns and more meditation.

Monks were allowed to speak to each other for one hour during recreation time. Even then, conversation tended to be as suppressed as the rest of their day. Only two monks were allowed to speak with outsiders or run errands for the monastery.

So much time was dedicated to prayer and meditation that Marcelo constantly tried to make sense of all that had happened to him. It was like solving a puzzle, piece by piece. As each piece came together from his past, the puzzle began to make more sense. But he was still confused. The only time he really felt at ease was when he was with Arif or the animals.

As months passed by, animals became their constant companions in this strange world of silence. Marcelo learned a lot about animals from Arif. Animals gave him contact with reality, one that existed only outside the monastery. Learning helped take his mind off the Inquisition and the fear of losing his family.

• • • •

Later that same week, Marcelo fell asleep in his room, as he often did following morning meditation. Noting Marcelo was late, Arif led Marcelo's favorite horse to his room's window. Dumping a bucket of water on the horse's head he then pushed the horse's head in through the window. As the horse shook his head, water sprayed over Marcelo. Arif, in a low voice, neighed, "You don't want to ride today? I'm hungry! Where's my food?"

Marcelo scrambled from his cot, shook off the water and in a loud whisper, "What kind of a friend are you!" as he pushed the horse's head back out the window.

Marcelo shook his fist at Arif, "I'll get even with you at the stable!"

Chapter 3
Remembering

Memories, buried long ago, barged their way through to his consciousness. Anguishing images came back to life. He tossed and turned in his cot, struggled to shut out those glowing, burning images. But he couldn't.

Marcelo shuddered! "A premonition? Could this be happening to my parents?"

Fully awake now, Marcelo broke out in a cold sweat! Those unspeakable images fluttered behind his eyes like a trapped bird beating against a window. They had the same intensity here in this desolate Catholic monastery as on that sunny Sunday morning when Marcelo was just fourteen.

• • • •

Marcelo and his four friends were playing, running through Madrid's cobblestoned streets. Inadvertently they ended up in the town's central plaza. There, they discovered a massive wood platform; workmen were finishing the structure.

Excited, Marcelo drew near and called out, "What's this? What's it for?"

"There's a *Quemadero* tomorrow! They'll burn the Jews, Muslims, and heretics! Another workman called out, "That'll take care of our Church's enemies! It'll be spectacular!"

Next morning, Marcelo heard the town's church bells pealing out their message: *Quemadero* today! Finding his four friends, they ran to the plaza and ducked into the shade of a doorway.

People began to arrive, some with young children. The plaza filled until it could hold no more. Soldiers opened a path through the crowd. Church and City officials came into view followed closely by Dominican friars. Lastly, the Inquisition's prisoners, those impenitent heretics condemned to burning at the stake.

Prisoners were dressed in a bright yellow tunic that reached down to their knees. Each tunic was decorated with figures of dragons and demons thrusting heretics into the flames of hell. On each head, a tall dunce hat decorated the same way. A rope hung from each neck; a burning yellow candle was in their hands.

On the platform, three priests in full clerical regalia celebrated a Mass to bless the event. Afterward, one priest, the Grand Inquisitor, faced the condemned prisoners. In a loud voice, he declared them guilty of disgracing the Church and themselves: they would pay for their sins with their lives.

Friars led each prisoner up the platform's steps to one of the waiting stakes. They were tied to their stake with hands behind their back. The Grand Inquisitor called out once again, offering prisoners a last chance to repent their sins.

Two prisoners confessed repentance and were immediately strangled, mercifully avoiding being burned alive. The others would suffer the flames alive and conscious.

Workmen lighted each of the big woodpiles heaped beneath the platform; flames quickly surged upwards. The mounting flames formed a pyre under each prisoner. Excruciating screams, the agony on each victim's face, the wretched smell of burning flesh!

Those horrifying images flooded back to Marcelo, replaying again and again. "There's no way that God could allow this to happen to my parents."

Seeking sleep, Marcelo closed his eyes. But, no! Another horde of memories shoved their way into to his consciousness.

• • • •

Marcelo left his friends and ran home horrified, nauseated. Barely making it to his house without vomiting, he rushed to the kitchen, found a bucket, and retched! He retched, on and on. His mother came running when she heard the sounds of Marcelo's sickness. She held him, touched his forehead to see if he was feverish, wiped perspiration from his face, tears from his eyes.

"Marcelo! What wrong? Are you sick?"

"Oh, Madre! I saw a something horrible! …the *Quemadero*! They burned human beings." Sobbing, as tears ran down his cheeks, he spilled out the whole terrible tale. He could still hear their anguished screams as flesh crackled in the flames; the smell of burning flesh still filled his nostrils.

Josefina led Marcelo to his bedroom. "Marcelo, please lie down, rest, and try to sleep." Leaving, she gently closed the door and hurried to find Antonio in the bakery.

"Antonio! Marcelo watched the *Quemadero*!

Even with his door closed Marcelo heard sounds of his parents talking in the kitchen. Anxiety in their voices told him something was very wrong. Curious, he got out of bed, opened the door. His

27

father signaled him to come in, sit at the dinner table. Both parents faced him. Their silence made Marcelo uneasy. Then, Antonio spoke.

"Your mother told me what happened today. I'm sorry you went to see that horrifying spectacle, the *Quemadero*. It's often given the misnomer, a Proclamation of Faith."

"You've been brought up, educated as a Catholic. We take you to Mass every Sunday. So what I'm going to tell you will be a shock, hard to understand. But please try!"

"Your mother and I are Jews. We're just like those you saw burned alive this morning. Before you were born, to keep you safe, we decided to profess being Catholic. Now, like us, you'll have to be very careful or we'll be in danger of meeting the same fate."

Marcelo was stunned! This can't be true: I am a Catholic; I've always been Catholic! I go to Catholic school! I learned the Catechism; I go to Confession and Mass! Is my father a madman, telling me I'm a Jew?

Antonio explained, "Years ago, the King, Queen and the Church wanted to keep our country's Catholic faith untainted. Jews and Moors were considered heretics and weren't welcome. So everyone had to be Catholic. Either you'd convert to Catholicism, leave the country or die the way you've just witnessed."

"Try to understand. When the Edict of the Expulsion was published in 1478 and later began to be strictly enforced by the Inquisition, my grandparents chose to become Catholics rather than leave Spain."

"With time, everyone saw them as devout Catholics. But, secretly they kept many of their old Jewish rituals. That was dangerous. If someone saw or heard about them keeping Jewish ways they would have been denounced to the Inquisition."

"That's how both our families survived: my Espinosa clan and your mother's Herrara kin. That's why you attend the Franciscan School and have been brought up a Catholic. We hoped to shield you from all this until you were older. But now you must fully understand, join us in protecting both our families."

Marcelo gaped in disbelief! Staring at his father, his mouth open wide.

"Padre, this cannot be true? I'm not a Jew! I'm a Catholic! I believe in our Savior Jesus Christ!"

"Marcelo, each of our hearts, soul and bodies are Jewish. No matter how we try to survive, we will always be Jews. That never changes. It's been hard for us to watch you grow up without our Jewish traditions. We even chose not to have you circumcised so you'd fit in with your Catholic friends."

Dumbfounded, Marcelo asked, "Why could it make any difference to God if someone is born a Jew?"

Antonio explained, "The Catholic Church teaches that Jews betrayed and killed Christ. Politics also plays a role. Many think of Jews as clever, shrewd materialists who have too much economic control over Spain."

Marcelo questioned, "Padre, how can Catholics preach God's love for His people, love for one another; yet sanction such intolerance and terror?"

It was a confusing reality for Marcelo, learning he was a Jew: Enrolled in a Franciscan Catholic school, his Jewish heritage coupled to the Inquisition's terror. If his teachers suspected he was not sincere in his Catholic beliefs, they could cause trouble for him and the whole family. It was frightening; he was torn between two religions at odds with each other.

His teachers had answers to spiritual questions, but he couldn't ask them about Jews or the Inquisition. As much as he wanted answers to those questions, he was muzzled by fear. His father urged him not to question, but simply blend into his surroundings. So blend in he did, and the friars found him to be a model Catholic student.

Marcelo turned again and again on his cot, mortally afraid of what was to come. He was alone; tears in his eyes, agonizing memories ran rampant in his head. Marcelo's thoughts wandered to happier times, memories that gave him peace in this time of unending fear and dismal loneliness.

• • • •

Marcelo's family lived in Madrid's bustling middle-class neighborhood. His father's bakery was conveniently attached to their home. Open seven days a week, they sold freshly baked bread, rich pastries and flavorful empanadas. Their bakery was a popular place for people to congregate.

When Marcelo's lessons and duties at the Franciscan school were finished for the day, he raced home through busy streets. He dodged vendor's carts, sidestepped puddles of slop thrown to the street from houses and shops. He tried not to jostle people going about their errands. He always felt happy as he entered the bakery's welcoming door. That unforgettable smell of freshly baked bread was intoxicating.

Early each morning before school, Marcelo worked at his father's side helping shape dough into loaves. He was learning the baker's craft just as his father had learned while working with his father. Someday, Marcelo would continue the family tradition, and take over the business.

Marcelo's father always made him feel important. As he grew older, he was given more responsibility. He loved working with his father who patiently taught him what he needed to know about the bakery. His father said, "Remember, there's always a need for a good bakery. So learn everything about our business now. It will be valuable for you in the future."

Again, Marcelo tried to sleep, but couldn't. He remembered when he began practicing Jewish rituals with his parents. His fears had grown; their observances were too obvious, easily subject to scrutiny. Marcelo questioned: "Why did they do it? Couldn't they just accept the Catholic way? Keep us safe, all together! Is being a Jew really worth risking our lives?"

• • • •

When just ten years old, Marcelo discovered his parents went to their cellar on Friday evenings, after he'd gone to bed. One Friday, he snuck down the cellar steps, crouched by the door to his father's study and peeked through a small crack.

Marcelo's parents were chanting strange words in front of burning candles. Shifting to get a better view, Marcelo nudged a small bottle that fell to the floor. Caught listening at the door, he was scolded, warned never to tell anyone. His mother explained, "Marcelo, we're just keeping old family traditions."

Later, as he began practicing Jewish rituals with his parents, he understood more of their observances. Gradually, they had become more obvious, easily subject to scrutiny.

Before Friday's sundown, his mother cleaned the house, added fresh linens to their beds and tables. At sundown, his father left the bakery not returning until very early Sunday morning. They changed into clean clothes and went quietly to the cellar; it was the Jewish Sabbath. On Saturdays, trusted employees ran the bakery.

Still awake, Marcelo thought about his parents. How difficult it must have been for them to include him in their Jewish traditions; their decision endangered his life. Angry, he muttered, "Why can't we believe what we want? Who gives the Inquisition the right to control people's beliefs?"

• • • •

Abbot Valdez was one of his father's best friends. Marcelo remembered the abbot as a big, hearty, vigorous person with a boisterous laugh. The Abbot Valdez frequently came to their home for dinner and usually ate portions fit for two people.

After the meal, those two old friends always retired to the cellar. For hours, they could be heard discussing philosophy. The abbot, dynamic and articulate, would invariably draw his father into a heated argument. Upstairs, Josefina and Marcelo heard them through the closed doors.

Once Marcelo heard the abbot speaking with his father in that strange, ancient language. Immediately, he understood the unspoken bond between the two; both were Jews in hiding.

He understood why his father took such care providing for the Abbey. Twice a week, Marcelo made deliveries to the abbot's monastery: dozens of large crisp loaves of bread, tens of oval brown buns. Over time Marcelo became familiar with the friars and their way of life, so different from his own.

Frequently, when leaving their house, Abbot Valdez would wink at Marcelo and encourage him to become a friar. Marcelo would laugh and tell him it was too late, he was already in love with a beautiful woman!

Still awake, Marcelo lay face down on his cot. Sleep still eluded him. Memories plagued his consciousness. Who had denounced his parents to the Inquisition? His father was sure it was Carlos, son of one of his best customers. Antonio had hired him as an apprentice.

• • • •

Antonio had never wanted to take on an apprentice. He feared someone working that close might become suspicious of his hidden Jewish practices. But eventually he grew weary. The bakery's endless hours and hard work finally convinced him he needed help. He also wanted Marcelo to have more time to pursue his studies.

Carlos turned out to be very helpful, principally because he managed the bakery on Saturdays while Antonio took a much-needed day off. Carlos opened the bakery's doors on Saturdays, greeted customers as if it were his own shop. This helped prevent any suspicion that Antonio might be honoring the

Jewish Sabbath. The bakery was always closed on Sunday mornings while the family went to church.

Carlos worked with Antonio for an entire year, learning everything needed to manage a bakery. He had never openly shown interest in any of the family's activities.

With his father's help, Carlos chose a location across town to open his own bakery. But his bakery wasn't successful. Carlos lacked the stamina, a work ethic strong enough to produce quality products, manage the bakery and compete for customers.

Later, Antonio discovered Carlos had stolen money and supplies during his yearlong apprenticeship. When confronted with the accusation, Carlos flew into a rage. If Antonio told his father, he threatened to denounce Antonio to the Inquisition. Later, Carlos' father pressed Antonio for the reasons why he was angry with his son. Without thinking, Antonio told him about the theft.

Clearly, Carlos had been far more observant of the Espinosa's way of life than anyone suspected. Seeking revenge, he denounced the Espinosa family to the Inquisition, a cruel solution to his personal problem.

Marcelo lay there on his cot, eyes wide-open, and his heart beating faster, teeth clenched! Seething with anger and hate: "If Carlos were here, I'd kill him without remorse!" Finally, a measure of calm returned, his breathing slowed, anger and hate faded but he knew it was lurking nearby. More memories fluttered before his eyes! This was his last day in Madrid.

• • • •

This was sadness Marcelo would never forget! That night when they sat down at the dinner table, Marcelo knew something was seriously wrong. He had never seen his parents so agitated; tears were in their eyes. Antonio blurted out, "We have been summoned by the Inquisition." Marcelo was stunned.

Antonio went on, "We have one month to respond to these accusations or prepare a confession. We are accused of being false Catholics, heretics who practice Jewish rituals."

Marcelo's father now spoke in a soft, broken voice, "Marcelo you must leave home immediately. There's no time to waste. Our lives are in great danger!"

"I'll try to explain as we pack your things. I can't reveal our plan. It must be kept secret. Our lives depend on making our plan work. I've made arrangements for us to leave together as soon as it gets dark. Then, we'll learn what lies ahead."

Antonio did not tell Marcelo the arrangements he'd made with Abbot Valdez, fearing Marcelo would panic and run away.

"My son, please understand why you must not be found and forced to testify. You'd be tortured until, despite yourself, you'd weaken, and tell the Inquisitors what they want to hear. You'd admit we openly appeared to be Catholics while secretly practicing Judaism. Then, the Inquisitors would make you incriminate us and many of our friends."

During those last hours at home, they hugged, kissed, and cried, hearts were torn apart. Within that sadness, Marcelo suffered the first angry outburst of fear and anger; it would grow beyond his imagination.

"I have to see Maria!" She was Marcelo's childhood sweetheart and best friend. Only recently had they discovered the wonder of holding each other, kissing. Then, finding a secret place away from her parent's eyes.

"I have to see Maria!" Antonio exclaimed, "Marcelo! There's no time!"

But, Marcelo ran to Maria's house. With her hand in his, he gave her no reason for leaving Madrid so suddenly. There was no rational excuse. Marcelo took her in his arms, kissed her tenderly. Then, he found courage enough to blurt out what he'd never dared say before: "Maria, I love you! I'll always love you; I'll never forget you!"

Maria stood there, stunned, confused; Marcelo ran away, in tears.

Turning again in his cot, Marcelo pleaded once again, "What's happening to my parents?" Would the tossing and turning never end? Would those fluttering images burning in his consciousness go away? But, this time when Marcelo closed his eyes, those fluttering images faded…then disappeared. At last, Marcelo fell asleep.

Would Abbot Valdez ever bring news of his parents?

Chapter 4
A New Beginning

Six months had passed; it was the summer of 1588. Abbot Valdez, weary from his journey from Madrid, found Marcelo kneeling in the chapel during morning prayers. When Marcelo glanced up and saw Abbot Valdez, his heart stopped.

The Abbot touched Marcelo's shoulder, signaled for him to rise, leave the chapel.

Softly, he said, "Let's go to your room where we can talk."

Abbot Valdez walked beside Marcelo keeping the monastery's silence. As they neared his room, Marcelo turned, in the early morning light; saw the abbot's face, drawn with red-rimmed eyes. A slash of fear struck Marcelo's heart! He knew what happened before the abbot spoke those crushing words. Marcelo's hands pressed hard against his chest, holding back a mounting pain that surged from within. A harsh sob of grief escaped his lips. He slowly felt pain transformed to a simmering anger.

Abbot Valdez slowly closed the door behind him so no one would hear. Minutes passed before he could speak. Tears flowed down his cheeks, his voice ragged, finally confirmed what Marcelo already knew.

"Marcelo, your parents have been put to death."

"Why? My parents never harmed anyone; they were good people."

Marcelo cried out, throat tight with anguish.

"Why? Why did the Church murder my parents?"

No words, but a deep thunderous sob, came from the abbot as he embraced Marcelo covering him with his tears.

Marcelo screamed.

"They killed my parents…they wouldn't tell where I was hiding! I'd rather die with them in the fire than live knowing they gave up their lives for me. Why am I alive?"

"Arif! Arif! I have to find Arif!"

Marcelo bolted from the room, ran desperately to the stables. Seeing Arif, he threw himself at Arif's feet, his agonized sobbing echoed through the stable.

"Marcelo, what is it? What's happened?"

Arif knelt down helping Marcelo stand up; his face blanched white. Marcelo wrenched one word at a time from his throat.

"*Asesinos!* They— killed— my mother— and— father! Oh *Madre*, *Padre*, what will I do, what will become of me now. I am alone!"

Arif placed his hands on Marcelo's shoulders, brought him forward until their heads touched. Marcelo's sobs slowed, then stopped. Only ragged spasms remained. They sat on the stable's straw floor, face-to-face.

"Hermano, let's run away together! We'll find a place to work with horses where nobody knows us or care about who we are. We'll look after each other. We both know enough to earn our way. Someday, we'll buy and sell horses. That's been my dream for a long time. We'll be partners and brothers."

"No, Arif, there's still hope your parents are alive. Nobody's told you differently. Someday soon, maybe you'll go home to those you love."

Abbot Valdez came into the stable, out of breath, red-faced. Taking Marcelo's hand he said, "Arif, please, I must speak with Marcelo privately."

"Marcelo, for both our safety, I must get you out of the country as fast as possible! Your uncle, your father's brother, was summoned by the Inquisition but then released. He fled to Mexico. Now, you'll go to Mexico, find your uncle and ask for his protection. Going there now is your chance to start a new life where there's no Inquisition."

"Abbot, I don't want to go without Arif."

Marcelo called out, "Arif! Arif! Come here!"

The abbot held up his hand to keep Arif away from Marcelo.

"Marcelo, we're all in danger. Please listen to me. Someday maybe you'll be able to get together. But now, it's best you both forget each other! Arif's parents have not been cleared. Besides, Arif doesn't have documents allowing him to leave the country. Marcelo, you do!"

Abbot Valdez took a firm hold on Marcelo's arm and spoke sternly, "Marcelo, go gather your things now; come back here to the stable. Arif you prepare our horses, get them ready go. Marcelo, as we ride, I'll explain where we're going."

The urgency in the abbot's voice, the fear on his face, made Marcelo dry his tears, set aside his anger and run off to do as he was told.

• • • •

Abbot Valdez found his friend, Abbot Martinez, in the library. Quickly they went to a corner table where they wouldn't be overheard.

"Martinez, the Inquisitors killed Antonio and Josefina Espinosa! Burned alive! They wouldn't reveal Marcelo's whereabouts. They wouldn't name their Jewish friends.

"The evidence against them was undeniable. My testimony, that they were good practicing Catholics, went ignored. It was Carlos that egotistic apprentice who denounced them. He stole their business."

"Valdez, my friend, we're trapped in this horrific system. There's no way I could live with myself unless we keep helping Inquisition victims."

Opening a cabinet, Martinez placed a wine bottle and two glasses on the table. He poured a generous amount in each glass.

"What's your plan now?"

Abbot Valdez tossed down half his wine before answering.

"Marcelo and I will leave immediately. Once I have him aboard a ship bound for Mexico, I'll return to Madrid. If our plan works, we'll do the same for Arif. God willing, we can save both young souls!"

Valdez nodded, "If it would help destroy the Inquisition, I'd gladly burn these robes and turn myself in. We'd burn on the stake for what we're doing. But, Antonio and Josefina's deaths will be avenged by saving Marcelo's life."

Valdez explained his plan. "I found Madrid's best forger and calligrapher to prepare Marcelo's travel documents. His documents show him to be a young Catholic man, son of a fine Catholic family.

Both his parents died of dysentery. He travels to Mexico City to live with his uncle. His ship sails next week from Cadiz, destination Havana, Cuba then Mexico. I had enough gold coins to pay for both the documents and the voyage."

"My God, Valdez, you've got a magnificent criminal mind! A genius! Should I hear your confession before you leave?"

Martinez added quickly, "Two Franciscan priests, friends of mine, are traveling on that same voyage. When you get to Cadiz, you must find them! Make sure they pledge to look out for our young friend. It's important they believe he is a Franciscan novice."

These two old friends sealed their plan with a strong embrace, tossed down what wine remained and Abbot Valdez returned to the stables.

Abbot Martinez mumbled, "I know God understands and forgives us both."

Marcelo had returned to the stable with his belongings. Arif had both horses ready to leave. The youths embraced each other, weeping. "Arif, I don't want to leave! Abbot Valdez ordered me to leave immediately. I don't know what will happen to me, or you! I'm scared, I don't know how I'll survive alone."

Abbot Valdez returned to the stables with blankets and food for their five-day journey. He carried a small leather packet containing all the documents needed for Marcelo's escape. Together, without speaking, they loaded the horses.

Riding off, Marcelo looked back just once. Arif stood alone; one hand raised high, and called out, "I'll find you, Marcelo! As soon as I can, I'll find you! I'll find you even if it's the last thing I do on this earth!"

. . . .

"Marcelo, This is our plan. We're riding to the seaport of Cadiz. Several ships there are being outfitted for a trip to Mexico. Two Franciscan priests, missionaries from a monastery near here, will be your companions. I'll tell them you've just finished training as a Franciscan novice. You're making the journey as a missionary. Documents have been carefully prepared allowing you to leave Spain."

The two riders followed the rushing waters of the Guadalquivir River until they saw the Moorish cupolas of Cadiz. A bustling port, they entered its narrow, cobblestone streets. Abbot Valdez located the Franciscan Abbey where they were welcomed. They arrived, dirty and exhausted. After bathing and a hot meal they slept until the next morning.

Then, Abbot Valdez began preparing Marcelo for his journey. "This is the robe you must wear. This prayer book confirms that you are Franciscan novice. This leather pouch contains the remaining gold coins your father entrusted to me. Hide the pouch beneath your robe; tie it securely around your waist. Protect it with your life; it's security for your future."

"Now, Marcelo, let me bless your mother's crucifix; pray for God to protect you. The New World is no place for the delicate of heart. But you'll find freedom to start a new life. Never forget, you have proof you come from a good Christian family, you have no Moorish or Jewish blood."

Abbot Valdez handed Marcelo a large cloth sack filled with things he had been able to gather;

clothes, food and utensils. Before leaving the Abbey, they found a quiet place to say their farewells. Both knew, once they left the monastery, there'd be too much commotion, no place to be alone. Facing each other, words didn't come easily. Abbot Valdez struggled; he wanted to share more of his own secret with Marcelo. He knew he'd never see Marcelo again.

"Marcelo, I want you to understand why I've done all this for you. My story is much like yours. The Inquisitors took my parents because they were secret Jews hiding their traditions. I never knew about their Jewish heritage. I was baptized, like you, in the Catholic Church. They never showed they were anything but devout Catholics. I was already a priest when my parents were discovered and condemned."

"Do you remember those nights your father and I met in the cellar? He was teaching me from the Torah the traditions of Judaism. I learned so much from him. I loved him dearly although we always argued. Your father was a good, decent, and kind man."

"I made my decision to stay within the Church. I wanted to save whatever lives I could. That's why I'm here now. If discovered, I'd be put to death for helping you. Remember, Abbot Martinez and I will do everything we can to help Arif escape. He doesn't know it yet but Arif's parents were both put to death."

Marcelo gasped and began to weep, "Will this insanity ever end?"

Abbot Valdez grasped Marcelo's shoulders firmly, looked him straight in the eye. Though burdened with angry tears he spoke clearly.

"Marcelo I am sad for all of us. Hopefully, you'll get to Mexico City safely. Then you can help Arif when he gets there."

• • • •

They embraced, left the Abbey and headed for the docks. As they made their way down hill, the Cadiz docks came into view. Marcelo got his first glimpse of the sea. He smelled the ocean; humid salt air filled his nostrils. Excitement grew as he saw the ships' masts reaching skywards. He heard commotion, sailors loading the ships. He saw that adventure lay ahead. But, suddenly, fear over whelmed him: going to the New World with nothing but a few meager possessions and the gold coins left in his secret pouch.

Approaching the dock, Marcelo caught sight of the sailing ship he was scheduled to board. The ship's crew had formed a chain, passing goods and equipment for storage in the holds below deck. Marcelo and Abbot Valdez gaped as sailors loaded water barrels, all kinds food and sacks of flour along with live chickens, three squealing pigs, two horses, and a cow.

"My God, Marcelo, they're really prepared for a very long journey. There are no stops to replenish supplies until you get to Cuba. Let's pray there's enough!"

They walked over to the ship's officer working at a makeshift desk at the foot of the gangplank. Two rocks weighted down his papers; a breeze kept trying to blow them away. He struggled to keep his records in order, the ship's manifest and list of passengers.

Marcelo and Abbot Valdez approached the officer's table, stood there for a few minutes before the officer looked up.

"Well now who do we have here?"

Abbot Valdez handed Marcelo's documents to the officer. Slowly, the officer examined each document's detail.

"How old are you, Brother Marcelo?"

Marcelo froze in fear. Was something wrong? Food from the abbey rose in his gullet, he swallowed hard, twice to keep it down.

"I'm nineteen years old…"

After what seemed an endless wait, the officer carefully folded each document, looked up at Marcelo, handed him his papers.

"All is in order. You may board the ship."

Marcelo thanked him. Both he and the abbot gave a hidden sigh of relief. Abbot Valdez asked the officer for permission to accompany Marcelo aboard.

As they reached the deck, they saw two priests standing by the opposite rail. They walked over to join them. Both priests smiled as Marcelo and the abbot approached.

"You must be Marcelo, the novice we were told about!"

"I'm Padre Chavez, and this is Padre Sanchez. Abbot Martinez sent word you'd be joining us on the ship. We're from Seville and we're pleased to have you with us on this mission."

"Yes, this is Brother Marcelo and I'm Abbot Valdez. We're from the Franciscan abbey in

Madrid. I'm grateful you've agreed to watch out for Marcelo on his trip to Mexico."

Turning to Marcelo, Valdez cautioned him sternly and lovingly.

"Brother Marcelo, you will obey Padre Chavez. He is the Church's senior representative on this mission. I've entrusted him with your safety."

Abbot Valdez handed Marcelo his sack filled with belongings. He gave Marcelo his blessing, and then, leaning forward, whispered…"May the life that you are about to enter bring pride to your parents. May your life count for theirs; may you never forget who you are."

Marcelo turned to Abbot Valdez and handed him one of the gold coins.

Valdez smiled, "Marcelo, There's no way I could take gold for helping my dearest friend's son. Knowing you're safe is my reward. But there is a favor, one that will help Arif leave Spain safely. When you arrive in Mexico, speak with the Captain before leaving the ship. When he returns to Cadiz, ask him to deliver a message to the abbot at the Franciscan monastery confirming your safe arrival. The abbot will get the message to me. Then, I'll try to arrange for Arif's departure for Mexico."

Sadly, Abbot Valdez turned away from Marcelo preparing to leave. He didn't want Marcelo to see his tears. He lumbered his way to the gangplank, descended and disappeared in the crowd.

As a Catholic priest hiding his Jewish ancestry, Valdez knew it would take Marcelo years to overcome the pain of living in fear and anguish. He prayed that he would find a way to be at peace with himself as a Christian, yet remain proud of his Jewish heritage.

. . . .

Feeling abandoned, Marcelo turned to the two priests. Padre Chavez was short, obese, had a stern expression and was the older of the two. His mouth curved downward in a way that made him look serious and, perhaps, unforgiving. Marcelo didn't relish having this man as his guardian. Padre Sanchez appeared to be in his mid-twenty's, had a soft, warm, and engaging smile.

"Are you frightened?" Padre Sanchez asked, placing a hand on Marcelo's shoulder. "We're about to begin a great sea adventure together. I hope that we can become good friends."

Marcelo returned his smile but walked away, looking for a place where he could be alone. He needed to adjust to the fact he was leaving Spain, possibly forever.

Later, both priests helped him carry his few belongings to their assigned space. It was a very small and crowded room for three people. Three sleeping mats were rolled up on the floor. In the far corner, a pitcher and bowl they'd share for washing themselves. They'd also share one latrine bucket. They agreed the bucket would be emptied and cleaned after each use so their sleeping space wouldn't be fouled.

"Now, Brother Marcelo, let's go up on deck and see what provisions they have for an evening meal," Padre Sanchez suggested.

Marcelo wearily climbed the ladder, not caring for food but glad for the cool breeze that greeted them as they came up through the hatchway. Marcelo managed to eat a bite of pork and cheese with a few swallows of wine but couldn't stomach more.

Afterwards, Marcelo wanted to be alone so he wandered to the ship's railing, watched the crew finish loading. Several other passengers arrived at the dock. He watched with envy as goodbyes were exchanged with friends and relatives.

Marcelo caught a glimpse of a young woman with long curly red hair. At the top of the gangplank she turned, waved her scarf. A female companion accompanied her. Looking at her, Marcelo felt a sudden rush of emotion. He hadn't felt these feelings since he last saw his girlfriend, Maria. Then, three families with small children boarded. Seven burly men followed them, each talking loudly to another as they made their way to the deck. No one was there to wave goodbye to Marcelo; he felt alone.

Several hours later, Capitan Perez summoned Marcelo and the two priests to his cabin. He introduced himself and thanked them for traveling on his ship. He told them their prayers were very important to the journey's success.

"We will need all the help from God we can get. It's not going to be an easy trip!"

Later that evening, when the ship's preparations were completed, Captain Perez sent his crew ashore for their last night in port.

Marcelo and the two priests didn't sleep much that night. Little doubt as to where the crew spent their last night before sailing. Ribald carousing reverberated from the nearby tavern and echoed in their cabin until dawn: singing, shouting, and cheering as fights broke out.

Next morning Marcelo awakened to the more of the sailor's shouts. But, this time, it was sailors casting the ship off from the dock. Dressing quickly he ran up to the deck to watch.

Padre Sanchez followed closely behind him. Marcelo turned to him. "I'm sorry, I don't feel much like talking. With your permission, I'd like to be alone."

Marcelo stood by the ship's rail, watched, fascinated, as sailors rigged sails out the yardarms. On deck, everyone was busy with assigned tasks. The ship slowly got underway. The captain's commands and sailor's shouts continued until they were safely out of port. There, a good wind greeted them, sails blossomed, and they moved smartly out to sea. Marcelo turned and saw three other ships about to join them. What a beautiful sight: Four ships heading west, sails pulling powerfully as they cut through the sea.

Bewildered, Marcelo held firmly to the rail, steadied himself against the ship's pitch and roll as the wind whipped around him.

Chapter 5
At Sea

Sailors said the ship's constant pitch and roll was not unusually rough but most passengers were brutally seasick. Passengers hung on the ship's railing, vomiting into the ocean. The stench was everywhere.

Marcelo was miserable. Days and nights were spent on deck; nausea alternated with diarrhea. Going below made it worse. Each ship's movement was like a body blow. Unable to eat, Marcelo grew so weak he could hardly stand. The two priests were no comfort; each fared worse than Marcelo. Slowly, he found his sea legs; nausea faded away, dizziness disappeared. He began to eat and gradually regained strength.

Marcelo and the priests slept on the floor of their ten-foot square cabin, huddled on rough burlap. Marcelo heard the rasp and scratch as rats scurried nearby; cockroaches crawled about looking for scraps of food.

Days dwindled on; ship's food was barely edible. As clergy, Marcelo and the priests fared somewhat better than others. Food supplies were carefully rationed but eventually were spoiled. Drinking water was in short supply; everyone was thirsty. Confinement and filth soured everyone's temperament. Days were interminable; nights even longer. There was no privacy. Searching out lice that shared their clothing and body hair became a constant pastime. When seas ran high, seasick vomit had to be cleaned. Stench from the bilge was vile.

Marcelo was curious about his fellow passengers. "Maybe they're like me, fleeing the Inquisition. Only fools would risk their lives sailing this ocean."

At night when he closed his eyes, he often saw his father dressed in a white shirt and flour-dusted black pants. Why hadn't he asked him to explain the Talmud? Now, he desperately wanted to know more about his Jewish heritage. Why was this age-old philosophy so important? While he believed his father to be a devout Catholic, he assumed he read the Talmud out of curiosity. Now, he understood. His father was a devout Jew unable to give himself over to Christianity and the Catholic Church.

Daydreaming, he remembered his mother's beauty, her tall figure, sapphire blue eyes, and long auburn hair. She made friends easily, knew everything about everybody in the neighborhood. When friends sought her advice, she was kind and soft. With a task at hand, her face was set with determination. Marcelo never heard her say a word against the Catholic Church. But, sometimes her eyes did reveal her true feelings.

A deep sense of guilt invaded Marcelo's grief. His parents had died because they refused to reveal his whereabouts. He was the sole survivor.

How could the Catholic Church be so cruel?

In his mind's eye Marcelo could see the *Quemadero* he witnessed as a boy. Now, those faces he saw above the surging flames were his mother and father. Marcelo was consumed by anger that stroked his depression. He withdrew to a lonely place within his soul, a deeper depression. Suicidal thoughts gripped him.

There is no God, only senseless terror! I should be dead!

. . . .

Everyone aboard treated the two priests and Marcelo with respect. They were asked to lead daily prayers for the survival of their fellow passengers and crewmembers. As the days passed, a passenger succumbed to the voyage's ordeal. Padre Sanchez had led the prayers as the body was lowered into its ocean grave. Marcelo knew his involvement with the church was misleading. But, he prayed in his own way and didn't feel dishonest.

Marcelo remembered being attracted to the beautiful redheaded young woman he had seen as they boarded the ship. It was her elderly chaperone that had died. He had offered the young lady his condolences, but she was too distraught to respond.

Three days later she finally appeared on deck, alone. Marcelo decided to approach, introduce himself. A sudden gust of wind pushed her cape's hood back from her face. The wind, fanning out her rust-colored hair, revealed her beauty. In an instant, her scarf blew free. A wind rushed it towards Marcelo who reached out and grabbed it. With a thumping heart, Marcelo walked towards her proffering the scarf. Holding fast to the railing as she saw him approach, a smile blossomed on her face.

"Senorita," he mumbled, holding out the silken scarf.

As their eyes met, Marcelo felt a rush of attraction.

"Thank you for saving my favorite scarf, it belonged to my mother."

Marcelo's heart fluttered nervously, his loins stirred.

"My name is Ana Aldones. And my quick–handed champion's name is?"

"I'm Brother Marcelo Espinosa."

Ana looked into Marcelo's eyes, instantly she felt a strong attraction.

How handsome! Pleasant brown eyes, firmly fixed on mine. Dark blond hair frames his face, a good strong jaw. He's on the thin side, not too tall. Too bad he's a novice monk! On the other hand, I might be able to trust him with my friendship.

Marcelo felt confident and spoke first.

"I was there at your chaperone's funeral service. I felt sad because there's no one else to look after you. How are you managing?"

"Thank you for your concern, Brother Espinosa. My aunt suddenly became ill and died soon after we came aboard this miserable ship. I try to make myself comfortable in that tiny closet they call a cabin. Coming up here on deck is so refreshing. So I'll continue on alone to Mexico City where I'll meet the man to whom I'm betrothed."

Marcelo's heart sank. Ana smiled and spoke again.

"Brother Espinosa, I've seen you here on other days. Your being a monk makes it easier for me to take the liberty of speaking with you."

"I'm so apprehensive when the crew follows me with their shameless glances. Several tried to make advances. Captain Valdez is my only protection. I've longed to find someone I could trust. Someone with whom I could speak, feel more protected. Captain Valdez is far too busy to notice everything that happens on his ship."

Marcelo looked at Ana attentively as she spoke.

"Could she be another Jew running from the Inquisitors? Is she telling the truth about having a future husband? Why would she risk her life on this difficult journey to be married?"

Just then, Father Chavez called out from an open hatch. "Marcelo! I need your help."

Marcelo didn't want to leave this charming new friend, but she understood. Ana gave him a sweet smile, tilting her head to one side, provocatively. Marcelo felt a burst of emotion. This sudden, intense attraction to Ana made him feel that life was good again, he was glad to be alive. He wanted to stay with her, but there was no other choice.

Noting Marcelo's hesitation, Ana quickly suggested, "Maybe we could enjoy the sunset together while we finish our conversation."

"Yes, I'll see you then!"

Watching Marcelo leave, Ana questioned her feelings.

"Why do I feel so attracted to him? Why do I feel so secure?"

• • • •

Father Sanchez said, "Marcelo, you will preside over today's funeral. Both passengers and crew will more closely relate with you as a member of the Catholic clergy." A crewman, sick for the last six days, had died in his sleep. The captain directed two sailors to wrap the body in canvas, place it on deck in preparation for burial.

Father Sanchez instructed Marcelo on the burial procedure. Read three passages from the prayer book. Pause for two minutes of silence, and then bless the body with the sign of the cross. Signal the sailors to lift the plank so the body falls into the sea.

Marcelo was nervous, uncomfortable reading prayers like a priest, but he did the best he could. Father Sanchez noted Marcelo hurried through the last prayer and wondered if it were only Marcelo's nervousness.

Indeed, Marcelo found the burial task more endurable anticipating his meeting with Ana. He wasn't aware that Ana watched the funeral service from behind the main mast.

At supper with the two priests, Marcelo realized he didn't fully understand the growing fervor of his infatuation with Ana…but he rushed on deck to meet her.

Chapter 6
Meeting Ana

Ana was waiting for Marcelo, one hand on the ship's railing. Shadows drawn by the late afternoon sun defined her face. Marcelo gasped; he'd never seen a woman quite so beautiful! Ana smiled and spoke as Marcelo approached.

"Brother Marcelo, I watched you lead the funeral service. You were so comforting to everyone."

"Gracias Ana that was my first funeral service, only God knew how nervous I was. If I'd known you were watching, I'd never have finished."

"Why aren't you wearing your monk's robe? You don't look like a religious from the Church."

Marcelo blushed as Ana laughed and took his hand. They stood fixed for several moments silently lost in their feelings, one for the other.

"Ana, I'm not sure I'll serve much longer as a religious. It's not really my calling. I'll see what waits for me in Mexico, then make my final decision."

Ana felt greatly relieved. She realized Marcelo had captured her heart and soul.

"Marcelo, I want to tell you something very personal; it must be kept a secret. I have doubts about my future, too. I'm worried about what awaits me in Mexico City."

The story of Ana's betrothal to Juan Benavidez, the *Alcalde* of Mexico City began the previous year. Benavidez sent two trusted friends, both merchants, to Cadiz. The two merchants had instructions to find a suitable wife for the *Alcalde* in exchange for a large sum of money. Their search found the Aldones family and Ana Aldones, a beautiful young virgin, the perfect choice for Benavidez. The Aldones family had lost almost everything when pirates sacked and sank their ship filled with a valuable cargo. The large sum offered by the agents for Ana's hand in marriage was more than her father could refuse.

"My father sold me as if I were just another piece of merchandise! I felt so ashamed. Once we were at sea, I was going to throw myself overboard. I tried…but I couldn't!"

Marcelo's heart ached for Ana. He remembered all too well the pains of wishing for death. Marcelo whispered to her in an urgent voice.

"No, Ana, I won't let you kill yourself!"

Ana paused, took a deep breath and said, "The *Alcalde* is much older than me…I'm afraid I wont like him. I have no other place to go. Maybe, he'll be charming and kind. I'm trying think of the good possibilities, but bad ones creep in all the same."

Marcelo felt a rush of hostility for the *Alcalde* but held himself in check, determined to be respectful.

"Ana, I want to know how your nightmare ends. Will the *Alcalde* be a handsome, dashing husband or a skinny-legged old tyrant?"

"And I need to know your decision. Will you keep your robe? Or burn it, burying its ashes with a prayer!"

They lapsed into an easy sharing of stories, teasing and laughter. Both were starved for the carefree lives they had back home, now so distant.

As the sun sank beneath the horizon, it colored clouds in the western sky; a sailor lit several lanterns on deck. As a strong wind hit, the ship's pitch, and roll made it difficult to hold onto the railing. Ana was frightened and reluctantly decided to return to her cabin. As she turned to go, the ship rolled, throwing her backward. Marcelo leapt forward to steady her.

"I'd better see you safely to your cabin."

Marcelo helped her cross the deck, down to her small cabin. As they reached her cabin's door, Ana whispered, "We'll meet tomorrow morning at the same place." She turned, allowed her lips to graze his, smiled and laughed, "Sweet dreams my dear Marcelo." She slipped into her cabin, gently closed the door. Marcelo was entranced!

• • • •

Padre Sanchez was waiting for Marcelo on deck. "Captain Valdez wants to see you now." Marcelo's heart skipped, could there be a problem with his documents. He quickly found his way to the Captain's quarters and rapped on the door.

"Enter!" barked the Captain's voice.

"You wanted to see me, sir?"

"Yes, my thanks for making friends with Senorita Ana Aldones. Unfortunately she's now traveling alone. I want you to make her safety your first priority, serve as her caretaker for the rest of our voyage. I've discussed this with both priests, and they agreed."

Marcelo was relieved, filled with joy.

"Of course, Captain, I'll do my best to assure Ana's safety."

"Then it's done! Good-night Brother Marcelo."

• • • •

Marcelo returned to his cabin smiling, happy at heart. He went to sleep anticipating sweet dreams. Then, he awoke with a start! Padre Chavez body was thrown against him. Marcelo sat up, pushed the snoring Chavez away, only to have him thrown back again. The ship's violent pitch and roll were tossing them around. They were in a serious storm.

Marcelo heard the captain shout orders; passengers screamed in fear. Hurriedly he put on trousers, lurched to the cabin door. His only thought was to find Ana, make sure she was safe. He clambered topside, thrown side to side. Reaching the deck, he was hit by torrential rain; huge waves crashed over the ship's railing. The captain saw him, ordered him to go below.

But, Marcelo was determined to cross the deck to Ana's cabin. He staggered and fell, slid on his belly, regained his footing. Several times he was almost washed overboard. He struggled against the waves but, each time, regained his footing.

When the ship lunged again, Marcelo was thrown the last few feet. He grabbed a loose line and pulled himself to the hatch that lead below. Clambering his way to Ana's cabin, he heard cries, passengers moaning, retching in fear and distress. Marcelo pounded on Ana's cabin door, yelling above the storm's clamor, the torrential rain, waves beating the ship's hull.

"It's me, Ana, Brother Marcelo, open the door!"

Ana managed to unlatch the door and, as the ship rolled violently, the door opened wide. Marcelo fell into the cabin, crashed into the opposite wall. Ana, sobbing, tumbled into his arms.

"I'm frightened! Are we going to die? Please don't leave me alone. Please!"

Marcelo gently turned Ana around, kissed her damp forehead and eyelids, calming her. Then both lost control, found each other's lips and kissed deeply. Both were lost in the moment. Another violent roll sent them crashing to the other side of the cabin. They landed in a tangle of arms and legs. Marcelo felt the full length of Ana's body beneath him, the fullness of her breasts, her soft round buttocks. Now, the storm didn't seem quite so terrifying.

Ana whispered, "If we're to die, I want to be surrounded by your love."

They were in each other's arms for the rest of the storm. Several hours passed before the violent storm passed. It calmed as quickly as it started. Marcelo left Ana sleeping and quietly made his way back to his own room. The two priests hadn't missed him; they'd been hearing passengers' confession.

• • • •

Marcelo snatched a few hours sleep before the sun rose. He awakened to sounds of passengers still seasick from the wild thrashing the storm gave the ship. Marcelo felt uneasy but not enough to keep him in the cabin. He threw water on his face, made his way to the deck where he was greeted by a stiff breeze of fresh air.

The crew was hard at work cleaning the deck with seawater. Others were attempting to get supplies back into storage. Slowly the ship returned to its regular pitch and sway, but the storm had left a horrific mess.

Marcelo looked for Ana. She wasn't on deck. He went to Ana's cabin to see if she were seasick. He stopped in one or two passenger rooms, said a hasty prayer and then quietly knocked on her door.

"Ana, are you all right?"

The cabin door opened to reveal Ana, a disheveled mass of red hair framing her greenish-white face.

"Marcelo, take me up on deck before I get sick all over my room, Hurry! Please hurry!"

He swept her up in his arms, carried her up the passageway and clumsily made his way to the deck. Ana ran to the leeward railing, leaned forward, and breathed deeply. Unsure if she would be seasick again, Ana looked at Marcelo. He stood there in a quandary, waiting for her to recover. Looking at him, she slowly gained control, smiled and then started to laugh.

So many crewmen were about she didn't dare reach out to Marcelo. But, suddenly she turned green again; clapped her hand over her mouth, holding back what was coming. She lost control, leaned over the rail, and couldn't stop retching for several minutes. Then, she turned to Marcelo who took her hand in his. Color returned to her cheeks. Both laughed! Then, Ana turned bright red with embarrassment.

"Marcelo, if you can stand seeing me like this, you must really love me!"

Both broke out in laughter.

"You're my guardian angel and I'm so grateful. I don't know what I'd have done if you hadn't been with me last night. And now you came to find me just in time."

Softly she whispered, "I can't help it. I am afraid that I have fallen in love with you."

Marcelo entranced, confessed, "Last night was the most wonderful night of my life. I have that same wonderful feeling. I'm in love with you."

Ana was silent for a few moments, deep in thought.

"Yes, last night was special for me too. I'm struggling with guilt. I'm promised to another, but I did want to be in your arms, even though I knew it was wrong."

"Ana, I don't believe it's wrong for us to be together. Life has taken so much from us both. But, now we've been given this great gift: Love. It's God's greatest gift! We shouldn't waste it. We're dear friends and do love each other. I feel alive, grateful for the first time since I left home."

They looked into each other trying not to be obvious about their feelings. Fortunately, nobody was nearby so they could talk openly.

"Ana, I want to tell you about myself so you have a better idea of whom I really am. Our future is so precarious; we don't know whether we'll reach Havana alive. So let's take advantage of being together. You must never reveal what I'm going to tell you."

"Marcelo, you're frightening me."

Marcelo moved closer, spoke in a low voice, carefully choosing what he would reveal and what he would hold back. He was not yet completely sure he could trust Ana, even though he knew his love for her was real. Marcelo explained he was not really a novice monk. His parents arranged the pretense to get him safely out of Spain. He was in danger because his parents had problems with the government.

"I'm going to Mexico City to find my uncle who has no idea I'm coming. Hopefully he'll take me in, help me find some kind of work. But if he doesn't, I'll have to find my own destiny alone. Either way, I'll be done with this novice monk deception. Some time later, I'll tell you what happened to my parents and why."

Ana looked at Marcelo in disbelief, "My God, Marcelo, we were both sent away from our home and family!"

Tears welled up in Ana's eyes, ran down her cheeks. Marcelo touched them gently. He turned to see if anyone had noticed them talking. Everyone on deck was busy with their work. Ana took Marcelo's hand and pressed it to her chest.

"Marcelo, my life was ruined by my father's arrangement of my betrothal. Now, only my anger is stronger than the sadness I felt when he ordered me to leave home."

As Ana spoke, Marcelo saw her eyes narrow; her nostrils flare with fury and frustration. Ana had told her father she would not go to Mexico and marry a man she had never met. But, she was not allowed to refuse the betrothal. Both her parents and her four brothers turned against her. If she refused, they said, she would be banished to a convent, inherit nothing. The bridal price paid off her family's debts, made them rich again.

"I hate them all! I'm so desolate. Even my poor aunt is dead, she was sent to make sure I arrived safely to Mexico."

"Now, all I have is you, dear Marcelo. Please don't leave me! In all this sorry mess, you're the one good thing that's come to me."

They stood there, facing each other, sorry for themselves. Both wanted to reach out, touch the other. Ana decided to go below and rest before dinner. They wouldn't see each other again until sunset.

Marcelo was filled with conflicting thoughts. Never before had he felt such turbulent emotions. He was elated that Ana cared for him, ecstatic about his feelings for her. His outlook on life was transformed from despair to joy.

But, she was not to be his! They could never plan a future together. He was elated and decided not to think about that now, leave it for later! His manhood had emerged; he'd never felt so strong or confident.

As Marcelo looked out over the ocean and its endless waves, he realized what a beautiful, loving woman does for a man. He thought of nothing other than Ana with some sadness, yet with so much joy.

How will I ever hide these wonderful emotions from those around me?

My dearest Ana! She's so comfortable displaying her attraction to me; such passion, she's so vivacious and demonstrative. She makes me feel I'm the most important man in the world. How could I ever live without her?

Days passed slowly. Marcelo and Ana only allowed themselves their sunset conversations. Once they reached Havana, they planned finding some way to be alone without constantly being watched. Ana explained she would be staying with the *Alcalde* of Havana, a friend of her future husband. Marcelo would be free to visit her, without suspicion, as long as he dressed as a monk.

One especially clear day Marcelo stood by the ship's railing gazing at the ocean's endless horizon. He saw a gray darkness forming where the sea met the sky. Squinting to see more clearly, could this be Cuba? Just then, a seaman, high up in the crow's nest sighting land shouted out, "Tierra! Tierra!"

Soon, they'd be safe on land in Havana. Marcelo was happy they'd arrived safely but sad knowing he'd soon be separated from Ana. She was the love of his life.

Would they find happiness on this side of the ocean?

Chapter 7
Port of Call - Cuba

Early next morning their ship sailed past the magnificent Castillo de los Tres Reyes Magos del Morro, the heavily fortified fortress guarding Havana's harbor from intruders. Now, their ship was tied safely to a dock along the waterfront's busy streets.

Marcelo packed his belongings and made his way to Ana's cabin. As he knocked on the door, Ana opened it, tears in her eyes.

"Marcelo, my heart is breaking! We won't be together during our stay in Havana."

"Ana, I promise we'll find a way to see each other. This ship has been our own small world. We've been lucky to have so much time together. Ana, I love you! I'll always love you!"

About noon, they lined up to go ashore. Marcelo looked around, counted heads and confirmed how many passengers had died at sea since their voyage began in Cadiz. They both were lucky to have made the passage safely. As they took their first steps on dry land, they both felt dizzy, looked at each other and laughed. They still felt the ship's incessant roll and pitch.

"My husband-to-be made arrangements for me to stay with his friend, the *Alcalde* of Havana. A carriage should be here to take me to his home. Please come call on me tomorrow. Surely, everyone knows how to find his hacienda. Marcelo, if you don't come visit, I'll go stay with you at the monastery." Both laughed.

"Don't worry, I'll find my way. I'll wear my Franciscan robe and ask about your wellbeing. So, keep thinking of ways we can be together."

Fortunately for Marcelo the two priests took their time leaving the ship. So, he walked with Ana a little way along the cobblestone street to a bench shaded by a large tree. Sitting together they were unaware of the commotion surrounding them: sailors unloading their ship, merchants hawking their wares.

This strange "new world" was much different from any they had seen before. The buildings along the waterfront were made of wood and mud. People's demeanor, their mode of dress lacked any sense of elegance. Both sensed a relaxed, invigorating atmosphere as refreshing as the breeze. Together, here, and now, everything seemed all right. They were both more confident and gained strength.

Several minutes later, an elegant carriage approached and stopped near by. The driver, a small man dressed in white, wore a large straw hat. He stepped down, tied the horse and walked to where they were sitting.

"*Permiso*, Padre can you help me? I'm looking for Ana Aldones who came from Cadiz. The *Alcalde* Ramon Garcia sent me to bring her to his hacienda. She'll be staying there until she departs for Vera Cruz."

Ana quickly responded, "Yes, I'm Ana Aldones. Please get my trunks. They're over there by the dock."

Marcelo accompanied Ana as she walked slowly to the waiting carriage. Once her trunks were loaded, the driver snapped the horse's reins. Their eyes met for a fleeting second. Then, the carriage rounded the corner and disappeared: Marcelo's heart was crushed.

• • • •

After gathering their few possessions, the two priests joined Marcelo and they went to find the Dominican monastery. They eagerly awaited a fresh water bath and a comfortable cot. Marcelo was exhausted; he didn't look forward to joining in prayers. So he ate alone and went to bed. He was obsessed with making plans for their meeting tomorrow.

The next morning, Marcelo put on his robe and set out to find the *Alcalde's* hacienda. Walking the streets of Havana, he was shocked to discover people living openly as Jews. Six-pointed stars were painted on the walls of the butcher's market. He stopped when he saw a long table filled with Shabbat candles and Menorahs. Apparently, the Inquisition had not yet reached Havana; Jews here were happy living their day-today lives.

As he came to the town square, Marcelo asked for directions to the *Alcalde's* hacienda. Eventually, he stood before a sizeable residence surrounded by lovely gardens.

"Surely, this must be the place," he said to himself. Mustering courage, he walked to the massive wooden door and lifted the heavy iron doorknocker. He let it fall three times; loud thumps resonated within. After a short wait, a soldier pulled open the heavy door. Marcelo explained he was the monk who made the journey with Senorita Ana Aldones. He asked if it were possible to visit with her. The soldier asked for him to wait in the entrance hall, and then left.

Marcelo felt lost in this magnificent foyer and the adjoining rooms he could see. They were elegant, far beyond anything Marcelo imagined could exist on this side of the ocean. He gazed at the elegant hand carved furniture, oil paintings framed in gold, large hammered iron candelabra filled with candles hanging from heavy beams. Mosaic floor tiles gleamed in the sunlight reflected by the bubbled glass windows. Rugs of rich wool carpeted other areas.

"Could I ever live in such luxury?" he wondered. "Could I ever offer Ana such riches? What a foolish thought! She is to be another's wife." Anguish stabbed his heart.

Marcelo heard voices, footsteps approached; there was Ana. His heart beat rapidly as she entered the room. Marcelo was stunned. She looked beautiful dressed in a simple dress that accentuated her figure. He couldn't believe how lovely she was. He just fell more and more in love with her.

Standing beside Ana, a tall handsome man dressed in a fitted black velvet suit; a heavy gold chain hung from his neck. Ana gracefully approached Marcelo showing the respect one gives to a priest.

"Brother Marcelo, I am glad to see you again. *Alcalde*, this is the good Brother Marcelo Espinosa, the novice friar who befriended me aboard ship. Marcelo, please greet my host, *Alcalde* Ramon Garcia. He is providing me with the safety and comfort of his hacienda until we set sail for Mexico City."

The *Alcalde* took Marcelo's hand in a firm handshake. "Brother Marcelo, welcome to my home. May I thank you for the considerate care you've given Ana. She told me all you did for her during the voyage. Would you please join us for lunch in the courtyard?"

Marcelo struggled to maintain his composure resisting the desire to take Ana into his arms. Calmly, he responded to the *Alcalde's* invitation.

"Yes, thank you, sir. I would be honored."

After exchanging a brief glance with Ana, Marcelo followed the *Alcalde* to the large, graciously appointed courtyard. Beautifully decorated ceramic pots surrounded the area, separated by a large expanse of grass. Each pot contained a different blossoming plant. They walked to the round wooden table, already set with three places and filled with dishes of fish, cheeses, garden vegetables, and wine.

Dishes were passed, goblets filled; then the light impersonal conversation stopped abruptly as the *Alcalde* inquired of Marcelo.

"So, Brother Marcelo, tell me of the Inquisition at home. Were you training to be an Inquisitor as well as a priest?"

Marcelo's hand began to shake; a few drops of wine spilled on the table.

The *Alcalde* leaned forward and spoke softly. "I could approve of sentencing a heretic to prison, even isolation. But, the Church is carried away with its power and vengeance. It has gone beyond its limits by burning people alive."

"It's shocking to hear you say that, sir," Marcelo croaked in a near whisper, looking from the *Alcalde's* eyes to Ana's and back. "Before leaving Madrid, I learned it's best to be silent rather than speak those words. Yes, there is a horrible force, one that grows without restraint. It's hard to tell where the fanatics are hidden within the Church, even here. Respectfully, sir, you're placing yourself in great danger by expressing defiance to the Inquisition!"

The *Alcalde* leaned back in his chair, looked out to the gardens, "Marcelo, I'm no longer a young man. I don't care so much for my safety as I do for what is true and right in the world. Here in Havana, we aren't bound so tightly to the Church. There is still freedom for other beliefs, for Jews and Muslims. As *Alcalde*, I want to keep that way of life. We don't need to terrify our people into obedience; capture, and control their minds with fear. We will not have an auto de fe, a *Quemadero*!"

Marcelo could barely keep from grinning with relief and pleasure. Instead, he spoke in measured tones. "Sir," he said, "Nor do I agree with the Inquisition. Several years ago in Madrid I came upon a *Quemadero* in the city square. That scene of unspeakable torture has all but turned me away from serving the Church."

Marcelo paused for a moment, fixed his eyes on the *Alcalde* and said, "I'm honored you have shared your convictions with me. You are a good man, people here in Havana are lucky to have you."

Ana's heart surged with love and respect for Marcelo as she quietly watched him interact with bold sincerity.

The *Alcalde* stood, raised his silver goblet. "Marcelo, now that our paths have crossed, may this day create a friendship between a young monk in training and an old politician ready for retirement. Ana, I toast your health. And I toast your good fortune in meeting Brother Marcelo."

"Now, please forgive me, I have business to attend before leaving on a short trip later this afternoon. Brother Marcelo, please feel free to visit Ana as often as you like." The Alcalde turned and quickly walked away, crossed the courtyard and returned to his office.

Marcelo looked at Ana; she guessed what he was thinking and said, "We've found a way to spend time together. What luck!" Both yearned to hold each other; their hearts pounded. Ana said, "Come, I'll show you the gardens surrounding the hacienda."

Ana led the way out the gate, turned to walk around the building and stopped beside a tall oak tree. Its wide branches formed a leafy umbrella, several sturdy branches almost touching windows on the hacienda's second floor.

"Which is your bedroom?" Marcelo whispered. Ana looked straight up, "That half-shuttered window is my bedroom. Thanks to the oak tree, my bedroom window should be easy to get to from the garden."

"Agreed! After dark I'll come back, climb the tree and join you in your room. This may be our only chance to see each other alone."

"That was my thought, but I am so afraid. Throw a few pebbles at the window so I know it's you. Please, Marcelo, be very careful."

"I have to wait until evening prayers are said and everyone goes to sleep. Hopefully, I'll sneak out without being caught. Don't worry, I'll be here somehow."

Marcelo left with a joyful heart but tremendous anxiety.

• • • •

That night, after all was quiet at the monastery, Marcelo put on his robe over his regular clothing and then warily found his way out into the night. When far enough away from the monastery, he took off the robe, rolled it up and carried it under his arm. His walk to the *Alcalde's* hacienda seemed to take forever. Even with moonlight, the road was lonely, every new sound frightening.

Marcelo walked as fast as he could until he recognized the hacienda, found the big oak tree outside Ana's window. He grabbed a few pebbles to throw at her shutter, put them in his mouth. Then, he began the climb, eager to find the branch that lead to Ana's window. He felt a sting on his buttocks as a branch ripped his trousers. Marcelo didn't stop. He kept climbing, searching until he found the sturdy branch leading to Ana's window. As he inched forward, his excitement mounted; his heart pounded. Near the window, he whispered, "Ana, I'm here!"

Ana hearing his whisper, ran to the window, opened the shutter. Marcelo threw away the pebbles, found his footing and jumped to the ledge. With one step he was inside the room and Ana was in his arms.

Marcelo covered her face with kisses. Wanting to see her face more clearly, he drew her into the moonlight. As they held each other, Marcelo saw tears streaming down Ana's cheeks.

"Ana, why are you crying?"

"Because I love you so much! I never want to be apart from you, even if it means dying." Marcelo whispered, "I feel the same way! There's no power on earth that can separate us."

"Marcelo be gentle, this is my first time. My body and soul are yours forever no matter what happens or where we go."

Her body was so firm, her breasts so full, and the passion between them was overwhelming. They could wait no longer. Marcelo began undoing the buttons of her dress. When it fell to the floor, he quickly took off his shirt and trousers. Kissing and embracing they fell onto the bed.

"*Mi amor*, kiss my lips gently, touch me with your soft hands."

Marcelo felt his excitement grow as he began to kiss her deeply. She moaned quietly as he smothered her with small kisses on her neck; moved down to kiss and caress her breasts. He knew he couldn't contain himself for long. When he felt that Ana was as ready, Marcelo whispered breathlessly.

"This is our time, Ana, are you sure, *mi amor*?"

"Yes, yes, now!" she cried out.

Their inexperienced bodies knew exactly what to do. She drew him into her. With one muffled gasp he forced himself through her barrier. She threw her legs around him, and they never stopped loving each other until their muffled sounds of ecstasy subsided. Then, quietly, they held each other; moonlight shined through the window; a gentle breeze cooled their passion.

Softly she cried in his arms, "Marcelo, my love, what are we to do? We know we can never be together once we reach Mexico. I know I'll never love another as I love you now."

"You are the love of my life, Ana. How can I plan a future without you?"

They held each other for what seemed to be an eternity. Both were lost in the amazement of this new experience they had just opened for each other. Moonlight shining through the window cast a beautiful soft glow on Ana's face. Marcelo could barely contain himself. He was so in love with her.

Talking quietly, nestled together, they decided Marcelo would come to call on Ana the next day. Marcelo suggested they might picnic on a quiet beach somewhere nearby. They agreed they'd find a chaperone if it were necessary.

"You must go now before it gets too late. Be careful climbing down the tree."

The walk back to the monastery was easy. Marcelo remembered each moment of their experience. He was lost in thought about what they would do tomorrow. His quandary: How could he leave the monastery without causing problems?

Entering the monastery Marcelo went to his room and to bed. But, Padre Sanchez was still awake. He asked Marcelo if he enjoyed his day exploring Havana.

"Padre, it was beautiful!" he whispered and quickly fell asleep dreaming of Ana.

• • • •

Next morning, Marcelo quietly left the monastery after breakfast and morning prayers without arousing any suspicion. He made it clear he wanted to explore the island alone, and nobody seemed to mind. With the *Alcalde* out of town, he knew it would be easier to be with Ana. The only problem might be a chaperone.

When he arrived at the hacienda with his robe under his arm, Ana greeted him at the front door. She was glowing with excitement.

"Marcelo, I have a plan and if it works it will be wonderful beyond your wildest dreams. I figured out how we can be alone. Follow me to the stables and I'll show you my plan. I told the chaperone we're going to take the Alcalde's horses out for a long ride. I offered to take her, but she's afraid of horses. Thank God. Lucky for us!"

"When we get to the barn let's saddle up, pretend we're going to out to exercise the horses, I've packed a picnic lunch and blankets in a way that nobody will suspect."

Marcelo glowed with excitement. "Ana, you're a genius."

They ran to the stables and quickly saddled two horses. Marcelo was surprised, "Where did you learn so much about horses?"

Ana laughed and said, "I've had my own horse since I was five years old."

Marcelo led the two horses to a path leading away from the hacienda.

Ana, in her long beige dress, mounted her horse sidesaddle, grabbed the reins and galloped away. Surprised, Marcelo fumbled with his horse's bridle, and then finally mounted his horse.

Ana stopped, turned around in her saddle to shout, "Marcelo, glad you could make it! Catch me if you can!" And off she galloped, her red hair streaming out behind her.

"*Dios Mio!* Is there no end to her surprises?" Marcelo galloped after her as fast as his horse would go. Finally, he caught up with her.

Ana laughed as she turned to Marcelo, "I thought you'd never get here."

Marcelo concealed his surprise at her riding talents. His horse was older and slower than hers. He was lucky to catch up. They kept on riding at a trot. Both felt the excitement of feeling free and filled with love.

Soon, the path ended at beautiful beach. There was no one in sight. They slid from their saddles and tied their horses to a sturdy tree. Quickly they fell into each other's arms. They held each other, lost in their love, happy to be together alone on this quiet, beautiful beach. Both turned and looked out at the sea; fresh salt breeze brushed their smiling faces.

"Marcelo, lets go into the water before we have our picnic."

"We can leave our things in that cove with overhanging branches, we'll have shade." They raced to the spot and tore off their clothes. Marcelo looked at Ana and mumbled.

"Ana, you're so beautiful! I love you so much."

"Marcelo can you believe this is happening? I feel as if we're in heaven."

They walked slowly, hand in hand, to the water' edge. Kissing they sank down to their knees in the shallow water. The ocean gently swallowed them. They rolled in the soft sand as waves lapped at their bodies. Waves rolled over them, time and time again. They consummated their love with the gentle rhythm of the ocean's waves.

They lay there in silence. Within their hearts, they realized what they would soon lose. The thought of separating was unspeakable. They talked about ways they might find to be together. Ana was hopelessly trapped by her family's threat of ruin and her upcoming marriage. Marcelo could think of no way to protect her from the dire consequences of their escape, if they chose to do so.

Suddenly, Ana burst into laughter shouting, "Let's be happy now and not think of anything but today!" They ran to the cove, dressed and ate their picnic lunch playing and laughing the whole time. As the sun began to set in the west, they rode slowly back to the hacienda; both wishing the day wouldn't end.

When the horses were fed and put in their stalls, Ana turned to Marcelo and asked whether he would join her the next day; the maid would show them around Havana. Marcelo agreed and left with a big smile, not caring what others at the monastery might think.

Marcelo arrived at the monastery just in time for dinner. Asked where he had been all day he told them that he had taken a horse and explored the island. Seeing Marcelo's excitement they didn't ask any more questions.

• • • •

The next morning Marcelo dressed in his monk's robe and joined Ana and her maid, Teresa, for a walk around Havana. There wasn't much to see near the docks other than storage bins loaded with items for transport back to Spain, others destined to Mexico, or other parts of the New World. Walking by the docks sailors were working on their ship, preparing it for its journey to Vera Cruz. Captain Perez greeted them from the ship's bridge, "Marcelo, if everything goes well, we'll be ready to sail in two days."

There was no way they could be alone later that day. They kept thinking of ways to get rid of the chaperone, but it was impossible. They didn't want to arouse suspicion. The hardest part was trying to be indifferent to each other. They wanted so much to speak of their love, find ways they could be together. At sunset, they slowly walked back to the hacienda neither wanting to say goodbye.

They were at the front door when the *Alcalde's* carriage pulled up. He waved and walked up to greet them.

"It's good to see you both. I hope you've both had a pleasant visit here in Havana. I heard your ship is leaving soon. Why don't we have dinner tomorrow Marcelo? There are some things we have to discuss."

Marcelo graciously accepted the invitation but wondered what the *Alcalde* had in mind. "Ana I'll be here tomorrow in mid-afternoon. Maybe we can think of something to do before dinner."

He secretly touched her hand and turned to return to the monastery thinking only of their next chance to be together. That night at dinner, Marcelo announced he was invited to the *Alcalde's* hacienda for dinner. Everyone scoffed. But, Padre Sanchez suspected he understood why Marcelo received the invitation. Sanchez said nothing but Marcelo saw a slight smile and a sparkle in his eyes.

• • • •

Marcelo joined Ana for a formal dinner with the *Alcalde*. At first, the conversation was light. The *Alcalde* talked briefly about the pirates who seek to capture Havana and sack their storage vaults.

"We have so much silver and gold here, it's no wonder they keep trying to overrun us. Thank God for the Morro Castle, the fortress that guards our port is invincible."

Then, he became more serious. "Brother Marcelo…Ana, I want to warn you of two very great dangers that may lie ahead in your journey to Vera Cruz."

The *Alcalde* described the danger of hurricanes that sweep thorough the Caribbean waters, especially this time of year. "There's not much you can do to protect yourself. So pray your ship's captain is a skillful navigator and that God will look down upon you favorably."

"The second danger is pirates; those I mentioned before. They swoop down upon flotillas like vultures. They board each ship and seize anything of value. Fortunately, your convoy has many heavily armed ships. They're needed for the return trip when they'll be laden with gold and silver from the Mexico's mines. Gold and silver aren't their only interest: they take the ship's maps and all the women on board. I want you both to be prepared for what ever might happen."

Marcelo thanked the *Alcalde* for his words of caution and assured him he'd be on the alert for signs of either danger.

The *Alcalde* paused, thought for a moment and then continued, "Marcelo, I've talked with Ana and Teresa, my housekeeper. Teresa will chaperone Ana on your journey to Mexico. Teresa has been with me for many years and is a wonderful person. I promised that one day I'd send her to visit her family in Mexico City. It's been years since she's seen them. So please, Marcelo, I hope you'll agree to look after them both."

Marcelo glanced at Ana and realized he should accept the *Alcalde's* plan.

"I'm sure your friend, the *Alcalde* of Mexico City, will appreciate your generosity as much as I do. Thank you for being so kind and thoughtful."

The *Alcalde* called for Teresa to join the conversation. She entered the dining room and stood by the table close to Ana. Teresa confirmed how pleasant it was to be with Brother Marcelo and Ana during their stay. She thanked both for allowing her to accompany them on their journey.

"Teresa, after Ana's aunt died suddenly aboard their ship, the ship's Capitan charged Brother Marcelo with Ana's safety. Now, he will look out for you both."

Marcelo responded, "Teresa, it's a godsend to have you with us. Ana will find life aboard to be easier and safer. Rest assured that I'd look out for both of you."

After dinner, as Marcelo prepared to leave, he respectfully repeated his warning: "*Señor Alcalde*, please be careful with the Inquisition." In return, Marcelo was counseled to do the same. They both smiled at its irony. The *Alcalde* embraced Marcelo, wished him well, said goodbye and returned to into his study.

Ana walked with Marcelo to the foyer, the massive front door was already open. They looked into each other's eyes: neither could speak. Both were saddened; fully aware this ecstatic chapter of their lives was at its end.

Marcelo kissed Ana's cheek. "Will I see you on the ship tomorrow morning?"

Chapter 8
Evading the Pirates

Their ship had been cleaned, fully repaired and restocked with food. Now, everything was ready for the final leg of their voyage: Vera Cruz, Mexico.

Padre Sanchez, Padre Chavez, Marcelo, and Ana were the only passengers continuing the crossing from Spain. Nine new passengers joined them; four were soldiers, but no other women besides Teresa. Then, the ship set sail, easing out of the harbor, headed west, and again passing beneath the protection of the magnificent Morro Castle. Three well-armed ships that made up their convoy joined them there.

Marcelo and Ana bore a new frustration: No longer could they meet on deck for their private conversations. Teresa, out of courtesy, stood just far enough away not to overhear their words, but close enough to see their every move. No way would they have any intimate time together. Finally, resigned to the situation, they spoke quietly of what was within their hearts. Their comfort came from being near to one another, sharing their hopes and dreams.

One moonlit evening as they looked out across the sea, Ana said, "Marcelo, I learned something troubling when Teresa took me to a fortune teller in Havana."

Teresa had taken Ana to a humble house and a darkened room inside. A wizened old woman, a fortuneteller, was dressed in black and sat behind a large table looking down. Candles were the only illumination. Teresa told the old woman that Ana was a friend, the Alcalde's guest. Finally, the old woman looked up, focused upon Ana's eyes, and quickly threw a handful of white seashells onto the tabletop.

The old woman gazed intently at the seashells before her, silently gathering information. She began talking in a low voice. Ana moved closer to hear her words. The old woman looked up and said with a smile, "You have a secret lover!" A few minutes later she looked up again, "One day your lover will be in serious trouble; your fate is to save his life." Ana's face had turned white with fright. She had hoped the old woman would tell her they would find a way to be together, spend their lives side by side. Then, Ana had asked if someday they would be together. The old woman had said it was possible, but she couldn't be sure.

Now, standing here with Marcelo, Ana was still frightened, troubled by this ominous prediction. "Marcelo, what if she could see the future? I can't stop thinking about her prediction."

"Ana, that old woman was lucky enough to guess one thing that was true. Nobody can predict the future! Please don't believe any of it!"

Ana, pensive, sighed, "I hope you're right."

To keep Teresa comfortable with their regular meetings on deck, Marcelo explained he was giving Ana religious guidance. But, a simple touch of their hands sent electric waves of passion charging them both. Marcelo was grateful for the loose robes of a monk. Ana was grateful for her abanico, an elaborate lace fan that hid her blushing.

Later on that afternoon both Ana and Teresa were on deck when they heard a cannon's roar. It came from another ship in the convoy. Ana was frightened, could it be that pirates were near? She sent Teresa to find Marcelo. Minutes later Teresa returned with Marcelo close behind. Once in her cabin Ana said, "Let us pray for our safety, Marcelo will listen to our confession. Will we survive this night?"

Marcelo replied, "Yes, we'll survive. Be calm, the Lord will protect us."

"Teresa, go find the Captain. Ask what's happening and come back to tell us."

Marcelo closed the door behind her. Once alone, Ana and Marcelo fell into each other's arms, suppressing the laughter that came bubbling from their lips.

"I'm sure that canon was fired by mistake, but it was clever of you say it might be a pirate attack." Quickly they smothered each other with kisses. Wasting no time for undressing, they sought the closeness they had been craving.

Teresa came back, knocked on the door when she found it locked. "Good news! One of our sister ships had a drill that required firing one of their canons. It was only a drill. Thank God!"

With a big smile, Marcelo quickly opened the door, "Thank you, Teresa. God bless you both."

• • • •

When it was impossible to be with Ana, Marcelo discovered a friend in Padre Sanchez. Only a few years older than himself, Marcelo found conversations with Sanchez more meaningful than talking with Padre Chavez.

One quiet evening, the wind was steady, sails were full; the ship plowed steadily through the waves, on course to Vera Cruz. Marcelo and Padre Sanchez sat together on deck.

"Padre, what possessed you to make this crazy journey to the end of the world? You could be in Spain enjoying all the comforts of life."

"Marcelo, I'm fortunate to have been chosen for this missionary assignment. Bringing the word of God to the Indians is important work for the Church. I only wish the Church would concentrate more on bringing people the Word of God rather than punishing those accused of being unfaithful."

"You mean you don't approve of the Inquisition?"

"I sense I can trust you, Brother Marcelo. Yes, I hate the Inquisition! I hate its killings and their punishments that surround everyone in Spain. I witnessed one *Quemadero*, or as the Abbot called it, an *auto de fe!* Those horrendous images seared themselves into my mind. I pray each day for them to fade, leave me in peace. So I spoke openly in opposition. As a reprimand, the Abbot got rid of me by sending me on this mission."

Marcelo was astounded. "Thank God that's how you think about the Inquisition. I've been afraid to tell anybody my thoughts."

Marcelo was silent, closed his eyes. Silently he prayed that his own visions of the *Quemadero* in Madrid would never return to haunt him as nightmares. Marcelo excused himself and went to bed.

• • • •

Marcelo was deep in thought as he arranged his bedding. Earlier, he'd aired it out on deck. The sun and sea breeze helped rid the stuffed burlap of vermin and the sour smells of sweat. He wanted to sort out his anger; all those reasons why he was here on this ship, so far from everything he knew and loved. He thought about his younger days when there was no reason for anger, fear or resentment.

Marcelo was thankful for having met Ana. She made both his heart and loins ache whenever he thought of her. He realized how lucky he was to have Padre Sanchez as a friend. He felt less lonely. He had found love, adventure, and friendship. Yet, he was always tense: danger might leap from any shadow.

Marcelo was confused by these fast moving crosscurrents of thought as they raced through his mind. Then, he thought about Ana…and soon dozed off to sleep.

Ana was half-asleep in her small cabin, thinking of nothing other than Marcelo. She wept silently, the thought of losing Marcelo. Other times she would smile, glow with the memories of the moments they had shared.

• • • •

BOOM! A burst of cannon brought Marcelo out of his slumber with a jolt. He heard the crew shout, "Pirates! Pirates!"

"The pirate ship is there, right over our port bow."

"They're coming in fast! Hurry, roll out the cannons!"

"Break out the extra swords— fast!"

Marcelo grabbed two of his robes and ran up on deck. He hardly saw the sails of the pirate ship. He ran full speed to Ana's cabin. As he ran past a sailor who had two loaded guns in his hands, Marcelo grabbed one of them, shouting, "I need this!" He was gone before the sailor could protest. Banging on Ana's door, he shouted her name. When she realized it was Marcelo, Ana unbolted the door and Marcelo fell inside.

"Quickly, Ana, put on this robe while I put on mine. Teresa, get into that big sea chest and pull the top down."

"Marcelo, I'm terrified."

"Ana, I have a loaded gun. So don't waste valuable time. Do as I say now, put on this robe!" Marcelo pulled his knife out from under his robe.

"Ana, I'm sorry, I have to cut your hair now!"

"No, please, I'll tie it back!"

But, Marcelo was already pulling Ana to him, a firm grip in her hair. He grabbed a hank of hair, his knife swept across until he felt it give way, then another and another. He stuffed her hair into a pocket under his robe.

He felt Ana's body trembling in fear. Marcelo was all too aware of men's voices approaching, coming down the passageway to the cabin. He pulled up both his and Ana's hood, shoved her down to kneel and began to pray in a loud voice.

Just then the door flew open and a huge foul-smelling pirate stood before them. "Well, what have we got here? Is this a chapel for scared, runny nosed young priests?" The pirate thrashed around the small cabin, found nothing of interest, then left, crying out, "Remember me to the Lord!"

As soon he was gone; they held each other close. Quietly, they moved apart when they heard Teresa stir in the trunk. Teresa peeked out to see Ana weeping; Marcelo was shaking, as limp as his robe.

Marcelo stood up and carefully opened the door. Seeing nothing, he slipped out closing the door behind. As he crept along, pirates were shouting.

"Back to our ship now, the armed boats are almost upon us."

"Hurry! There's no gold or women here!" "We found some provisions— help me carry this crate." They left the same way they had come.

Suddenly, everything was calm aboard the ship, as if nothing had happened. Only the sound of cannons was heard as two of the convoy ships gave chase to the pirates.

Marcelo returned to Ana and Teresa. Later, the Captain came to check on his two women passengers. As the door opened Marcelo rose to his knees, pointed the gun at the door.

"*Dios Mío*, Brother Marcelo, give me that gun before you blow my head off. Do you realize that it's loaded and cocked? With one nervous finger, you'll put a lead ball between my eyes!" With that, he took the gun from Marcelo hand.

The Captain looked at Ana and said, "Senorita Ana! Did one of those pirates get close enough to cut off your hair? You're dressed in a monk's robe! That must have made them feel guilty!" Then, winking, he said to Marcelo, knowing full well why Ana's hair was cut, "Good work, young man, fast thinking!"

"They might have stolen one of your trunks from the hold, Senorita Ana. I saw them throw one across and onto their deck. I'll find out when I have time and let you know. Have to go, there's lots more to do."

It took several days before everyone felt calm and at ease again. Ana, in a dismal mood about her hair, was seen only with a variety of scarves on her head. Several colonists had adventurous pirate tales to tell, and then it was forgotten. Five days passed with gentle winds and perfect weather. Then suddenly, a shout came from the crow's nest above, "*Tierra, Tierra*" — land was in sight.

Everyone came running to the ship's railing, shouting and pointing.

"Land, there's land ahead, do you see it?"

Ana found a place at the railing beside Marcelo. For a moment, they forgot this would end their time together. In a one moment, that reality hit them; they suddenly looked at each other. As the others rejoiced, they mourned.

"Marcelo, we have been together almost every day for the last three months. I'm dying inside at the thought of being separated. I love you more than I love my own life. I feel trapped; my life is out of control. Can't we run away and live together in some far, out of the way place?"

"I know this is painful for us both. I'd gladly run away with you," said Marcelo. "But, if we did run away, the *Alcalde* would surely find us and kill us both."

Hand in hand, they agreed, somehow, they must find a way to be together.

Chapter 9
Arrival in Mexico

Their convoy's four ships dropped anchor off the beach at San Juan de Ulúa, landing spot for the city of Vera Cruz, Mexico. Small boats came to ferry passengers and cargo to shore. Confusion, a sense of panic, and fear, filled the air as the convoy's passengers disembarked. No one seemed to know where to go or how to claim their belongings.

Ana and Teresa stayed close to Marcelo, hoping he would sort out the confusion. Marcelo soon found two soldiers, a sergeant and corporal, sent by the Alcalde to accompany Ana to Mexico City. They had been waiting several weeks for Ana's ship to arrive.

The sergeant greeted Ana formally and informed her they had hired two Indian porters and purchased two mules for Ana and Teresa. Ana requested he permit both the priests and Marcelo to travel with them for their protection. The sergeant reluctantly agreed knowing if more mules were needed they would be hard to find.

Waiting in Vera Cruz was both miserable and uncomfortable. Since there was no inn or boardinghouse, the sergeant had set up tents: three for the men and one for the women. It took two days for their baggage to be brought from their ship. Indeed, the pirates had stolen one of Ana's trunks. Luckily, the stolen trunk had her fancy clothes, not needed until she got to Mexico City. The remaining trunk, smaller and lighter, was full of her necessities.

Their clothing was much too heavy for this tropical climate. But, it did protect them from mosquitoes. To make things worse, almost everyone was frantically trying to buy provisions needed for the journey to Mexico City. Indians offered meals of fish and native fruits, but almost everyone failed to find them tempting. Each evening, the Indians lit fires of green wood and manure to fight off the bugs. Even so, sleep was difficult because of both humidity and constant noise. All were irritable and disheartened.

When finally all their belongings had been brought to shore, they all went to say farewell to Capitan Valdez. Before leaving, Marcelo gave Valdez a letter, asked him to deliver it to the Abbot at the Franciscan Monastery in Cadiz who would forward it to Abbot Valdez in Madrid. Valdez would learn that Marcelo had arrived safely in Mexico.

• • • •

Marcelo was fearful of the dangers that lay ahead in this primitive land. He had heard others talk about the treacherous mountain road that led to Mexico City. The small group left together in a column led by the sergeant. The corporal walked behind overseeing the porters and the mules carrying their baggage

They walked uphill until the road entered a densely overgrown jungle. There, strange sounds and the songs of beautiful birds surrounded them. The serpentine trail continued leading upwards. It was frightening. Ana screamed; she saw an enormous snake slither across their path. Everyone slapped at flying insects and sensed strange animals were prowling nearby. At night, they camped around a bonfire. As they climbed upward, the jungle gave way to green valleys and they glimpsed steep mountains in the distance.

As day as they came closer to their destination, Marcelo saw Ana grow more and more despondent. Teresa was very concerned for her. The priests and soldiers were very attentive. But, there was no way for them to talk privately.

Occasionally, they would look into each other's eyes: agony for both! They were trapped, frustrated by their love for each other. Desperation slowly overpowered their emotions. Then, slowly, each understood the truth… parting was now a reality.

After climbing this seemingly endless road, they broke out of the jungle onto a green plateau surrounded by steep, snow capped mountains. It was late in the afternoon so they decided to rest for the night. The sergeant found a clearing close to a small pond. After tending to the animals, they gathered for their last supper together. Before noon the next day, they would be in Mexico City. All were exhausted but each washed away the grime with fresh water from the pond.

When supper was finished, Ana said, so all could hear, "Brother Marcelo, please walk with me. I want you to lead me in my prayers. I want to thank God for all his blessings on our voyage. I want to thank Him for bringing you, such a fine monk, to guide and protect me during these past three months. They've been most dangerous of my life."

"Of course, Ana, we will see the heavens fill with stars. Then, we'll pray together."

Slowly, they walked away from the campsite, each holding a rosary, both mumbling in prayer. When they had walked far enough so they couldn't be seen or heard by the others, Ana turned to Marcelo. She touched his cheek with her hand. He took her hand kissed it, held it to his face.

"Ana, my love!" he said, tears in his eyes, "What I really want is to keep walking until we are far from everyone!"

Marcelo could see her tears in the moonlight as she began to speak. But, he hushed her by kissing her lips, and continued telling her the sadness that filled his heart.

"Ana, I wish we could be together. But I know it's impossible! We would be hunted down and punished, most likely killed. Your safety and security would be gone forever. I could never let that to happen. My love for you has grown so much. You are the most beautiful, most endearing, most precious person I'll ever know. But we must part, do our best to deal with life as we find it ahead, each on our separate path."

Marcelo hesitated and then affirmed, "Ana, I don't know how I'll find the strength. But I must! We both must! You've given me my life back. When we met I was dead inside. Our love made me realize how precious and good life really is. I could never forget you! I'll always hope, pray that someday— somehow— we might be together."

As Ana and Marcelo embraced, she felt his growing hardness.

"Oh, Marcelo!" she moaned, not wanting to release him. And lust overcame caution. Holding tight to each other, they dropped down to the soft grass cover. They made love silently as not to give evidence of their passion. After too brief a time, they moved apart and returned to camp in silence and sadness.

• • • •

Entering Mexico City the next day, they learned that the city was built on an island! The city was in the middle of a crystal blue lake. Tall majestic pine trees grew along the shore. It was a beautiful sight, more than any had envisioned. The air was cool and clean. The people seemed clean and well dressed. Buildings were made of huge carved stones, different from what Marcelo and Ana had ever seen. Teresa smiled at coming home.

They continued through to the center of town, a large square on whose border was the construction of a Catholic church besides the remains of an Indian temple. The sergeant explained to them that the church was built on top of the Indians' temple, using some of their bricks for the structure. The native Indians seemed more civilized than those they saw in Vera Cruz. Marcelo breathed a sigh of relief. He might just survive or even flourish in this new place.

Marcelo and the priests thanked both soldiers and the porters for all their help. When it was finally time for them to go their separate ways, Marcelo embraced Ana and whispered in her ear.

"Ana, I love you. I'll never forget you! God willing, someday, somehow we will be together again."

Ana was devastated. She couldn't speak, emotion clamped her throat shut; she was barely able to squeeze Marcelo's hand. Then, she turned, walked away with the two soldiers to the *Alcalde's* mansion. Her chest was so tight she could barely breathe. She was scarcely aware of moving her feet or arms. Her emotions suddenly and mercifully shut down.

Marcelo, again, felt the sharp pain of abandonment. He was sure, should he ever see her face again, he would abandon his resolve, lose self-control, and surely ruin both their lives. That sharp pain felt was like a dagger thrust into his chest; he wanted to die. It was the same pain he experienced when told that his parents had been burned. He turned away, raised his right hand, and waved over his shoulder to hide his pain and tears.

• • • •

Padre Sanchez asked Marcelo if he would go with them to the monastery. Marcelo thought for a moment — "Padre, It's best for me to find my uncle now. I hope he'll accept me into his home. Would you please stay with me until I find his home?"

Marcelo asked a passing soldier, "Do you know of a Capitan Tobias Espinosa?"

"Of course, he's a very well-known officer of the Spanish Brigade."

The directions to the Captain's residence were easy to follow, and they found it without difficulty. The two priests escorted Marcelo to the front courtyard of a grand home. Padre Chavez, happy to be rid of his charge, hastily departed for the monastery.

Padre Sanchez gave Marcelo a good-natured hug. He blessed Marcelo, wished him well and assured him he would be at the monastery if needed.

Marcelo finally took courage and said, "Padre Sanchez, it's not my calling to be a priest. If my uncle takes me in, I'm sure I'll find my way. Thanks for your friendship."

Padre Sanchez was not surprised by Marcelo's declaration. As he waved goodbye, he said, "Good luck, Marcelo. May God bless you for all you've done for His Church."

Marcelo turned anxiously, walked to the imposing entrance of his uncle's home.

Chapter 10
Captain Tobias Espinosa

Marcelo walked up to his uncle's elegant home, firmly grasped the doorknocker and rapped three times. He felt forlorn, gripped with the fear. Would his uncle take him in, offer him help? This man was the only family he had left in the world.

A uniformed soldier opened the door, glared at the dirty Franciscan monk and barked, "What businesses have you here?"

Marcelo blurted out, "I've come to see my uncle, my father's brother. I've come from Madrid and just arrived after a voyage from Cadiz to Vera Cruz."

"Wait here!" The soldier left Marcelo standing outside the heavy door.

The soldier tapped lightly on the door of Captain Espinosa's study.

"Enter," a deep voice responded.

"Capitan, there's a poor, dirty monk standing at the front door. He says he's your nephew from Madrid, that you are his father's brother! Most likely he's a beggar. Should I chase him away?"

"I have no relatives in Mexico. Get rid of him! Wait! Did you say Madrid?"

"Si, Capitan, the monk did say Madrid."

The Capitan thought twice. No one in Mexico knew anything of his family in Spain. As the soldier turned to leave, he thought better of his order and decided to see this strange monk.

"Take the monk to my reception room."

The soldier opened the front door and ordered the monk to follow. Reluctantly, he took Marcelo to the reception room.

"Wait here for Capitan Espinosa!"

Marcelo stood there in silence searching his memory for any recollection of his uncle. He had met him only a few times when a small child. In a back corner of his mind Marcelo remembered Uncle Tobias didn't like to play with children. They had never been close.

Marcelo remembered his parents told him why his uncle had left Madrid. He had been summoned and questioned by the Inquisition. His parents believed his testimony had been so convincing, the Inquisitors confirmed he was a good practicing Catholic. However, the Inquisition experience was so traumatic that, after his acquittal, he left for Mexico hoping to be safe.

Over the years, Marcelo's parents had received several letters from Tobias. He was well, happy and had built a successful life in Mexico City. His father once mentioned his Uncle Tobias had become a very important person. He never married, but made his military career his life.

A door to the reception room swung open, and a fine-looking uniformed man brusquely entered the room. He approached, stood uncomfortably close, staring angrily at Marcelo with fierce dark eyes. Marcelo's heart almost stopped. The man said nothing, but examined Marcelo head to toe. Then, his eyes narrowed to study Marcelo's face. His suspicion was obvious. A bead of sweat rolled down Marcelo's brow, dripped on his soiled robe.

The Capitan moved back three steps and said firmly, "So! You claim to be my brother's son...I can't imagine any relative of mine dressed in a monk's habit!"

"Come to my office!" he commanded.

Marcelo followed him through the door. As the Capitan closed the office door, he ordered, "I am not to be disturbed!"

Capitan Espinosa looked at Marcelo squarely in the eyes.

"Tell me now! Can you prove you are my nephew? Or are you just another beggar?"

Marcelo mustered his courage, stood tall and spoke quietly, "My name is Marcelo Espinosa. I am the son of Antonio and Josefina Espinosa of Madrid. When I was a child, my father spoke of you often, told me many stories about you. I vaguely remember your visits to our home."

Marcelo began to stutter, tears came to his eyes; but then he spoke clearly. "The Inquisition killed my parents, burned them at the stake! I'm alone in the world except for you."

The Capitan's face was a blank; his eyes fixed on Marcelo in disbelief.

Marcelo, overcome with grief, couldn't control his tears. He paused, took a deep breath, looked up, fixed his eyes confidently on the Captain's face, and continued.

"I know your secret: My father told me you were questioned by the Inquisition and were fortunate enough to be released. If we had left with you, my parents would still be alive. They made it possible for me to escape. Abbot Valdez sent me here as a novice monk. That, in itself, was a miracle."

In an instant— hearing Abbott Valdez name—
Tobias knew Marcelo's story was clearly the truth.
This same close friend had helped him immigrate to
Mexico City.

"Marcelo, I do believe you."

Then, as his brother's death hit him, he
exploded in pain and anger. His fist slammed loudly
upon the desk. He cried out, shouted obscenities
condemning the Inquisition, the Catholic Church.
Now sobbing, hands pressed to his face, Tobias
lowered his head to rest upon the desk. Minutes
later, regaining restraint, he stood, turned to
Marcelo, firmly placed his hands on Marcelo's
shoulders and embraced him.

Marcelo breathed a deep sigh of relief and
dropped to a chair. His uncle moved a chair and sat
before him. Capitan Tobias explained that, when he
first saw Marcelo, something was familiar. Later, in
his office, he saw several resemblances to his
brother, whom he loved deeply. The key was his
mention of Abbott Valdez.

"Marcelo, please tell me more."

"When my parents received the Inquisition's
summons, we went immediately to Abbot Valdez."
Marcelo explained how Abbot Valdez, his father's
best friend, arranged his entry to a cloistered
monastery under the guise of a novice. Months
later, when Valdez learned of his parent's death, he
also found out the Inquisition wanted Marcelo for
questioning. To save his life, Abbot Valdez worked
his plan: Marcelo was given identity as a Franciscan
monk and put aboard a ship bound for Mexico.

"Marcelo it was Abbot Valdez who arranged my
passage to Mexico." Tobias explained. "Abbot
Valdez tried to persuade your father and mother to

leave with me. But, your father cast aside all his arguments. He was confident his family would all be safe in Madrid." Now, Marcelo understood why Abbot Valdez was so sure his uncle would help. Tio Tobias would point him to survival; he was another Jew in hiding.

"Marcelo, the first thing we have to do is get you cleaned up!"

• • • •

That evening, when Tio Tobias and Marcelo had finished supper Marcelo gave him the documents Abbot Valdez had forged. They declared he was a Catholic in good standing and came from a good Catholic family. Tobias carefully examined each page of the forged documents and declared, without a doubt, they erased Marcelo's entire Jewish heritage.

"Marcelo, you'll live here with me until you establish yourself in the community. I'll do all I can to help. But in return, you must do exactly as I say."

"Tomorrow morning, go to the monastery. Inform the abbot of your decision to end your status as a monk. You have decided upon another calling. It's important you sound sincere. Since you're only a novice you've taken no vows. Leaving the religious order should not pose any problems."

Marcelo breathed a sigh of relief. He wouldn't have to live at the monastery.

Tobias continued, "If they should ask, say your parents suddenly took ill, died and left you orphaned. You came to Mexico hoping to find your uncle. Fortunately, you found me and I will take charge of your future. It's important to say, at first, you felt that you had a calling to be a priest, but that changed. We don't want their asking too many questions, but we do want to be on their good side. The Catholic Church here is very powerful."

"One more thing. You will not put me at risk by loose talk or foolish behavior. Is that clear? I can help you if you join the military and dedicate yourself to becoming a fine Christian soldier."

"*Sí Tío*," Marcelo promised. "Thank you for your advice and protection. I'll do exactly as you say. I'll make you and my parents proud."

Tobias and Marcelo both stood and approached each other. Tobias placed his both hands on Marcelo's shoulder. "Marcelo, I'm sorry you've lost your parents. Working together, I'll help you build a future here in Mexico. Now, you are all the family I have left!"

• • • •

Marcelo adjusted slowly to his new life in Mexico. The Spanish customs he had grown up within Madrid were somewhat different in Mexico City. So he had to be careful not to offend anyone. He found it difficult to trust anybody so making new friends was not easy. He felt somewhat lonely, but knew it was safer this way.

Marcelo thought of Ana every day and desperately wanted to see her, if only from a distance. He learned where she lived, the *Alcalde's* hacienda. Marcelo was careful to keep his word. He avoided anything that might possibly reveal their secret, place them in danger's way. He never saw Ana again.

He did, however, visit the monastery frequently to see Padre Sanchez who became his best friend. Marcelo learned that the Inquisition was not yet a strong force in Mexico. But, he suspected it would soon grow bringing fear and slaughter.

Marcelo began his military training in 1589 when he was 20 years old. He moved out of his uncle's house into the military garrison's barracks, glad to be on his own. But, each time he met his uncle, he was reminded to never let down his guard.

"Marcelo, be careful. Careless talk or behavior can cause suspicion. Nobody is to be trusted!"

Marcelo assured his uncle he understood his warnings. His uncle's concerns blotted out any idea of approaching Ana. His officers considered Marcelo an attentive and respectful trainee, a responsible soldier and a devout Catholic. Still, there wasn't a day Marcelo didn't think of Ana and their love.

Three years later, in 1592, Marcelo completed his training and was commissioned a Captain at the age of twenty-three.

• • • •

Many Sephardic families lived in Mexico City; some practiced their Jewish traditions openly. Others, having learned to fear the Inquisition, lived as Christians keeping their Jewish faith secret. A few had truly converted to Christianity, abandoning all their Jewish faith and customs.

In time, leaders of the Catholic Church became aware of the many Jews who had fled Spain and Portugal to live in Mexico. Their concern was placed in the hands of the Inquisition whose tentacles had already reached out to encircle Mexico. It wasn't long before suspects were reported, summoned summarily for hearings.

Luis de Carvajal was one of the first to suffer. Born a Jew in Spain, he became a sincere convert to Christianity. Later, he moved to Mexico City and became a businessman and soldier having fought with valor against the Indians in Xalpa and Huasteca. As rumors circulated that his family was secretly practicing Jewish rites, Carvajal's economic and political fortunes gradually reversed; his businesses failed.

Carvajal was summoned by the Inquisition's tribunal to respond to twenty-two charges. Under torture, Carvajal not only confessed to abandoning Christianity and reverting to the Jewish faith but denounced friends and members of his family. On January 8, 1596 Luis de Carvajal was burned in the Zocalo along with his mother and three sisters.

• • • •

Marcelo was assigned an unthinkable task, one impossible to refuse. He was responsible for the delivery of the dreaded Inquisition summons to suspect Jewish families. Naked terror was visible on each face of those accused. His anger, so closely linked to that terror, arose each time he presented a summons to those unfortunate souls. His duty was unthinkable, never painless.

Marcelo had never learned exactly how his parents had died. But, he saw what happened to those condemned here— the torture, the *Quemadero!* That was agonizing! Imagining how the Inquisition killed his mother and father.

As time went on, Marcelo became more depressed, concerned for his own safety. It was late in the afternoon when his commanding officer called him in to give him his next assignment: The ceremonial *auto de fey* scheduled for the following day.

"Captain Espinosa, tomorrow you will command the escort of those accused by the Inquisition from the church to the town square."

He went on to explain the event, how it would be conducted. Church bells throughout the city would ring for one hour calling everyone to the plaza. Once the prisoners were there, the sentences decided upon by the Inquisition would be announced to the community. Those found guilty would be punished immediately; the innocent set free. Officials and clergy from throughout the region would be present. Some eight thousand people were expected to attend.

"Marcelo, this *auto de fey* is a spectacle everyone will want to see!"

Hearing this, Marcelo suffered a severe cramp in his stomach; he wanted to vomit. But, he held firm and responded, "*Si, Señor*," saluted, turned away and returned to his quarters. Later, as he lay in bed staring at the ceiling it suddenly occurred to him that Ana and the *Alcalde* would probably be there. He broke out in a cold sweat, was lost in his thoughts, unable to sleep. He hugged his pillow, remembered Ana, how much in love they had been.

"*Dios Mio*, why am I unable to forget this woman? I love her now as much as I ever did. The thought of her watching a *Quemadero* revolts me— I 'm sure it will upset her."

Early the next morning Marcelo dragged himself out of bed and reluctantly followed his orders. He rode on horseback stopping at various parts of the city to announce there would be an *auto de fe* at the town square starting at noon.

As he made his rounds, Marcelo felt foolish calling out, "Rewards in heaven will be granted by the Church for those who attend today's burning ceremony, including women and children. Bring the whole family."

By noon, Marcelo was back at the cathedral awaiting the procession. He worked hard to control his emotions. The possibility of seeing Ana with the *Alcalde* filled him with both excitement and fear. Would she look the same? What does the *Alcalde* look like? So many years had passed.

Suddenly trumpets sounded. The church bells had been ringing for almost an hour. The square was filled; people were excited about the event.

Now, a lone priest appeared; he carried a large crucifix, draped with a black veil. Then, twenty-four high officials of the Church and the Inquisition followed, each carrying a lighted torch. They sang the Deus Laudem Tuam as they walked.

A Dominican priest walked in front of the prisoners, holding aloft a large silver box. It held the Inquisition's verdict for each prisoner. Marcelo rode behind the priest. Then the prisoners, fifty in total; each accompanied by two witnesses, usually family members. Marcelo's soldiers, all on horseback, rode at the four corners of the group, guiding them into the town square. Prison guards made sure none escaped.

When the procession arrived at the town square, it was already crowded, but they opened up a path for the procession. The priest placed the crucifix into fittings behind the altar; the church officials placed each torch surrounding the cross and the altar. A large table was in front of the altar; the silver box was placed in its center. Two large bleachers had been built, each with ten rows and were located on either side of the altar for the Church officials.

The soldiers and guards opened an area for the prisoners. The stood facing the altar, witnesses at their side. Prison guards stood in a semi-circle behind the prisoners.

The *auto de fe* ceremony always began with Mass, this time led by the Archbishop. Marcelo and his soldiers remained mounted. Marcelo scanned the crowd looking for Ana. He found her seated with the other government dignitaries. Her elderly husband sat at her side. As their eyes met, his heart pounded— she was so beautiful. Hidden behind her elegant black lace fan, Ana blew him a kiss. Marcelo nodded in reply. Ana couldn't take her eyes off Marcelo. Their emotions, pain and excitement, were discreetly hidden. Neither the *Alcalde* nor anyone in the crowd would have noticed.

When the Mass was over, the church and government officials gathered at the table. The Inquisition's Dominican bishop made an impassioned plea to each prisoner: repent and accept Jesus Christ as your Savior. Some did, and others did not. At last, a priest took his place with the Inquisition's silver box. With great ceremony, he lifted the top of the silver box, set it aside, and took the first verdict from the box.

"Diego Marron is hereby sentenced to 200 lashes for bigamy."

Then a second verdict:

"Juan de Estrada is hereby sentenced to 100 lashes for terrorizing a priest."

Marcelo watched as prisoners sentenced to lashing were tied to posts and flogged according to their sentence. It was a horrific scene to behold: the prisoner's screams, their blood, the whip's sharp crack, and the crowd's cheers. Marcelo felt nauseous, he glanced to Ana; her face was hidden behind her fan.

When the flagellations ended, a priest called out a second list of prisoner names; each was sentenced to banishment from Mexico City for two to five years. Finally, the priest held up another list of prisoners: each person named was declared innocent and ordered released. They left quickly with their witnesses.

The group remaining wore the *Sanbenito*, a bright yellow tunic that reached down to their knees. Each tunic was decorated with figures of dragons and demons thrusting heretics into the flames of hell. On each head a tall dunce hat, decorated the same way. A rope hung from each neck; a burning yellow candle was in their hands. These were the prisoners accused of crimes against the Church.

The crowd became quiet anticipating announcement of those who would be burnt. This group included six Jews and a British pirate captain.

Marcelo could not bear to watch the burning. He knew all too well, if anyone learned his secret, he would die in the flames. When he looked across to see Ana, her chair was empty. The smell of burning flesh, the pitiful victim's screams had driven her away.

After returning his soldiers to their barracks, Marcelo quietly took leave and spent the night at his uncle's house. He was deeply disturbed by the event; it brought back memories of the *Quemadero* he had seen as a boy. Marcelo was extremely upset realizing his parents had died this same cruel, horrifying way.

• • • •

Marcelo began to fear for his own safety. No matter how well he played the role of a Christian soldier, he constantly worried. Somehow somebody could discover his Jewish background and denounce him to the Inquisition. He would suffer death burning on a stake at a *Quemadero*.

Marcelo remembered the efforts his parents had taken to appear as devout Catholics. And look what happened to them. Feeling paranoid, he decided to change his appearance and grew a beard. He felt older, more mature with his new facial hair.

Marcelo made up his mind he wanted to leave Mexico City. He had no idea where he would go. But, he did know he wanted to live his life in safety and peace. His uncle mentioned that a close friend, Don Juan Perez de Oñate, was forming an expedition. They planned to establish a new colony in an unsettled place north of New Spain. Oñate's plan included conversion to Christianity of the Indians in the area. He needed soldiers to protect the colonists and to preserve order.

His uncle suggested this expedition would be a great opportunity for Marcelo to advance his military career. Now 24 years of age, Marcelo would be able to start a new life, maintain his hidden identity on the outskirts of civilization.

Marcelo felt his life was going out of control again. Being a Jew while pretending to be Catholic was disrupting his life. Marcelo was angry and dejected.

"Will this suffering, hiding from persecution, ever end?"

Chapter 11
Meet the Alcalde

Ana would never forget the day she arrived in Mexico City, the afternoon she met the Alcalde, Juan Benavidez, and his mother, Maria. Ana was dismayed when she saw the old man who was to become her husband. But, she carefully suppressed her feelings and politely greeted them both.

"*Buenas tardes*, I am Ana Aldones from Cadiz, Spain. I bring you greetings from my father, Enrique Aldones."

The *Alcalde* quickly took her hand, "I am Juan Benavidez, welcome to my hacienda." Then, he slowly turned Ana around, measuring and appraising every inch of her body.

"Your father has sent me a most delicate and beautiful woman to be my wife. Come closer, my dear." Drawing her near, Benavidez first kissed her hand, and then leaned forward— she smelled his sour breath— to kiss Ana's lips. Ana used all her self-control to keep from recoiling.

I don't believe it! He's much worse than I'd ever imagined. He is short, thin, and ungainly! His hair is gray! He's much older than I was told. Madre de Dios, what am I to do? I will never be able to love this man!

Then Maria, her mother-in-law-to-be, took Ana aside, looked her over with severely critical eyes and declared, "Ana, you'll do just fine once we have you dressed properly. Come along, I'll show you the hacienda and then a maid will take you to your room. You have much to learn."

As they toured the hacienda, Maria spoke with a precise tone, "Juan's first marriage ended when his wife died at childbirth. He was cheated out of a wife and a son. I was very proud when Juan asked for me to take charge of his social affairs and be his escort to political events. I have worked out a perfect system, and we have an excellent relationship. Juan relies on me, and I do not disappoint him."

Maria paused, looked squarely at Ana, and took both her hands, "Now about this wedding, I have made all the arrangements. Juan has waited much too long for your arrival."

A servant girl showed Ana to her room. She found it spacious and comfortable but too garishly decorated for her taste. Exhausted, she slumped into the first chair she found. The servant dragged her trunk and belongings into her room. Maria entered, looked at Ana's possessions with disdain and turned to leave the room. As the door closed, Maria haughtily told the servant, "You make sure she is cleaned up! Dinner will be served in two hours."

Ana was heartbroken! Her mother-in-law's sharp tongue made her cringe. She had hoped to plan the wedding ceremony herself. Obviously, Maria had done everything without any consideration for Ana's taste or preferences. Ana prudently decided to ignore the complex situation between mother and son hoping she could eventually turn things around.

From that first night, Benavidez, the *Alcalde*, revealed himself to be an egotistical, emotionally immature son of a mean-spirited and dominating mother. That same afternoon, he sent her word that he expected her to be in his bedroom after their evening meal. This skinny old man wastes no time trying to claim my flesh! How could this be happening to me? Ana returned a note, with a playful tone, saying she would be in his room on their wedding night, and not before.

When Ana was called to dinner, she discovered the *Alcalde* and his mother had both been sipping wine for some time. Their faces were flushed, and conversation excessively animated. Soon both appeared tipsy, arguing about the promotion of a member of the *Alcalde's* political circle. Very little conversation came Ana's way.

When there was a pause, Ana hurriedly said, "Thank you for making me comfortable in my quarters. The rooms are so large and well arranged."

They both nodded to her, the *Alcalde* filled her wine glass, and both returned to their previous conversation. When the meal was finished, both the *Alcalde* and his mother were quite drunk.

Listening, Ana tried to understand their conversation. She wanted to become familiar with some of the names and positions, but soon she was just bored.

Is this going to be my new life in Mexico City?

• • • •

Several days before the wedding, Ana realized she was not her usual self. She tried to ward off any sign of depression. But one morning, awakening, she felt uncomfortably nauseous; shocked, she realized she might be pregnant.

Oh, *Dios Mio*… I'm not pregnant! Please God… I can't be!

Oh my God…Yes I could!

Ana's thoughts returned to that last time Marcelo had filled her with warmth, a quiet joy as well as apprehension. If I am with Marcelo's child, I'll have part of him in my life forever. Is this God's gift to me?

Ana decided she had to find a way for the *Alcalde* to believe it was his virility that would produce a child. Ana would have to solve a difficult and delicate problem for the wedding night.

Surely, my husband will examine the bedclothes for the sign of my virginity.

Ana decided to hide an embroidery needle on the underside of her wedding gown. At the right moment, she would prick her finger; draw the blood needed to stain the bedclothes. It could be done easily; both Ana and the *Alcalde* would be satisfied.

Ana smiled... Maria thinks that she's the only 'event designer,' but I've learned how to do some designing of my own.

• • • •

The *Alcalde* was impatient for the wedding to take place. His mother had gone to great expense to have a proper, yet lavish gown, created for this important event. Maria invited only the most important politicians and the highest-ranking church officials.

The Archbishop himself celebrated the wedding Mass. Ana was beautiful standing at the altar next to her half-drunk groom. The reception that followed included the only finest musicians and the most delicious foods and wines. Ana had started to greet and speak with some of the guests. The *Alcalde* came to her side, took her firmly by the arm and, walking rapidly, led her away from the festivities.

Ana protested she had not yet spoken with many guests

"I have waited far too long for the taste of you, my bride. Now it's my time for my feast!"

The *Alcalde* took a firm hold upon Ana's arm, pulled her up the stairs directly to his chamber. The door had no sooner closed than he turned, placed a wet kiss on Ana's mouth, and began to strip. Then, Juan Benavidez, the *Alcalde* of Mexico City, launched his assault. There was no persuasion, no gentle caress, not even one sweet word.

So it was that way Ana was initiated into her marriage. Her husband, satiated, snored loudly. Ana's body was bruised, raw and misused; one shoe still on her foot, her left arm still inside her gown's sleeve. But, Ana kept her head, found the hidden needle, managed to prick her finger and wipe blood on the bedclothes.

Limping back to her room, Ana prayed for the baby's protection: Marcelo's baby!

Chapter 12
Don Juan de Oñate's Expedition

"Marcelo, have you given serious thought to joining Don Juan de Oñate's expedition to the north?" "Yes, Tio, I have— but I'm concerned with the risks. Several explorers who have gone to the northern wilderness, say they were lucky to get out alive. They told me about three dangers: get killed by the Indians, get lost or starve. The truth is that I fear the Inquisition more than the dangers of Don Juan's expedition."

Hearing Marcelo's concerns, Tobias paused, considered them thoughtfully. "Marcelo, I've known Don Juan de Oñate for many years. He is a good man, one of the few people I would trust with my life."

Tobias explained that Oñate's father, Cristobal de Oñate, had become a wealthy man by developing the Indian silver mines in Zacatecas. Don Juan had learned from his father how to achieve his goals and had already served as the Crown's Governor of New Spain. Over the years, Don Juan had survived many Indian attacks and dealt effectively with Indian issues. King Phillip II had personally ordered Oñate to lead the colonization of the northern frontier.

"Marcelo, be sure that I will support whatever your decision may be. Perhaps you should talk with some of those people who have already signed on for the expedition."

Next morning Marcelo went to where Onate's people had set up a place, recruiting volunteers for the expedition. He spoke with the person in charge and explained his interest and concerns. He learned that the main objective of the expedition was to establish new missions and convert Indians to Christianity.

Since he was a military officer, Marcelo was soon surrounded by a small group of enthusiastic men, each trying to convince him to volunteer. Marcelo was an important person for them to recruit.

Marcelo learned how difficult it was to interest colonists, recruit soldiers, and gather missionaries, as well as amass food, arms, livestock and supplies for the expedition. Marcelo sensed that many volunteers sought to escape the uncertainty of life in Mexico City. The Inquisition was growing stronger day by day.

Some had volunteered for monetary gain, others for adventure, or status. Everyone knew that rich silver mines had been found north of Zacatecas. Going further north into the wilderness, there were excellent prospects for finding more mineral riches.

Recruiters added the promise of royal titles, large tracts of land and spurred hopes of financial gain. Surely, Indians would be eager to work their plantations. They would welcome the Word of the one true God as well as the gift of Spanish civilization.

King Phillip II in his orders to Oñate had emphasized the primary purpose of the expedition was to regain the trust of the Indians; convert them to Christianity. Early Spanish explorers had slaughtered Indians either through conquest or disease. The Franciscan missionaries were an important part of this expedition's evangelist objective.

Since the expedition was assembling in Zacatecas, Marcelo would have to leave Mexico City, his uncle, and his lost love, Ana. Although he never saw her, knowing she was nearby had comforted him. He hated his present duties; he was an instrument of the Inquisition. Each time he delivered a summons for the Inquisition it struck fear into their hearts and his heart as well.

Marcelo questioned, "Is this my fate? Always leave everything behind, always be among strangers in strange new places!" Taking a deep breath, he pushed those thoughts aside, regained the confidence of his military training. He recognized the noble part of the expedition; bring a better life to the Indians. Nonetheless, he would assure his own safety.

Marcelo decided, "Yes, Tio, it is time for me to move on. I will join Oñate and distance myself from the Inquisition." Early the next day they prepared their horses and left for the three-day trip to Zacatecas.

Don Juan de Oñate graciously received them at his beautiful hacienda. Oñate had an overpowering presence. He was tall and handsome; had an aquiline nose, a broad brow, heavy eyelids but a kind expression. He radiated self-confidence and enthusiasm for the prospects of his expedition. Marcelo sensed Oñate to be an effective leader, worthy of his loyalty. He also saw that his uncle and Oñate were very good friends. And, Oñate was genuinely elated that Marcelo had decided to join his expedition.

That night Marcelo took the final step required to join the expedition. His uncle had prepared all the papers necessary for his transfer, signed them and handed them to Oñate. Now, Marcelo was under the direct command of Don Juan de Oñate.

· · · ·

Moving from the comfortable relationship he had in Mexico City to the primitive conditions of Oñate's camp was not easy. Some provisions had been made for military personnel. Marcelo was assigned to live with his eight soldiers in a crude mud hut plagued by an assortment of unwelcome bugs and rodents.

Their stables were located just behind their hut so the smell of manure wafted to their living space. Soon, Marcelo made friends with other officers and members of the expedition. They all shared the same desire; make any necessary sacrifice to better their lives.

Marcelo found an Indian who, for a little money, would cook, wash his uniforms and keep his section of the hut clean. He renamed him Mateo because it was easier to pronounce than his more difficult Indian name. Mateo was a quiet little man who spoke broken Spanish. Marcelo was grateful for his help and his wiry strength.

Every morning Marcelo's troop would meet with Oñate to make plans for the day. Their responsibility was to see that the camp was kept orderly, that new colonists were cared for as they joined the expedition.

· · · ·

The Viceroy, Luis de Velasco who had confirmed the King's order for Oñate to lead the expedition was transferred to Peru. His replacement,

Don Gaspar de Zuniga y Acevedo, declared Oñate unfit to lead the expedition. This was a cruel humiliation for Oñate just three days before the expedition's departure. Shock and disappointment ran through the camp; departure was postponed indefinitely. A new leader had to be appointed.

Oñate immediately dispatched a protest to the King in Spain. But in the months it would take to receive an answer, Oñate faced huge financial losses. He was responsible for feeding the colonists and their animals as well as all the expenses related to the expedition. The expedition was stuck in Zacatecas with no chance of help from the new Viceroy.

Rumors abounded. Many said the Viceroy wanted one of his own people to lead the expedition so he could share in the riches. Others whispered the Viceroy had created a question for the Inquisition, Oñate's true religious beliefs. Maybe it was something about race. Oñate had married an Indian, Isabel de Tolosa Cortes-Moctezuma.

Marcelo learned that Oñate's wife had died at an early age leaving him with two children. His young son would go with him on the expedition, but his daughter would remain behind. Oñate's wife had been a woman of prominence, the granddaughter of Hernan Cortez who defeated the Aztecs in Mexico City in 1521. She was also the great-granddaughter of the Aztec leader, Montezuma. Her father Don Pedro de Tovar had accompanied Coronado on one of the first exploratory expeditions to the Northern Territories in 1535.

As days turned into weeks, weeks into months, the original group of enthusiastic adventurers became disgruntled and restless. When a year had passed, many colonists left; some of the soldiers deserted. Marcelo decided he was safe in Zacatecas, so he remained. Mateo stayed with him and became his faithful servant and friend.

Marcelo helped with the herds during the day and tried to encourage the frustrated, unruly colonists from abandoning the expedition. But, he knew that, day-by-day, the expedition was falling apart. All the enthusiasm disappeared. It became increasingly difficult to reorganize and sustain the expedition. Still, Oñate never doubted the expedition would soon be on its way under his command.

While they awaited the King's response, the colonists took out their frustrations on the military officers. They knew they were closest to Oñate. Marcelo constantly received complaints, "This is preposterous! We're living in squalor while the Viceroy decides to appoint a new leader." Then again, they all knew the Inquisition had increased its purge of Mexico City.

Marcelo had no time to think about that ever-present danger. He was busy helping Oñate manage the out-of-control expedition. It was a major undertaking to keep alive four hundred colonists and some seven thousand livestock.

Marcelo's only relief was at night. He got together with other officers, drinking or playing cards. That quelled some of the boredom and frustration. Many became his friends. They didn't care who he was or where he came from. Rarely did they talk about their families. Mostly they were single, each looking for a better life and the prospect of finding riches.

As the colonists waited, livestock died of disease and supplies began to run out. Single men complained there were not enough women. Those with women in their family had to protect them. Bouts of dysentery ran rampant. Crowded living conditions turned the camp into a rancid slum. A blanket of despair lay limp over the camp.

Oñate made it clear; the Viceroy would be forced to reappoint him as leader of the expedition. Each morning, people gathered hoping for news of their departure to the north. But, even some of the most loyal colonists, tired of waiting, gave up hope and left.

As the months passed, Oñate formed a great respect for Marcelo's abilities. One evening, after inspecting the camp, he said, "Marcelo, your uncle was very generous transferring you here. I appreciate your loyalty to our cause. Both Tobias and I are sure we will find wealth in these new territories. Marcelo, I hope your dreams will come true."

As he spoke, Marcelo was troubled. Does Oñate think Tobias reassigned me here for my administrative and leadership abilities? What he doesn't know is that I'm fleeing the Inquisition.

Oñate had been deeply wounded by the Viceroy. But, he never once showed or voiced his thoughts. Instead, he made his daily rounds in full dress uniform mounted on his beautiful horse, Helicon. He rode with dignity, treating everyone with respect, always giving encouraging words. The Franciscan missionaries were reminded of the countless Indians waiting for their conversion. The colonists were told of the land and wealth that awaited them in this new land. His presence and leadership helped hold the camp together.

• • • •

More than two years elapsed before Don Juan de Oñate prevailed. The order from King Phillip II finally arrived in Mexico City. He ordered the Viceroy, Don Gaspar de Zuniga y Acevedo, to reappoint Oñate head the expedition.

By the King's order, Oñate was immediately given the prestigious title of Adelentado, Governor and Captain General. This title had never been granted before in the New World. He also received the right to distribute land to those settlers in the new colony who accompanied him.

Now, it was the duty of the Viceroy to ensure the expedition was adequately supplied and funded. The Spanish Crown helped Oñate finance part of the revitalized expedition, but he had the responsibility of paying salaries and providing the necessary animals and food. Oñate had full control over the colonists, the missionaries, and the soldiers.

A final inventory was ordered to make sure that supplies were replenished. Once the Viceroy was satisfied that Oñate had enough hardware, clothing, seeds, medicine, weapons, gifts for the Indians, books, paper, equipment, and the necessary tools for the journey, the expedition was finally on its way.

An updated contract was prepared for all members of the expedition. It stated that they had volunteered of their own freewill; abandoning the expedition would be considered treason. They all knew treason would be strictly enforced with severe consequences, including execution.

The week before they were due to leave, the Viceroy appointed a priest to join the expedition, one who was said to be involved with the Inquisition. Oñate refused to accept the priest asserting, due to the priest's age, he could never endure the journey's physical challenges.

Later Oñate confided to Marcelo, "With all our problems, I do not need an Inquisitor looking over my shoulder, finding faults or making demands. So I appeased the Viceroy suggesting he send a younger priest more suited to our journey."

Marcelo's respect for Oñate grew even stronger. Oñate was a devout Catholic, but he would not allow the Inquisition to be part of his expedition.

The Viceroy's replacement priest arrived. When Oñate introduced the priest to Marcelo, the two greeted each other with boisterous, back slapping abrazos. It was none other than Marcelo's friend, Padre Sanchez. Marcelo remembered his dislike of the Inquisition. Unquestionably, there was no connection to the Inquisition.

Padre Sanchez took Marcelo aside, "I've brought someone to join the expedition you may know." Sanchez explained that a young man had approached him and asked whether he knew a Franciscan monk named Marcelo Espinosa. Sanchez told him he knew a Brother Marcelo Espinosa who had made the voyage with him from Spain. But, the Marcelo he knew had left the Franciscan Order and was living with his uncle in Mexico City. The young man visited Marcelo's uncle who must have trusted him. Tobias told him to search for you here in Zacatecas with the expedition.

"I'll point him out to you. His name is Juan Carlos de Castro."

Marcelo's mind raced; he couldn't remember any Juan Carlos de Castro. He was suspicious, wary of any stranger.

Padre Sanchez pointed across the clearing. "That's the man, over there, leaning against the second wagon. It's the man with dark skin and black hair. He's been very persistent trying to find you."

Marcelo raised his hand, shaded his eyes, "Oh my God!"

Marcelo ran towards the wagon, whooping and hollering.

"Arif! –Arif! – Is it really you?"

Arif turned, recognized Marcelo and ran to tackle him. They both were shouting, pounding each other until, at last, they stood up and looked at each other. Both recognized the changes five years had made to their appearance.

Marcelo took Arif aside so that they could speak privately. "Arif, remember we have to guard our secret carefully. Be very careful of what you say."

"Yes, I understand. Your uncle stressed the importance of secrecy. So be careful! Don't call me Arif; he no longer exists. I am now Juan Carlos de Castro."

"Juan Carlos, tell me how you got to Mexico! I was sure I'd never see you again."

"After Abbot Valdez told me my family was killed by the Inquisition, he put me on a ship with forged papers, just as they did for you. He changed my name so I wouldn't be suspected as a Muslim. I never thought I would survive that voyage across the ocean or ever have the chance to look for you."

Juan Carlos continued, "That was the worst experience I've ever had— I was sick the whole way. I recovered at the monastery in Mexico City. I stayed there for a year but couldn't stand that way of life. Before leaving, I met Padre Sanchez. He knew you and sent me to your uncle. Marcelo, first, your uncle was very suspicious and I was afraid to tell him my story."

"But, I decided to take the risk. I told him that the Inquisition had killed my parents. When I said I was a Moor, he began to soften. He remembered your telling him how hard it was to leave your Moor friend behind. Then, I mentioned Abbott Valdez and that did it! He recognized me as your best friend from the monastery. He told me I'd find you here with Oñate's expedition. So here I am!"

"Have you thought about joining the expedition?" Marcelo asked. "I'm determined to go to the northern territories. The Inquisition is making its way here, and I want to be as far away from them as possible.

"Sure, Marcelo, I want to go with you. How do I sign on?"

Marcelo could hardly believe his luck. Not only was Padre Sanchez was with him, but now his best friend Arif, now Juan Carlos de Castro, would also volunteer.

"I'll go talk with Don Juan de Oñate now!"

Marcelo told Oñate of Juan Carlos' knowledge and experience with managing horses. Oñate quickly recognized his value and approved his joining the expedition. Then, Marcelo helped Juan

Carlos take care of the paperwork and found him clothes and equipment for the journey.

"Juan Carlos, always be vigilant; trust no one with secrets of our past."

Chapter 13
Departure to the North

It was January of 1598: Marcelo was awed by the spectacle! Don Juan de Oñate's expedition had finally been given the Viceroy's approval to leave Santa Barbara. A complete inventory was ordered to ensure everything needed was ready to travel. Wagons and carts had to be repaired, wheels greased. Supplies were taken from warehouses for loading.

At long last, Oñate's order for departure: "We leave Santa Barbara and head north."

At last count, there were some four hundred men, women, and children plus seven Franciscan priests and two lay brothers. After so many months waiting, fewer men remained who brought their families. Most men sought riches and status: the promise of hidalgo, one of Spain's royalty titles and new discoveries of gold and silver.

The day before departure, following tradition, priests offered Confession then celebrated Mass. All present were granted absolution of their sins and given a special benediction asking for God's blessing upon the expedition.

Then, everyone joined in a gran fiesta, a boisterous celebration that lasted well into the night. Settlers wore their best clothes and the soldiers their uniforms. The food was good, and drink was unlimited. Marcelo celebrated with his two old friends. The mood was set for the exciting adventure ahead.

An enormous train of eighty-three motley lumbering wagons and two wheeled carts assembled, all eager to go. Don Juan de Oñate took his place at the head of the caravan, proudly mounted on his horse, Helicon. His field commander, nephew Juan de Zaldivar, rode slightly behind and to the right. A second nephew, Vicente de Zaldivar, his third ranking officer was to the left of Juan de Zaldivar.

Following the three, Oñate's son Cristobal, just ten years of age, rode with Marcelo and two other officers. Marcelo knew this place of honor confirmed Oñate's trust in him.

Soldiers came next, followed by the brown-robed priests and a long line of ox carts and wagons. Some had wheels six feet high; all carried a full load of supplies. Then, came the settlers and their families. Following the train, Juan Carlos' men herded seven thousand head of cattle and five hundred horses. Together the caravan was more than four-miles long.

Now, as he rode, Marcelo suffered from a throbbing headache; too much drink. He felt loneliness mixed with excitement and apprehension. Here he was, 29 years old, riding into the wilderness. Gone forever were his parents and home in Spain. Left behind: his uncle and beloved Ana. No more than memories remained. Marcelo reassured himself, "My parents and Ana would be proud of me."

Sounds of the caravan could be heard for miles. Ox carts groaning and creaking forward, shouted commands and warnings. Most walked, carrying meager supplies, weapons, and gunpowder. Without a doubt, anyone seeing this caravan from a distance would be awed by its sheer size.

Marcelo had brought an ox cart to carry his possessions. His military kit included a captain's lance, and three suits of armor with a Toledo made sword, dagger, and three pistols. Matching powder horns plus fire locks, and bullet molds completed his armament. For his horse, there were three sets of buckskin armor and three Cordovan leather saddles. Finally, there was a bed with two bedrolls, his non-military clothing and hand tools. Marcelo packed as much food as possible: barrels of dried fruit, meat, lard, flour, water, and a few bottles of wine.

Mateo was responsible for leading the oxcart, keeping Marcelo's equipment safe and in order. Considering his short stature, he was incredibly strong handling heavy loads and animals without difficulty. He also cooked meals for both Marcelo and Juan Carlos. Mateo had lost all his family to a disease that swept through his tribe. Even so, his brown wrinkled face revealed how happy he was working for Marcelo.

• • • •

Don Juan de Oñate was fully aware of earlier expeditions to the north. Coronado's twenty-three month exploration trek in 1539 departed from the Pacific coast. Coronado searched for Cíbola; the rumored Indian city made of gold, and had no intent of establishing a colony. He also hoped to find a northern water passage connecting the Atlantic and Pacific. Finding neither, Coronado began his return leaving behind two dedicated Franciscan priests. One of Oñate's challenges was to find these priests, if any had survived.

Oñate decided on following the already known route to the north. They would cross the east-west flowing Conchas River in the central part of New Spain and later the Rio Grande del Norte. This route should ensure an adequate water supply as well as provide good grazing grounds for the livestock.

The journey from Santa Barbara to the Conchas River accustomed everyone to an easy daily routine. However, crossing the river loomed as a hopeless task. The river flow was high and the current fast.

Oñate gathered his officers to work out a plan. They found logs on the river's edge that, when bound to extra cartwheels, formed a bridge. The task was difficult and exhausting.

Two days later, the makeshift bridge had reached the far bank. Miraculously the first heavy-laden cart wobbled across the bridge to the other side. The crowd of onlookers roared in approval, celebrating success. Then, all the carts and wagons slowly made the crossing successfully. Building this makeshift bridge had sealed a bond of achievement between everyone in the expedition.

Next day, Juan Carlos and his drivers brought the horses and livestock to the bridge. They selected a lead horse, gently coaxed the horse to take the first step onto the bridge. When the others saw the lead horse move ahead and cross, usually most would follow.

One frightened horse resisted taking the first step onto the bridge. In desperation Mateo mounted the horse thinking the horse would be more confident with a rider. He succeeded in getting the horse onto the bridge. But, then the horse reared up in fear, throwing them both into the river's fast flowing current.

Marcelo shouted, "Mateo, let the horse go! He'll swim! Save yourself!" Mateo struggled in the water, gasping for breath each time his head breached the water. Marcelo saw the problem. Mateo's foot was caught in a rope that he couldn't shake loose.

Marcelo dove into the river, swam to Mateo. He got close enough to pull Mateo to the surface, but the struggling horse pulled Mateo under again. Marcelo dove down and found Mateo's trapped foot, struggled to pull it free, but couldn't. Rising quickly to the surface, Marcelo gulped air, and dove down again, reached for his knife and cut through the rope freeing Mateo.

Mateo shot upward to the surface, made his way to shore and held fast to a branch growing out from the riverbank. Several hands helped pull Marcelo on shore. The horse, still afraid, struggled for his life. Juan Carlos and two drivers calmed the horse and brought it ashore.

As Marcelo recovered, Mateo stood nearby. He looked at Marcelo, placed his hand over his heart, bowed his head, and called out, "Patrón, Gracias! Thank you for saving my life!" Slowly, Marcelo approached, placed his hands firmly on Mateo's shoulders and responded gruffly, "Mateo, I'm just glad you're alive!"

Juan Carlos came running, "Marcelo, you could have drowned!" Marcelo turned to his friend, "Mi amigo, you'd do no less for me! Hey, we still have Mateo to look out for us both."

• • • •

Don Juan de Oñate moved the caravan due north and halted when they found the smaller, easier to cross San Pedro River. Oñate knew that continuing north from the Conchos meant blazing a new trail through the desert, a forbidding obstacle. An earlier expedition had avoided the desert by heading east, following the Conchos until it merged into the Rio Grande. Then headed north again along the Rio Grande's banks.

Oñate wanted a shorter, more direct route. After easily fording the river and topping off their water supply, the caravan entered the barren desert region. They trudged forward for more than a month, always heading north. The desert terrain made it more difficult to pull the wagons' load; each day the wagons covered less distance. Water was needed for livestock; their reserves were practically gone. There was no wildlife to hunt for food.

Still, there was no sign of the Rio Grande del Norte. Oñate knew he was in serious trouble; he had to find his way out of the desert.

That evening, Oñate sent for Marcelo. They sat together, alone, by his campfire. "Marcelo, I want you to scout what lies ahead. Confirm we're on the right course to the Rio Grande. Choose a small group, men you trust. Take care making your selection; I don't want others to be alarmed. We will camp here until you return."

Marcelo confided in Juan Carlos that Oñate had given him a scouting assignment. "Marcelo, you know I can't go with you. I'm struggling just to keep the horses alive. But, if anything happens to you, I don't think I'd go on."

"Juan Carlos, *mi hermano*... don't worry! Mateo will look out for me. I'll be back in three or four days. Just work your magic on the horses. We need them!"

Marcelo chose three of his best soldiers and included Mateo for his Indian knowhow.

Chapter 14
Lost in the Wilderness

At daybreak, Marcelo and his scouts left the caravan riding due north. As the sun rose, there was a brilliant blue sky, not a trace of clouds. Marcelo scanned the horizon; there were no mountains now, no landmarks. He saw only hummocks, small hills or mounds of light brown sand. Yucca plants were intermingled with the cactus, each leaving space one for the other. The distance between them created paths in the sand that led nowhere.

Marcelo followed several dry riverbeds that headed north. But they also led nowhere. By noon on the second day Marcelo was almost sure they were lost. During the morning, a windstorm had covered the marks they'd left to find their way back to the caravan. By day's end, their water was gone and none had been found. Marcelo questioned if they weren't traveling in circles.

On the third day thirst set in— mouths were parched, tongues swelling, horses too exhausted to carry them. Mateo selected a cactus and showed them how to cut the succulent leaves, catch drops of water with their mouth. This helped relieve their thirst, and dizziness from the blazing sun beating down.

For the first time in years, Marcelo found himself praying to God, asking for His help. Marcelo was scared. But even so, he was determined they would survive!

Just then, Mateo called out, "Look, smoke, over those dunes, there!"

Mateo pointed to a faint column of smoke in the distance. They mounted their horses and cautiously made their way to the smoke. When near, they quietly dismounted, tied their horses and approached with swords drawn. Four Indian hunters were fast asleep. With surprise on their side, they captured all four without a struggle. Marcelo ordered them tied hand and foot.

Marcelo and his men saw the Indian's leather water bags and slaked their thirst, then ate what food they found. The Indians were afraid for their life; they had never seen a Spaniard nor their armor, swords and knives. Marcelo ordered them untied. But, each soldier kept his sword drawn. Fortunately, Marcelo had brought trinkets, small mirrors, and eating utensils that aroused the Indian's curiosity.

Mateo, using sign language and crude drawings on the ground, succeeded in conveying that they meant no harm. They were lost and needed the Indian's help. One of the Indians seemed to understand and chattered to the others. Marcelo wondered if they weren't in the same predicament themselves.

Marcelo gave each of them a gift in hope this might assure them of their good will, though they had taken their food and water. The Indians nodded and smiled and appeared willing to help. Again Mateo, using signs and gestures, promised them greater rewards if they would lead them back to the caravan and show them a viable route to the Rio Del Norte.

Early the next morning they began their search for the caravan. With the Indians' help, by late afternoon they saw signs of the caravan in the distance. When the Indians first caught sight of the caravan, they were afraid, started to turn back. They had never seen anything so enormous.

As they came closer to the caravan, Marcelo was concerned. "Will Oñate honor my promise of rewards for the Indians?" By now, Marcelo strongly believed that if they treated them well, they would lead the expedition to the Rio Grande. Still apprehensive, the four Indians rode into the camp closely behind Marcelo. They stayed close to him as Marcelo went to Oñate's wagon to give his mission's report.

"My God! Captain Espinosa, I'm glad you returned safely!" Oñate, then more formally and with concern in his voice, "I feared you were lost. We were ready to move on without you. So tell me who are these Indians?"

"*Commandante*, we could not find a route but I believe these Indians may know the way." Marcelo presented the Indians to Oñate who gave them more gifts, as was the custom, before attempting to communicate with them.

"Marcelo, can these Indians be trusted?"

"Sir, taking the caravan into the desert is dangerous. There are no landmarks and it's easy to get lost. I believe we have to trust the Indians. We saw no sign of water or food for the animals. Mateo has worked hard to help us gain their trust, but we barely communicate with them."

After hearing his story, Oñate instructed Marcelo not to alarm the others telling them how they were lost without food or water. "Just say these Indians will show us the way to the Rio Grande."

As Marcelo left Oñate's wagon, Juan Carlos came to him. Marcelo could see anger in his face. "It's bad enough I'm losing horses to starvation and thirst," he hissed at Marcelo, "...I have to carve them up for food. I was worried you were lost!"

Marcelo threw his arm around his good friend, "Juan Carlos, there will be hard times for everyone. But we'll just have to find our way past them. I'm confident we will survive this journey. We can't turn back. So, let's be strong for each other."

Oñate agreed to reward the Indians in exchange for their assistance as Marcelo had promised. The journey to the Rio Grande was not one the Indians had ever made themselves, but they knew many stories about the Great River to the north. They drew a map in the dirt showing two possible routes. The first was the rougher mountainous route to the east. The other, more direct going to the north through the desert. Oñate again chose the desert, because, according to them, there would be enough water and better terrain for the wagons.

Now, Oñate insisted on their route being marked with stone mounds so that future caravans, especially those bringing supplies, would be able to find their way. He also reasoned that should they perish, eventually, someone would find their remains.

• • • •

Mateo and the Indians led the column until they were well on their way across the barren desert. The Indians gave everyone courage teaching them how to find water holes and hunt for food. Several weeks later, the Indians conveyed they were no longer familiar with the region and could be of no further help. They said the present northeasterly route would eventually lead them to the Rio Grande. As they signaled their leave-taking Marcelo gestured his gratitude. The Indians rode off, leaving them to find their way as best they could.

Each day the heat was unbearable; food and water needed constant replenishing. Many livestock became sick. When an animal died, every scrap was used. The hides gave cover, fat was used for candles and meat was sun dried for jerky, viscera used for stew, bones added flavor to the soup. Gradually, that familiar sense of desperation returned, the caravan was running out of food, water…and hope.

Oñate and the priests encouraged everyone, reminding them, "We are on God's mission! There are Indian souls to be saved, gold and silver to be found for Spain. God will not abandon us!"

Oñate instructed the priests to celebrate Mass daily, to offer thanks to God for their survival and ask for His guidance. Many received courage to keep on and helped others. But, Marcelo longed for the comfort of a responsive God. Even so, he found himself joining in their daily prayers. Later, he would hate himself for his hypocrisy.

As Marcelo settled himself on his pallet to sleep for the night, he ached for the arms of a woman. But, there were no single women for him to choose. Thoughts of Ana were there, always wondering about her life. Would this New World offer them a time and place to be together?

A few days later, Marcelo was awakened at the crack of dawn by Juan Carlos' favorite cattle-herding dog. The dog stood over Marcelo licking his face. Marcelo remembered the dogs often went on early morning explorations. But, the dog was dripping wet!

Marcelo shouted, "Get up! Get up! The dogs have found water!"

Then, Marcelo saddled his horse and followed the dog tracks back to the water hole the dogs had found. This water hole surely saved the caravan. After they drank, filled their jugs and washed, the caravan trudged on, eating whatever roots they could find.

Several more weeks passed and, again, the caravan was struggling to keep moving forward. The relentless blazing sun scorched the sand. Their shoes were worn so thin sand burned their feet. Some ripped clothing into strips and used them to bandage their blistered feet. Juan Carlos saw his horses starving, unable to carry either supplies or their riders. Day by day, moving the caravan forward became more difficult. Only the oxen were strong enough to keep pulling their carretas forward.

The priests led their prayers, "Merciful God, in your infinite mercy, please give us rain." Would their prayers be heard?

As the sun sank below the distant horizon, Marcelo sat down on the sand, exhausted. Hearing a rumble, he looked up to see massive black clouds flickering with lightning forming to the north. The clouds were moving in their direction. Minutes later he felt the first drops of rain on his face. The storm drenched the caravan with enough water to sustain them a few days more.

Slowly the caravan crawled forward as problem after problem pummeled their progress. Many wagons had broken down, toppled over in the sand or fallen into gullies. Eight wagons were damaged so badly they had to be abandoned until extensive repairs could be made. A camp was set up at a watering hole nearby; volunteers would remain behind to make repairs on the damaged wagons. They would survive until soldiers came back to guide them to the caravan. The carretas were needed to save critical supplies.

One week later Marcelo caught sight of a thin green line on the northern horizon. As they drew closer, he could make out trees; it had to a river. Then, sensing water was ahead, the livestock became restless; the herd began moving faster.

Juan Carlos shouted, "No! No! The livestock will burst their bellies if they drink too much." But, nothing could be done to hold back either the livestock or the caravan. The colonists and soldiers ran ahead, threw themselves into the river and drank their fill. Livestock joined them, some drank until bloated and were swept away by the river's current.

After four months struggling through the desert, Oñate's caravan had finally found the great Rio Grande Del Norte!

That night, after making camp, the priests celebrated Mass giving thanks to God. Marcelo, feeling God's presence, joined the others to receive Holy Communion. Marcelo was confident this great river would lead them to their destination. The caravan rested for several days on the banks of the Rio Grande. A small group was sent back to bring the volunteers, and wagons left behind. Near the river, fish, and game were plentiful. Little by little people regained their normal selves. Marcelo and Juan Carlos especially enjoyed a roasted goose Mateo had hunted.

Now, Oñate focused all his attention on crossing the Rio Grande del Norte.

Chapter 15
Journey of Death

Crossing the Rio Grande safely was a challenge; the river was deep, the current swift. The caravan continued north for several days until they found a spot where the river was wide and shallow enough for the entire caravan to cross safely. The crossing took several days as they carefully made their way to the other side without loss of life.

By April 30, 1598, when the caravan was safely on the other side of the Rio Grande del Norte, Oñate orchestrated a lavish celebration. The soldiers strapped on their armor, and the colonists dressed in their best, albeit tattered, clothing. In a brief ceremony, Oñate declared official possession of the land north of the Rio Grande del Norte in the name of King Philip II of Spain, and named it the Province of New Mexico.

When all the preparations were completed; the caravan continued its journey north along the riverbank. After several weeks the heat became unbearable, there were few trees to provide shade. The terrain along the riverbank was too muddy and unpredictable for the wagons. They had to go back to the flat desert route. Soon, the caravan was again running out of food and water. This desert was the roughest, and most challenging they had encountered. Soon, they found themselves dealing with dry riverbeds and deep arroyos, while enduring the blistering sun and blinding windstorms.

As the days wore on, Marcelo became more and more depressed. He considered the prospects of an early death and became obsessed with dying alone in a strange and lonely place. The only souls close at hand to provide support were Mateo, Juan Castro and Padre Sanchez. But, his dream— one day having a family— gave him strength to go on. It was this stubborn hope that sustained him when death might have appeared easier than continuing.

• • • •

The journey across this desolate desert was long and unbelievably cruel. As the wagons and carts pushed forward, a smoldering loneliness accompanied each person. The bleak landscape, sand much whiter than before, reflected the heat from the blazing sun. They could no longer ride their horses; they were too weak to carry a rider. Everyone conserved energy in any way they could. They barely spoke with one another, throats afire, and lips dry, and cracked. Every step forward brought them closer to hopelessness and death.

During the hottest hours of the day, the caravan stopped and everyone rested seeking shade under the wagons. Marcelo noticed that people dared not venture very far from the others, afraid of what might be waiting to harm them. In the late afternoon, they would continue walking until it was dark and cold. Everyone was weak and starved. Almost every day there would be a death. The caravan would stop; a priest would say a prayer as the corpse was lowered into a shallow unmarked grave.

Marcelo met with Padre Sanchez after one funeral and asked, "Padre, so many have died. Do you miss your home? Do you wish you'd stayed there? You could be doing important work for the Church back in Spain."

Padre Sanchez put his hands on Marcelo's shoulders, looked at him eye-to-eye, "I know God has brought us here for a reason. It's one we don't yet know. We must do our best to stay alive until God discloses His reason. Marcelo, look around carefully. Can't you see God's love everywhere?"

With that said, Sanchez began to laugh. As Marcelo looked around at the desolate desert, he understood Sanchez' sarcasm— and laughed along with him.

As the caravan trudged on, the terrain abruptly became easier to navigate. There were trees; foliage to give them shade. The ground was firm making it easier for the carretas wheels to navigate. The river curved back into their path, and everyone gave a great sigh of relief; the desert was behind them.

• • • •

Several days later, Oñate saw a large yellow building in the distance. The caravan had found their first Indian Pueblo. Coronado had described these Indian buildings on his previous journey. The Pueblo was built two or three levels high with small square opening for windows. Retractable ladders, made of notched logs, provided access to rooms on the second and third levels. The first floor had no windows but provided a wall of defense against enemies. Observing the cultivated fields surrounding the Pueblo, it was apparent to all in the caravan that these Indians had a good understanding of farming and knew how to store their crops.

Oñate called his officers together, "This is an excellent opportunity for us to trade for provisions. It is very important not to frighten the Indians. If they are alarmed, they will hide their food in the hills. The sight of our huge caravan would frighten anybody unaware of our intentions."

Oñate selected four soldiers to ride ahead, scout the trail and return to the caravan. Under no circumstances were they to enter the Pueblo. But, the scouting party ignored Oñate's orders and went into the Pueblo asking for food. The Indians willingly shared their food; unaware the four Spanish soldiers were part of a large caravan. When the soldiers returned, Oñate was furious to learn they had disobeyed his orders. Without hesitation, he ordered their execution for this serious breach of discipline. But, Father Sanchez was able to persuade Oñate to put off punishment since the caravan's morale was already so low.

Oñate knew that once the Indians spotted the caravan, they would move quickly. By the time the ragged caravan reached the Pueblo, most all the Indians were gone taking their food with them. Later, smoke from campfires in the surrounding hills could be seen but there was no way to pursue them. Fortunately, several older Indians had stayed behind. Marcelo suggested to Oñate that Mateo might be able to communicate with them. Using gestures and hand signing, Mateo was able to communicate that they came in peace, meant no harm. All they wanted was to trade for food and water. Then, the older Indians sent for their people to return to the village. Oñate offered rewards if they could supply food and water but was disappointed with the small quantities they had to offer. Just the same, he kept his word and gave them gifts of mirrors, beads and metal knives that were gratefully accepted.

• • • •

The caravan continued its journey after several days rest. Marcelo rode alone, deeply concerned about why he was here in this punishing desert. Lonely and depressed, he turned back to find Juan Carlos who was riding near his horses. Marcelo's heart lifted at the sight of his best friend. He waved in greeting and fell in quietly beside him.

"You know, Juan Carlos, one thing that keeps me going is knowing that the Catholic missionaries are suffering just as much as we are!" At that thought they both gave out a hearty laugh.

As they rode on together, Marcelo reminded Juan Carlos of their days together at the monastery, "Would you have believed we'd be here together in this wilderness, not knowing where we're going or if we'll survive?" Marcelo rationalized how others in the caravan had found confidence in God's protection or they surely would have been dead by now. Marcelo's belief in God was not the God of his childhood or of those Catholics who killed their parents. His belief was in a living God. "If I don't survive, Juan Carlos, my parents' death would have no meaning."

"Marcelo, dear friend, I don't suffer physically as you do, my people come from the desert." Over the centuries, Moors have wandered the deserts and learned how to be comfortable. City people don't have the body, mind or culture to cope with the desert's environment. "Don't worry; I'll help you through this difficult time. After all, where else could I go?"

"I'm fortunate to have you as a friend." Marcelo explained his anger. "Together, a Jew and a Muslim, we are both hiding from the Inquisition. I'm tired of running! Most likely there are many others in our caravan running from the Inquisition for the same reason. It's like the story my father told, Moses and the Jews crossing the desert, fleeing Egyptian oppression."

• • • •

The caravan approached the next Pueblo cautiously, not knowing what to expect. Much to their surprise, the Indians hesitantly came out to see the giant caravan. The Spanish soldiers were dressed and armed for battle. Again, using gestures and offerings, Mateo was able to communicate they were not enemies; they came in peace. As a result, they were allowed to enter the Pueblo. Marcelo saw that these were strong and healthy people. Their plentiful crops demonstrated their skill as farmers; their structures proved their expertise as builders. Marcelo was intrigued by the drawings on their walls and the beautiful, carefully crafted pottery.

Don Juan de Oñate wanted to demonstrate to the Indians that his men were strong warriors. So he decided, once they had eaten and rested, the soldiers would stage a mock battle. At first, the Indians were terrified to see the Spaniards in full armor, firing at each other. Finally, the Indians realized they were not trying to harm each other. After the performance, the Oñate gave the Indians many beautiful trinkets and tokens of appreciation for sharing their provisions.

As they were leaving the Pueblo, Oñate was surprised when one of the Indians addressed him in broken Spanish. Struggling for words, the Indian told Oñate about two other Indians, Tomas and Cristobal who lived a while with other Spanish explorers.

Both Tomas and Cristobal lived in a Pueblo through which the caravan would pass as they continued the journey north. Desperate for a good interpreter, Oñate took great care to secure the accurate directions to find the two Spanish-speaking Indians. He hoped they would remember enough Spanish to communicate with them and would also know enough Indian dialects to ease their communication problems with other pueblos.

Again, the caravan packed their provisions and continued their journey north along the Rio Grande del Norte. Small game was plentiful and the travel conditions easier. Now, they were able to move at a faster pace.

• • • •

At first glance, the next Pueblo they found seemed friendly enough. They were welcomed as if word had come before them. Marcelo wanted to see some of the Pueblo's buildings from inside. As he entered one of the larger buildings, he discovered a mural, covered over, depicting the stoning of two priests. Marcelo remembered that Coronado had left behind two dedicated Franciscan priests and that one of Oñate's challenges was to find these priests. When Marcelo described the mural, Oñate assumed that it described the fate of those missing Franciscans. Oñate immediately ordered a hasty departure, and the caravan gathered their belongings and departed.

Again heading north, Oñate followed the directions to the Pueblo where he hoped to find Tomás and Cristobal, the two Spanish-speaking Indians. Oñate planned to ask them to join the caravan and act as guides and interpreters.

Once there, Oñate learned these two Indians had come to the Pueblo with an earlier expedition led by Castaño de Sosa. Oñate offered generous rewards and both Indians accepted. Now, with Tomás and Cristobal, they would be able to deal peacefully with the Indians they would encounter on the way further north.

The caravan of colonists, soldiers, and clergy continued to follow a northerly course close along the Rio Grande del Norte. After several days, they came upon a recently abandoned Indian Pueblo. When they saw the caravan approaching, many had fled to the hills taking most of their provisions with them.

Oñate called his officers together, "We must help them understand we are not like the cruel Conquistadores searching for gold and silver. They had treated them badly while passing through their Pueblo."

Tomas and Cristobal suggested that Marcelo and two soldiers accompany them into the hills to find the Indians. Together they would assure the Indians no one wanted to hurt them. Their efforts proved successful; the Indians accepted the Spaniards as friendly visitors. Returning to their village, they agreed to trade for some much needed food and provisions. Oñate named this pueblo Socorro meaning "Help."

Going further north, with God's guidance, they would find rich soil watered by a mountain river.

Chapter 16
Journey's End

July of 1598: Don Juan de Oñate declared, "This is the ideal location for us to settle! Here lies a valley with excellent farmlands, an awesome backdrop of snowcapped mountains. Two rivers join and then flow to the Rio Grande del Norte." It had been seven months since they left Santa Barbara; they had traveled some fifteen hundred-miles. Everyone in the caravan was worn-out, discouraged and exhausted.

With great anticipation, Oñate called his captains together to appraise the area. "This land is flat and can be easily irrigated from the river. There are already several Indian villages in the area. If they agree to share this land with us, I think it's the right place to stay. We are centrally located to many pueblos, a perfect location to begin spreading Christianity to the Indians."

Oñate and his interpreters went to meet with the leaders of the valley's tribe. First Oñate offered gifts. Then, the Indians saw the soldiers were weak, hungry, and no threat to them. With a good deal of difficulty communicating, finally the chiefs understood what Oñate wanted. They agreed to let the caravan stay.

Later that day, with great joy, and hope for the future, Oñate announced to everyone in the caravan, "These Indians belong to the Tewa tribe. Until we build a permanent home, their chiefs have given us a nearby abandoned Pueblo, Oh-ke. It's on the east bank of the Rio Grande del Norte. We will name this Pueblo San Juan de Los Caballeros— Saint John of the Gentlemen— to honor these Tewa Indians who have been so generous."

Now, the entire expedition lacked food and clothing. They were beggars, entirely dependent upon the Tewa Indians for survival. Their grueling journey had not allowed either time or the place to replenish provisions. By now the colonists had slaughtered most of their hardy Churro sheep. Most of the cattle had succumbed to either starvation or thirst and had been eaten. They barely had sufficient animals for breeding.

Thankfully, during that first year in the northern territory, it was a good year for rain. So, abundant crops grew from the seeds brought from Mexico. And the Indian's food stores were large enough to share until the colonists became self-sufficient.

Although San Juan was well suited for them, the caravan soon moved across the river to be nearer the other Tewa villages in the region. They found more space on the high ground that was easily fortified. It also provided more room for expansion and land for planting crops with access to water for irrigation. This first Spanish settlement in New Mexico was called San Gabriel.

The Spaniards felt comfortable as neighbors of the peaceful Tewa Indians. Marcelo admired their contentment with meager material possessions. He found them curious by nature and, in time, his fear and distrust disappeared. Marcelo found Tewa women to be attractive and graceful, their movements quiet and dignified. They wore beads of dried seeds over undecorated clothing. The men were lean, muscled and wore buckskin breeches or square loincloths.

Marcelo also recognized their successful agriculture knowledge. Meat was preserved by sun drying on their rooftops. In response to the frequent shortage of rain, they had also devised an effective system of irrigation by flooding ditches with river water. Their crops consisted mainly of corn, beans, and squash. They had also learned how to raise domesticated turkeys. The women made pottery to be used for cooking and storage, while the men cultivated cotton that women used for weaving.

• • • •

To establish a productive community, Oñate gave first priority to organizing the colonists and his troops. During the journey, he had given considerable thought to how this could best be accomplished. Oñate wanted the colonists to learn and adopt the Indian methods in order to help the settlement survive.

Juan Carlos was summoned to a meeting with Oñate soon after they had moved to San Gabriel. Oñate called out as Juan Carlos approached, "Aha! Here comes the Horse Master!"

"Juan Carlos, I commend you for your excellent work with the animals during our long journey. You have become one of the most valued people in our new colony. I'm sure you'll agree we need to build sufficient enclosures for the animals, especially the horses. We cannot afford to lose any more animals to disease or theft."

Juan Carlos received the authority to select ten men to help cut trees, and vines needed to fence in a stable yard. Then, make smaller corrals for the horses and the domestic livestock. There was no doubt; horses were an essential part of their survival.

Given that the territory was now officially part of Spain, Oñate established a yearly tax to be levied by the Spanish Crown on each Indian family. The Tewa Indians would pay for their protection from Apache and Navajo raiding parties who frequently pillaged their pueblos.

Payment was made with a basket of corn or beans, a cotton blanket, buckskin or a buffalo hide. These goods were stored for use by the colonists when needed. Tewa families who helped the Franciscan missionaries build their churches were exempt from payment. Since payment was so easy, the Indians readily accepted the Royal Tax. Both corn and beans were easy to plant and grow, and these crops were indispensable when there was rain and the harvest was good.

Marcelo was assigned the task of scouting the region to chart the location of each Tewa Pueblo. Then, each Pueblo would be assigned to one of the Franciscan priests. Marcelo welcomed the task since the Indians had no animosity for the Spaniards. The Tewas usually tried to help and be friendly.

Oñate knew it was critical to build a fortification surrounding San Gabriel. His design included four entry gates, one in each direction. Inside the fort, a church, Oñate's residence, a meeting hall with barracks, storage rooms, an enclosure for horses and a stable. All the colonists, along with many Indians, took part in this construction.

Once the fort's construction was nearing completion, Oñate declared it was time to assign the promised homesteads to the colonists. He gave each colonist two weeks to look over the surrounding land and select an area to be claimed.

Marcelo chose a land grant along the Rio Grande del Norte — flat land that could be easily cultivated. He found this location attractive mainly because of the many Cottonwood trees that grew along the riverbank. Juan Carlos selected his land grant adjacent to San Gabriel so he could be close to his horses and have a safe place for breeding.

When Marcelo started marking the boundaries of his farm, his Indian helpers did not understand. Indian tribes did not believe in individual ownership of farmland; land belonged to the Indian nation.

For centuries, Indians had lived a communal life. It was beyond their comprehension why one person would choose such a large tract of land. It could not be defended or farmed by one person alone. Oñate's assignment of land grants created one of the first resentments among the Indians to the Spaniards.

So, Oñate dedicated much of his time and effort reconciling the chiefs to homestead land distribution. It was agreed no land would be assigned near any Tewa Pueblo or in an area where Indians were already cultivating crops. Nor would sacred Indian land be touched. It was understood that, in return for the land, the colonists would be responsible for the protection of the Tewa Indians. Each homesteader would be responsible for collecting the yearly tribute from the Tewa families assigned to them.

• • • •

Marcelo's Indian helpers came to him voluntarily from Picures, a nearby Tewa Pueblo. Marcelo needed their expertise and experience for he knew nothing about farming, or for that matter, survival in this part of the world.

Standing on his riverside land grant, Marcelo could see a beautiful mountain range to the west, other snow-capped mountains to the east and the Rio Grande del Norte in the valley between them. Beautiful Cottonwood trees growing along the riverbed framed the view.

Marcelo spoke, "This must be life on earth and in heaven, both at the same time!" There was a special aura of spirituality in this quiet, peaceful place. He felt very close to the spirits of his parents. At night, the stars were so bright and seemed so close he felt he could almost reach out to touch them. He felt safe on his homestead, free from the Inquisition's constant threat. Only the distant howls, yips and yelps of the coyotes disturbed the night's silence.

Oñate, as the *Adelentado*, had been given the power by the King and Queen of Spain to confer the title Hidalgo to each settler. Regrettably, some presumed that this title, the lowest of nobility, exempted them from working their large tracts of land. They expected their welcome to nobility gave them the right to enslave the Indians. They would do the heavy work needed to build their haciendas, plant and harvest their crops.

With great courage, Oñate invoked the Crown's law prohibiting the enslavement of Indians. Thus, it became mandatory; each colonist did the work or paid their Indian laborers a just salary. This edict angered the newly titled Spaniards and sowed new seeds of discontent.

Once the fortified town of San Gabriel was completed, and the colonists had taken possession of their land grants, seven priests and two lay brothers went out to the nearby Indian pueblos to begin the task of saving the Indian's souls for Christ.

Marcelo was deeply saddened as he watched Padre Sanchez mount his horse, then turn to wave farewell. He was very fond of Sanchez and feared for his safety. It was a wonder to Marcelo that Sanchez' faith in God could be so strong as to overcome the dangers he certainly faced. "I will surely miss him," he muttered to himself and even said a prayer for his friend's safety.

Marcelo marveled at the courage of these Franciscan priests. Leaving the fort's security to venture into the Indian pueblos, they trusted in God's protection for their quest. To explain God's word, each priest would have to gain his pueblo's trust.

In the San Gabriel area, there were some seventy-five pueblos or approximately forty thousand Tewa Indians. And, each Tewa Pueblo had its own dialect and customs making communication difficult, even the translators were discouraged. Saving souls would be far more difficult than expected.

Once the missionaries got used to the pueblos, they started their first task, building a church in the assigned Pueblo. At first, Indians did not resist learning about this Christian God, one with "big medicine" that matched the strength of Spanish weapons and tools. Later, it became clear to the Franciscans that, although accepting a new God, they would not give up their own gods, traditions or culture.

At the end of the first year, Marcelo was assigned to collect the Royal Tax going from Pueblo to Pueblo with three of his soldiers. It was an enjoyable experience since the Indians were very hospitable. He got to know many Tewa families and collecting the Tax was easy due to plentiful rain and abundant crops.

The sky was unbroken by clouds as Marcelo gazed out over this beautiful land so full of life, but often dotted with hidden danger. Vultures wheeled over a distant hill, occasionally one would drop down, out of sight. He felt a sense of adventure astride his horse; cool air in his nostrils while the sun warmed his back. During these trips, Marcelo took time to look for pueblos not included on his original map or explore for signs of mineral deposits. On his early travels, Marcelo went as far east as the Pecos Pueblo, as far west as the Jemez Pueblo.

• • • •

The Indians told Oñate tales of the great buffalo herds roaming the vast plains east of the mountains. So, Oñate decided to mount an expedition to explore the area, looking for signs of gold and silver; and, for buffalo in preparation for winter. Oñate believed it might be possible to domesticate the buffalo providing a continuous source of meat and hides. He appointed Vicente de Zaldivar to lead the expedition who then selected some sixty soldiers, including Marcelo and Mateo. Vicente's brother, Juan de Zaldivar, remained with Oñate to help protect San Gabriel and the colonists.

As predicted, they did encounter huge buffalo herds but failed to find any trace of gold or silver. A large corral was built to capture some of the buffalo. Marcelo and Mateo were assigned to ride into the center of the buffalo herd then stampede the buffalo towards the corral. The stampede technique worked well with horses and cattle, but they had no experience with buffalo. They had not been warned of the dangers involved.

When they came upon a buffalo herd they quickly and quietly set up the corral. Then, they circled around the buffalo herd and charged into it shouting, forcing the buffalo to stampede toward the corral.

Mateo quickly realized they could not control the panicked buffalo stampede; the plan was too dangerous. He shouted to Marcelo, "Get out! Get out now!" Mateo's voice could hardly be heard over the roar of the crazed buffalos' hooves. Mateo forced his horse closer to Marcelo; then, shoved Marcelo's horse to safety outside the thundering wave of frenzied buffalo. In a moment of horror, Marcelo saw Mateo and his horse disappear under the tide of snorting, bellowing beasts.

Once outside the herd, there was nothing Marcelo could do but stand high in his saddle, desperately trying to find Mateo. The rampaging herd leveled the corral in seconds as the buffalo wave ran onto the open range.

Marcelo saw what remained of his dear friend Mateo! He leaped down to embrace the limp and broken body, and screamed. *"No, No, NO!— Mateo!* Oh God, why did this happen?" Soldiers pulled Marcelo from the body; he sat dazed, watching with glazed eyes as they wrapped Mateo's remains in a blanket. Other soldiers dug a grave for this brave and steadfast Indian.

That night Vicente de Zaldivar sought out Marcelo. "I am sorry you lost your friend. His death taught us very important lessons." They had learned the hard way what most plains Indians already knew. Never ride into a buffalo herd, select a buffalo from the herd's edge for the kill. A few buffalo calves were captured, but they soon died without their mothers. So, the idea of domesticating buffalo was abandoned.

Yes, they did kill enough buffalo to take home many hides and meat to help survive the oncoming winter.

Chapter 17
The Seige at Acoma

Vicente de Zaldivar returned to San Gabriel from the buffalo hunt. They had been away for two months. Oñate had agreed with Vicente that he would assume responsibility for protecting San Gabriel when his expedition returned. His brother, Juan de Zaldivar, would then leave to join Oñate near the Zuni Pueblo. After a week's preparation, Juan gathered his soldiers and headed west to join Oñate.

Don Juan de Oñate had journeyed to the Zuni Indian Pueblo, a four-day horseback ride to the west, hoping to find new mineral deposits. He had discovered a rich salt deposit as well as good prospects for mining silver. Oñate also learned that pearls were rumored to be plentiful in the South Sea— now known as the Gulf of California— and might be the commodity he needed. Oñate also wanted to establish a deep-water port, vital for future trading purposes. Everyone knew he was desperate to establish a significant commercial value from the land he had claimed for Spain.

• • • •

Marcelo was with Juan Carlos in the stables when a messenger found him and delivered a message from Vicente de Zaldivar ordering him to report immediately. Marcelo noted that the messenger was pale and uneasy, "What's going on?" The messenger said, "We are in great danger from the Indians!" A sense of dread swept over Marcelo and Juan Carlos. Something must be seriously wrong.

Later, meeting with Vicente de Zaldivar, they learned two of his brother's soldiers had returned to San Gabriel, both seriously wounded. The Acoma Indians had rebelled! Juan de Zaldivar and ten of his men had been slain.

Juan had stopped at Acoma to obtain supplies from the Indians. Initially, they seemed friendly but suddenly they attacked. Those few survivors decided to go in three directions. The first went to the Zuni Pueblo to warn Oñate of the Indian's rebellion. The second returned to San Gabriel to alert the fort's defense. The third went to find the missionaries at other Indian pueblos with the message to return to San Gabriel for protection.

Four days later, Oñate galloped back into San Gabriel. His haggard face, covered with sand, and sweat was, in turn, sad then angry. He signaled his officers to follow him to a table under a lone tree. Oñate was genuinely alarmed; the Indians could easily attack and annihilate the entire colony.

"Due to the treachery of the Acomas, I have lost my nephew and many of his men. Now, we must punish those Indians responsible for this heinous crime." Oñate ordered the officers to gather colonists, soldiers, and priests for a meeting in the fort in two days time. He cautioned, "If the Indians start a revolt, we are in great danger. They are so many, and we are so few."

When they gathered, Oñate confirmed their colony was completely isolated; there were no reinforcements for their protection. After a spirited debate, they agreed the guilty Acoma Indians had to be severely punished. If the Indians ever understood the vulnerability of the small Spanish colony, they could be easily overwhelmed and destroyed.

Retaliation with a significant show of force would demonstrate to all the region's Indians that Spaniards were now in control. Retaliation had to demonstrate their supremacy; disobedience to Spanish law would not be tolerated.

Seventy soldiers led by Vicente de Zaldivar were chosen to go to the Acoma Pueblo. Oñate knew from a previous visit the Acoma Pueblo was built upon the top of a Mesa, four hundred feet in the air. It was accessible only by a hazardous sequence of hand, and footholds carved out of the Mesa's steep sandstone walls. At the far end, the Mesa's top was cut in two by a deep gorge.

Oñate gave Vicente orders to demand the surrender of all those Indians who had been involved in the massacre. If the Indians did not comply, the soldiers were instructed to attack and take the Pueblo by force. Oñate decided not to accompany the strike force. If he were killed, the entire colony would most certainly fall apart. Vicente's retaliatory group of heavily armed soldiers mounted their horses and, towing two cannon, headed out to the Acoma Pueblo.

Marcelo remained in San Gabriel with fifty-nine soldiers to defend the colonists and the missionaries in the event of an Indian attack. Their fortification consisted of adobe buildings built around a large central plaza with four heavily gated entrances.

Juan Carlos brought the horses and livestock into the walled fortification for their protection. The men prepared for the expected attack positioning the remaining cannon. Women, dressed in men's clothes, joined them on the rooftops to create the illusion of a large defensive force. Several small groups of Indians were seen approaching San

Gabriel but when they saw so many armed soldiers on the rooftops, they quickly withdrew. Priests heard confession, including both Marcelo and Juan Castro, giving absolution and the last sacrament. They all prayed for God's protection in this dark hour.

• • • •

"We were victorious!" Ten days had passed when a lone soldier galloped back into San Gabriel's west gate. Oñate shouted excitedly, "Dismount, tell me everything!"

On the way to Acoma, the retaliatory group was wary of being ambushed as they rode through freezing winds and snow. On the way to Acoma, they stopped at a small Indian Pueblo. With uneasiness, they asked for and were given food and some supplies. When they arrived at Acoma in late afternoon, the group made camp in a protected site at the foot of the Mesa's cliffs.

The Acoma Indians were reputed to be fierce warriors who had never been defeated. As Vicente evaluated the Acoma Mesa he recognized their advantage; four hundred feet of sheer walls protected their Pueblo from attack. But, he saw the Mesa had two parts; the Pueblo inhabited one, and the other was empty. Both parts were separated by a deep gorge.

Vicente's plan of attack was hazardous. The first assault group would scale the cliffs using the Indians' hand and toe holes dug into the sheer sandstone, leading upward to the Pueblo. A second group would climb the uninhabited Mesa's walls taking the two cannon to the top. A plan was developed to span the gorge, enabling a surprise attack from the rear.

Any Acoma submission was doubtful right from the start. Sounds of the Acoma war dance filled the night; drums, yips, yells and chants were heard as they prepared for battle.

At dawn the next morning, Vicente demanded the surrender of tribe members who were responsible for killing Juan de Zaldivar and his men. The Indian interpreter shouted his demands to the Acoma chiefs. This was their last chance to surrender peacefully.

As the first group started climbing the cliffs, the Indians launched a barrage of spears and arrows downwards. Fortunately, their metal helmets and breastplates protected them from mortal wounds and they were able to reach the Pueblo.

The battle was frenzied; every Indian, man, woman, or child, had a weapon. All were trying to protect their lives and their homes. As the main battle developed, the second assault group, undetected by the Indians, successfully scaled the walls of the deserted Mesa. Once there, they found a fallen tree trunk that served as a bridge, enabling them to take the two cannon across the gorge. The Indians had not protected their rear.

Intense fighting lasted two days until finally the Acomas realized that they could not win. Some committed suicide, jumping off the cliff while others surrendered. The Acoma Pueblo was destroyed; body parts and blood were everywhere. There were some three thousand Indians living in Acoma when the battle was launched. After the battle, only six hundred or so were still alive, many of them wounded. Amazingly, only two Spanish soldiers lost their lives.

"The Acomas were no match for us!" Oñate embraced the soldier with tears in his eyes. "I am proud of what has been achieved. Now, get some food and rest while we prepare for the return of the troops."

· · · ·

Oñate gathered his officers and soldiers in the town square and explained the problem they faced. "We're here, without any hope of reinforcement, surrounded by angry Indians who outnumber us. The Indians now recognize our strength. But, if we show any sign of weakness, they could easily unite to kill us all. Our advantage is the Indians are not organized. So I have sent word to Vicente to take the surviving male Indians prisoner. They will be tried at the Santo Domingo Pueblo. Once there, we will decide how to punish those found guilty."

During a three-day trial, two colonists provided representation for the Indians' defense. All were found guilty of murder. There was an impassioned disagreement between Oñate, the colonists, priests, and soldiers on how punishment should be determined.

Some felt that the Indians had been punished enough because so many of their Pueblo had died. Others suggested that prisoner enslavement would be a meaningful symbol for the Indians. The angriest, including Oñate, wanted an extreme punishment, one that would characterize Spanish domination.

Finally, Oñate's wishes prevailed...

Acoma warriors over the age of twenty-five had one foot amputated; twenty-four would never fight again. Indian warriors saw this as the ultimate humiliation, shamed forever. Other surviving

Indians were sentenced to twenty years servitude under Spanish supervision.

The elderly and some of the women were exiled to live forever with the Querechos Indians, a distant tribe on the Great Plains. Children under the age of 12 were placed under strict supervision of the missionaries. Two Hopi Indians, that just happened to be at Acoma when the battle began, had their right hand cut off.

Oñate's purpose was to establish Spanish strength and domination. Amputations were performed publically, striking fear into every Indian. Messengers took word of these sentences to each of the area's pueblos.

• • • •

Marcelo, Juan Carlos and Father Sanchez were angry and saddened by the cruelty inflicted upon the Acoma Indians. They gathered at Juan Carlos' home and were seated around the dinner table, each looking intently at their hands.

Marcelo looked up, glanced at each friend and broke the silence, "I remember the look of hate on each Indian's face! Should they band together, they could easily kill us all in just one day. There would be no escape!"

Juan Carlos couldn't hold back his anger and blurted out, "What gave Juan de Zalvidar the right to go to their Acoma Pueblo in the first place? Demand food? He knew the Acomas weren't friendly. They resented our interfering with their religious traditions. Paying tribute meant nothing to them— they didn't need our protection. They've always been secure on top of their Mesa."

Catching his breath, Juan Carlos declared, "There's no excuse for this cruelty! It's barbaric!

Our people are more savage than Indians could ever be! Soldiers believe their lives are more valuable than those of the Indians! The Acoma Indians were just trying to defend their way of life..."

Marcelo sighed, "I understand why Oñate had to establish Spanish domination. But I'll never feel safe on my farm surrounded by Indians! I'll forget about having a family."

Padre Sanchez reached out, placed his hands on theirs, "It's true— Zalvidar should have stayed away from the Acomas. We knew they never wanted to accept Christianity, and they resented other pueblos accepting our missionaries. Now, Zalvidar's arrogance has endangered our mission. Oñate's attitude toward the Indians has always been severe. If Oñate had sought conversion in a kinder, gentler way perhaps we would have had more cooperation."

"You're right, Padre" Juan Carlos broke in. "There's no doubt Oñate believes he must establish his strength and power here in the New World. He needs to plant respect for the Crown and the Viceroy. Of course, he also seeks immense wealth."

Sanchez hesitated, "While living in the pueblos, I've learned Indians are a proud people; their way of life has served them well for centuries. After what we've done to them, I don't know how can I go back to my Pueblo, face those Indians and encourage them to learn about Christianity. Anger and revenge could easily make them want to kill me!"

Marcelo had heard enough, "Padre, I have to leave, go back to work my farm. I'll pray for your safety. Juan Carlos, if you can, come visit my farm, stay with me a while."

"Marcelo, Please be careful. It would be a tragedy if anything happened to you." They each embraced the other. Then, Marcelo left, mounted his horse and rode off.

Padre Sanchez also departed, returning to the Jemez Pueblo. What would he say to the Indians? He had no words to justify the amputations or the exile of women and children and enslavement of so many.

Anger quickly spread throughout the Indian pueblos. Neither the Indians nor the Spaniards felt safe.

• • • •

Marcelo returned to his farm with intense feelings of shame and guilt. It was hard for him to work with the Indians; he couldn't talk with them about Acoma. Would they judge him to be like those who were so cruel? Could they understand he was powerless to stop the carnage at Acoma? Or the severe punishment imposed upon the Acoma survivors? Marcelo believed Oñate's use of extreme force might restrain the Indians for a while. But, over time, they certainly would seek revenge.

Rumors circulated among missionaries and colonists. Several wanted to return to Mexico City, report to the Viceroy what happened at Acoma. They were confident the Viceroy would be angry and report Oñate to the Crown. The task of converting the Indians would be more difficult, if not impossible, when controlled by fear.

After a few weeks, the Indians working with Marcelo slowly returned to their usual routine. Sometimes he thought he saw anger or hurt; he vowed to regain their trust. He couldn't blame them if they sought revenge upon the colonists and soldiers. Marcelo's long held feelings of frustration returned. Why hadn't he sought revenge when his parents were needlessly put to death in Spain?

After the Acoma revolt, the troops were afraid to leave the protection of the fortress to explore for new lands and mineral resources. They prudently determined that in the wilderness, Indians would have the upper hand and could easily annihilate them.

They had been in San Gabriel for just seven months. But, they all knew survival was impossible without the Indians' help and good will. And, since exploration was postponed, the colony was now in danger of bankruptcy.

Marcelo wondered how the Indians felt now about payment of the Crown's tribute. Fortunately, the Indians in many pueblos were docile when they learned how the Spaniards had dealt so severely with the Acoma Indians.

Some Indians conjured up that the Spaniards had a supernatural strength. So few soldiers conquered a seemingly impenetrable stronghold while wearing armor, fighting with rifles and two cannon. They had defeated so many with so few. Marcelo hoped, for their own safety, the Indians would see the Spaniards' God as the most powerful.

Marcelo was frightened and lonely. What would his future hold in store?

Chapter 18
A New Life at the Farm

Spring arrived! Lots of work had to be done to prepare for the planting season. By now, Marcelo had begun to build relationships with his Indian workers, especially Dancing Bull and his sister, Little Evergreen. Gradually he was gaining their trust working side by side in the fields. Marcelo attempted to teach them Spanish while, at the same time, he was trying to learn Tiwa. Communications were difficult, sometimes frustrating, and at times humorous. Marcelo succeeded mostly by drawing in the dirt with his hands and feet.

Marcelo thought about building a house on his land grant. He was living in a temporary Indian shelter. In the Indian culture, women built the homes while men built their kivas, or temples. Since he had no wife to build a house, and no need of a kiva, he asked the Indians to help him construct a house.

The house he built used both Spanish and Indian construction methods. The one story adobe house had walls that were very thick with small windows. Logs placed a few feet from each other provided support for the roof. A large fireplace was in the kitchen. The floors were made of clay and painted red with sheep blood.

When Marcelo suggested building a fence around his property, Dancing Bull firmly rejected his idea. "Indians will never believe you own the land your house is built on. We learned that land is a gift of the Great Spirit for all to share."

Construction was completed in about a month. To celebrate, the Indians gave Marcelo a dog and a several turkeys. Then, Dancing Bull presented him with a prayer stick. Marcelo had noticed these ornamental sticks in some of the Indian homes and fields. He could see they were carved with great care. This prayer stick was exceptionally beautiful. Dancing Bull explained, "I passed this prayer stick through sacred smoke and then breathed a special prayer into it to give you long life."

Then, sadly, Dancing Bull told Marcelo, "I'll bury your prayer stick in a secret place. Your priests say prayer sticks are the devil's things." Marcelo understood Dancing Bull's disappointment and was sad for them both. He knew the priests considered prayer sticks as idols whose worshipers must be punished. The Inquisition had made him bury so many valuable parts of his own life.

Now, Marcelo wanted to share the enjoyment of his new home and farm. So when he heard Padre Sanchez was in San Gabriel, he sent an Indian helper with a message inviting him to bless his home and farm. He also invited Juan Carlos to join Father Sanchez for the trip. When the messenger returned, he delivered a note from Padre Sanchez: "God willing, Juan Carlos and I will be with you in three days."

• • • •

Looking out from the front of his house, Marcelo saw four riders in the distance. As they came closer, he knew it was Padre Sanchez and Juan Carlos flanked by two soldiers. As they arrived at Marcelo's house, Padre Sanchez swung down from his horse and threw his arms around Marcelo.

Juan Carlos jumped down from his horse and embraced Marcelo. "I've brought you a special gift, the first horse born in San Gabriel!" The colt was a brown and white pinto mare. They stood admiring the small beauty, grinning at each other.

Marcelo thanked God for bringing his two dear friends safely. That these two friends could share in his happiness had great meaning for him. He proudly introduced the Indian helpers who had worked with him building his home.

Padre Sanchez exclaimed, "Marcelo, when we were together aboard that rat-infested ship, could you have imagined we would be together now, here on your farm. Well, thank God— we are here!"

Marcelo said, "You must be thirsty! Come in and you'll enjoy the clear, cool water from the river on my property. We'll have lunch and then, Padre, I'll want you to give God's blessing to my new home!"

Little Evergreen had prepared a meal of corn, rabbit, and berries she had picked by the river. They drank a bottle of wine Marcelo had brought from Mexico City just for a special occasion. When they finished their meal, Padre Sanchez put on his vestments, took out a carefully wrapped bottle of Holy Water and began the blessing ritual.

Shortly after Padre Sanchez had finished the blessing, Marcelo saw Dancing Bull on the other side of the house. He was chanting Indian words and scattering corn over the ground. It was puzzling, but Marcelo believed this was a good omen and truly felt twice blessed.

Padre Sanchez said sadly, "Marcelo, I'm sorry but we have to go back to San Gabriel tonight. Tomorrow morning I must go to the Jemez Pueblo.

Juan Carlos also has to get back to his horses." But, before leaving, they decided to share their thoughts about this new country. They walked to the river, found a shady spot under the Cottonwood trees and sat looking at the river's flow.

Marcelo said, "I'm impressed with the innate dignity of these Pueblo Indians. Their temperament and humor is different from what I've seen in other people. They show respect for each other and honor their gods. Their gods are inseparable parts of nature and permeate every aspect of their lives. I've never seen greed or materialism. Once in a while I've noticed signs of arrogance or jealousy, rarely any cruelty. Padre, how evil can their religion be?"

Padre Sanchez had also developed empathy for the Indians and agreed with Marcelo. "When we first arrived in this land, we Franciscans didn't try to change the Indian religion or culture. We hoped that, as they accepted Christianity, they would eventually abandon their former beliefs and practices."

"But, this isn't happening," Sanchez said. "Indians are happy to take on our Christian God and Catholic concepts as long as they don't have to give up their own. Recently, I attended a clerical meeting in San Gabriel. The senior Franciscan missionary ordered us to be much more punitive, use harsh punishments, when persuading the Indians to fully convert to Catholicism."

Padre Sanchez paused, "You know, Marcelo, I'm not in agreement with this kind of treatment. I'm worried about what may happen. The Indians are just beginning to forget our cruelty at Acoma. I'm concerned that adding more punishment will only encourage another revolt. Then, we'll suffer even more bloodshed!"

Juan Carlos added, "Padre, I can't accept forcing others to agree with beliefs that are not held in their heart. A different belief doesn't necessarily make someone an evil person. I've found the Indians quick to learn many of our ways. They have a deep respect for their animals and their spirits. I can relate to this because of my love for horses."

Walking back to the house, they talked even more and then said their goodbyes. As Padre Sanchez and Juan Carlos rode off, Marcelo already felt lonesome, alone in the wilderness. Not wanting to dwell on these thoughts, he went to find Dancing Bull.

"What were you doing tossing corn seeds around behind the house?" Dancing Bull explained that corn is a sacred gift from the gods. "We use corn seeds to bless a person, a special place, or even an animal. First, we bring a handful of corn seeds to our lips and breathe a special prayer into them. Then, while chanting sacred words, we scatter the seeds."

• • • •

Now, Marcelo felt he was safe from the Inquisition. He was simply Capitan Marcelo Espinosa, peacefully working his farm while carrying out his military duties. His Indian helpers had become close friends.

When Don Oñate needed Marcelo, he would send a soldier to escort him to San Gabriel. Depending on the task assigned, Marcelo could be away for days or months at a time. In his absence, Dancing Bull was responsible for running the farm.

Marcelo was confident everything would be all right when he returned.

Dancing Bull was about Marcelo's age. His solemn brown eyes, coppery brown complexion were framed by long, straight black hair. His lean, muscled body stood erect and he moved with masculine grace. Dancing Bull rarely smiled and was usually alone. He handled the farm animals, livestock and pets with authority and gentleness. He never rested while there was work to be done. Marcelo suspected that Dancing Bull believed these foreigners, thrust into his life, would have a hard time surviving on their own in the Indian world.

Marcelo and Dancing Bull worked side by side, month after month, developing a strong bond of trust and respect for each other. Dancing Bull was one of the few Indians who had made an effort to learn Spanish. Out of respect for him, Marcelo continued his struggle to learn the Tiwa language.

Dancing Bull often told Marcelo, "In Indian life the woman owns the house and takes care of the food." A woman was essential to an Indian man's survival. Over time Marcelo developed a close relationship with Little Evergreen. She was much younger, just fourteen. She was quiet and graceful, with dark penetrating eyes and a shy smile. She spoke only Tiwa and had no desire to learn Spanish.

Little Evergreen and Marcelo worked well together, doing tasks where little language was needed. She prepared flavorful meals for him, taught him to prepare and enjoy foods that he had never eaten before. In a quiet gentle way, they developed a deep affection for each other, one that was nurturing for them both.

Marcelo was always amused when Little Evergreen would come to him; pull on his sleeve signaling him to follow her. Something needed his attention. She was happy caring for Marcelo and asked for nothing more. It was a great friendship that Marcelo did not allow to develop into anything deeper.

Soon, Marcelo learned to be self-sufficient. He provided his own food and did his own cooking, gathered wood and found salt to season and preserve his food. With the help of Little Evergreen, he learned how to make his own clothes, weaving his own cloth. Marcelo learned to live comfortably under the hot summer sun as well as winter's frost and freezing cold. He repaired his own weapons, armor and all the gear he owned.

Occasionally, Dancing Bull left the farm for several days without a word of warning or explanation. Marcelo was curious but didn't want to antagonize him by asking where he had gone. In time, Dancing Bull recognized Marcelo's concern and offered an explanation.

"Marcelo, your priests don't like our Indian gods. They only like their God. They punish us if we keep our old beliefs and traditions. But, there are times when I must go back to my Pueblo to participate in our religious ceremonies. They are part of my Indian life."

Marcelo explained to Dancing Bull that he would respect his Indian beliefs if Dancing Bull would, in turn, respect his beliefs. Dancing Bull couldn't know that Marcelo was tormented with doubts about Christianity ever since the Inquisition had murdered his parents.

As Marcelo learned more and more of the Tiwa language, he and Dancing Bull were more comfortable talking about ideas. Marcelo felt he now had a friend and shared some of his own fears and doubts. Dancing Bull learned to trust Marcelo allowing him entry into his own spiritual world.

Dancing Bull explained he had to use some words in Tiwa. There were no words in Spanish that could easily describe Indian beliefs and customs. The Pueblo Indians compensated for their lack of a written language with an enduring memory. Their stories of creation, their laws and traditions, and the feats of their heroes were recorded in oral history and in drawings that had been passed on from generation to generation since the beginning of time.

"Marcelo, I want to take you to see our ceremonies, but our chiefs say no. Your missionaries tell us not to have ceremonies, so we do them secretly. If they discover us we get into trouble, much trouble."

Marcelo couldn't help but see the parallel. Just as Jews had to hide their ceremonies, so did the Indians. "My friend, I hope that someday I'll be able to see your gatherings. Can you tell me about your ceremonies?"

Dancing Bull explained that the Shaman, or medicine man, has special powers of healing and leads the ceremonies. The tribe is divided into clans. The secrets of each clan are never shared even though they belong to the same tribe. Each clan leader gathers his people and, with the direction of the Shaman, prepares their part of the ceremony.

"I've been a clan member since I was a child. It's the same clan as my father, the father of my father, and father of his father. Our dances are the way our tribe asks for our gods to bless our Pueblo; bring good weather, crops, and good hunting. My clan's job is to see that the right dances are performed properly during the ceremonies of each season of the year."

Marcelo encouraged Dancing Bull to tell him more about their customs. How their ceremonial dress, instruments, songs, and dances were selected. A location was chosen in the Pueblo square for all to see; or in a kiva, a round, underground ceremonial room where women were not allowed.

Religious objects such as *kachinas*, spiritual statues dressed in ceremonial apparel, were usually kept in the kivas and were taken out for all to see on special religious occasions. Each *kachina* was different in its body and dress representing a single survival need. They were messengers of the Pueblo Indians to their gods. The *kachinas* were used to ask for both spiritual and practical advice such as how and when to plant crops. The Shaman provided another way of talking to with their gods. During their ceremonies, he wore a sacred mask that gave him power to speak directly with the gods.

• • • •

Several days later, while working together clearing rocks for a kitchen garden, dark clouds covered the sky, a violent thunderstorm approached. They decided to wait inside until it passed them by. "Dancing Bull, please tell me more about your way of understanding life. How did man come to be here on earth?"

Dancing Bull went silent, withdrawn, almost as if in a trance. Perhaps he was asking his gods' permission to share his beliefs with an outsider.

When he spoke, his voice was low, a mere whisper, "Before this world existed, the elders of my tribe taught us that the maker of all things created the Sun Father and then created Water. From the seeds of these two, Mother Earth came into being. Later, Man was created in the womb of Mother Earth, known as the Underworld."

Dancing Bull looked up at Marcelo. "The Underworld is a dark place, with no comfort, and is difficult for man to leave. But it's from this place all life comes." Dancing Bull likened the process of emerging from the underworld to that of a child's birth. He explained that his ancestors learned to respect every part of Nature once they were on the earth's surface. If Mother Earth saw disrespect for Nature, she could make life on earth harsh and unforgiving.

"My people know they must live in harmony with Nature, always taking time for sacred prayers and ceremonies. These beliefs became a central part of our lives." Dancing Bull, his voice low and halting, and repeated words he had been taught long ago. "Acts of evil were done by ancestors in the bowels of Mother Earth before they emerged to the surface. These acts caused human deformities in subsequent generations. It slowed their ascent into the light. Father Sun then gave them light to help them find their way."

Dancing Bull believed that his ancestors, after a long struggle, had worked their way to the light with the help of their spiritual guides, the *kachinas*. They taught them the true way to live harmoniously. "Those who became disorderly or violent were cast back into the subterranean underworld and punished." Dancing Bull emphasized this with hand gestures pushing downward. Now, Marcelo began to understand why Indians respected all aspects of nature and had come to trust one another.

Marcelo asked Dancing Bull about death and afterlife. "When I die, I will pass into the spirit world. I'm sure that, one day, my spirit will return to earth and live again." Dancing Bull explained he would be buried fully dressed in his ceremonial clothes; all his personal belongings would journey with him.

"Why do you say a prayer when killing an animal?" Marcelo asked. "We kill animals only when necessary for food or clothing. When we take a life we must pray and honor that life, giving thanks to the animal's spirit for its sacrifice."

Dancing Bull paused, then spoke – his voice on edge, "The priests can make me build their churches or even pretend to receive their Catholic God. But I cannot accept the idea that there is a hell, a place for all time that punishes men for their sins. Nor could I accept one God who died for our sins."

Instead, Dancing Bull declared he believed that famine, disease, and drought are a result of Nature's gods being angered. Indians had always known their religious leaders could restore balance to their lives through our gods and their spirits.

Dancing Bull's voice was sharp, "I know our way of life has faults that bother me." Several respected friends had been identified as 'witches,' killed because they were outspoken. Their ideas did not coincide with the tribe leader's beliefs. As a result, he kept any creative thinking to himself, even knowledge he had gained working with Marcelo.

Dancing Bull accepted control by the culture and customs of his people.

As the thunder receded in the distance and the rain ended, work called them back to finish the kitchen garden. They agreed their conversation would be best kept as a secret.

• • • •

Like Dancing Bull, Marcelo buried his feelings and beliefs to survive. The Inquisition had deadened those deeply ingrained teachings of the Catholic Church. He didn't know enough about Judaism to accept it as a religion. All he knew was that Judaism was in his blood. He sensed that God had abandoned him.

Marcelo couldn't accept Dancing Bull's beliefs as his own. But he could understand why those beliefs had served the Indians so well for so many centuries. Marcelo sensed it was wrong to compel them to destroy their beliefs. He had chosen to live in this part of the world as a Christian Spanish soldier, seemingly dedicated to the Spanish throne and the Catholic Church in order to avoid the Inquisition.

Marcelo did everything necessary to hide his secret: going to Mass on Sundays whenever he could, honoring the Christian Holy Days. He did nothing that might suggest his Jewish heritage. Even so, on Fridays he felt compelled to light a candle at sundown; try to remember who he was and where he came from. He prayed to his parents whom, he felt, were spiritually linked with him. He trusted they would help him find a purpose to his life as a way to honor their deaths.

During times of extreme loneliness Marcelo dreamed of living with a woman like Ana. One with whom he could be honest about his past; one who would understand his deep spiritual wounds. In his heart, Marcelo knew this could only be a Jewish woman, one who had experienced a situation similar to his own. How could he trust a Spanish Christian woman? There were times when Marcelo fantasized about marrying an Indian woman, as many of the soldiers and colonists had done.

Passionate memories of Ana haunted him. Ana was always present in his thoughts. He kept those memories in a special place, never mixed with anything else. When very lonely, just like receiving a carefully wrapped gift, Marcelo would unwrap those very precious memories. He would relive each memory of Ana, one at a time. Then, carefully, he'd wrap them all up again, close the package and tuck it away deep in his heart.

News from the outside world was rare. When it came, it arrived with the caravan from Mexico City, once every one, two or three years. His uncle always wrote; he was still looking for an appropriate wife for Marcelo. Perhaps one day he would have his own family.

Marcelo often wondered, "What happened to my sweetheart in Madrid?" Did she ever learn why he left Madrid so suddenly? Had she married? One day, if he went back to Spain, would he find her? Would she still love him? Even if she knew he was Jewish? Had she learned the Inquisition had burned his parents alive?

Threatening storm clouds were forming on the settlement's horizon. Could they be resolved?

Chapter 19
Sowing the Seeds of Discontent

The Franciscan missionaries returned to their assigned pueblos after the Acoma incident. They resumed their efforts to Christianize the Indians, gently first, then as time went by, with even greater fervor. Soldiers were assigned to each Pueblo's mission to protect the missionaries. They also ensured that the Indians were not conducting their own religious ceremonies. If Indians were caught, they were accused of witchcraft and idolatry and punished.

Missionaries were directed by their superiors to eliminate all vestiges of Indian religion; kivas, kachinas, masks, costumes, and prayer sticks were destroyed. Religious dancing and singing, as well as painting religious murals, were also forbidden.

Marcelo said to himself, "This persecution is so much like the Madrid of my youth!"

One day, as Dancing Bull and Marcelo rested from their labors, Dancing Bull spoke out in a clear but distressed voice…he formed each word carefully.

"Priests say we worship idols! Our dances and ceremonies are called the devil's work! They are killing people! Some are sent away from their tribes."

Marcelo couldn't speak but he did understand. He knew Dancing Bull was very angry and deeply hurt. The missionaries had dishonored their sacred objects and rituals. The missionaries' effort to bring

Christianity to the Indians had started so innocently and with sincerity. Now, they were trying to destroy the Indians' ancient beliefs.

Marcelo questioned himself— Why? Is this the Inquisition? Is Catholic teaching the only one that's acceptable? His anger with the Catholic Church came back and began to grow.

Dancing Bull told Marcelo many Indians refused to become Christians. They fled to distant pueblos or hid in the mountains to escape from the Spaniards and their missionaries. They wanted to keep their religion sacred, live their lives in freedom. They were willing to relinquish the comfort of their Pueblo to keep their traditions.

Marcelo recognized his own situation was all too similar. The difference was that he fled the Inquisition because he was Jewish, albeit with little allegiance or learning. These brave Indians fled because they loved their gods, knew their teachings, and practiced their way of life.

Marcelo's crushing moods of depression and anger came from this realization. He felt that his life had little purpose or value. He found very little in common with the Spanish colonists. He felt isolated and out of place. He mulled over, "Where could I hide if I have to leave my farm?"

Marcelo decided to lessen his pain by working his farm. He concentrated upon his crops and animals, and cared for the Indians who helped him, especially Dancing Bull and Little Evergreen. The comradeship of his Indian helpers, the real affection he had for them; this was the part of life that meant most to him. These thoughts kept him from recognizing that relations with the Pueblo Indians were rapidly deteriorating. His Indian helpers made veiled comments about the missionary's abuse in their Pueblo.

Despite Don Juan de Oñate's reprimand, many colonists continued to abuse the Indians as servants and laborers. As a hidalgo, they considered it a given right. Indians were paid poorly or not at all. Indian labor was used to build their haciendas, raise crops and tend livestock. The Indian's resentment grew even more when forced to pay their annual tribute to the Spaniards. Even more dissension was created when those Indians working for the missionaries were given an exemption from paying their tribute.

• • • •

Marcelo's parents had taught him very little that could be helpful in the wilderness other than baking. Marcelo's cooking and baking abilities amused Indian men. In their culture, only women prepared the food.

Little Evergreen showed Marcelo how to gather wild plums, acorns and piñon nuts. She taught him how to cook cactus, yucca, sunflowers, dandelions, mustard plants, and cattails. His Indian helpers taught him how to grow beans and squash and to use other plants for medicines and dyes.

Marcelo learned how to preserve and sundry food on the rooftop, to be stored and eaten when food was scarce. Marcelo had brought wheat seeds from New Spain and planted them in his fields. Once the wheat was harvested he began baking bread the Indians enjoyed.

When work in the fields was over for the day or when the weather kept them under cover, the Indians shared their crafts, making baskets, pottery, and weaving cloth out of cotton for clothing.

The Pueblo Indians had been farming this area for centuries so there was much for him to learn. Marcelo learned to live within the rhythms of the land on its own terms. Indians knew how to protect the soil by rotating certain crops. Their most important crop was corn. When the rainy season was good, there was an abundance of corn to make into cakes and bread in the big domed outside-ovens. Constructed out of mud, the Spaniards called the oven "*horno.*"

Marcelo and his Indian helpers worked as a group. The women had their specific jobs and the men their assigned tasks. With time, they all understood that to be productive on the farm everyone had to share in the work. This included gathering food and preparing meals, working in the fields and keeping the house in order.

Dancing Bull spent many hours helping Marcelo learn how to track and stalk wild game— deer, bear, turkey, and mountain lions. Wild rabbits, squirrels and gophers were plentiful and were easy prey even in winter. Marcelo's hunting skills gradually improved, and he was able to provide meat all year long. Wild animal carcasses and other food for winter were seen on his roof, drying. Marcelo and his Indian helpers always ate small amounts and preserved and stored the rest.

Marcelo was proud Spaniards had made contributions to the Indian culture. Sheep, unknown to the Indians, were brought from New Spain and provided mutton as well as wool. Indian weavers learned they could use their traditional looms to weave warm woolen garments. They also introduced oats, barley, chili peppers, onions, peas, watermelon, peaches, apricots and apples. Perhaps most important, Indians learned how a horse works better when coupled with four wheels.

But the Spanish seeds of discontent had already been sown— discontent was growing rapidly— their fruits would soon ripen.

Chapter 20
Sharing Secrets

Marcelo realized Dancing Bull had become the brother he'd always longed for. Accepting this, he felt less lonely so far away from the childhood comforts he left behind in Madrid. Marcelo mulled it over, "Maybe people can be connected by more than blood relationships." He surely felt connected to this Indian brother.

One day, Dancing Bull again asked about Marcelo's past and his spiritual beliefs. "You're not like the other soldiers. You are like an Indian. But, I sense you carry a heavy heart."

Marcelo decided this was the right moment to share his past with Dancing Bull and swore him to secrecy, though he knew it wasn't necessary. "My ancestors come from a tribe called Jews who existed centuries before Christianity came into being. Many Jews did not accept Jesus Christ as Son of God but instead believed he was a great Jewish prophet."

Then, Marcelo told him about Moses: "God gave Moses the Ten Commandments; laws everyone should obey." He also explained the Jew's Covenant with God; if they loved Him and obeyed His laws, they would be protected.

Dancing Bull interrupted, "Missionaries talk about those Ten Commandments. But, you seem to be the only one who lives by these laws." He sensed something had happened to Marcelo; had his God abandoned him?

"Dancing Bull, let me show you something sacred my mother gave me in our last moments together." Marcelo showed him his crucifix, hanging on a cord around his neck, concealed beneath his shirt.

"This was my mother's crucifix. It's different from others you might have seen." He pulled up on the vertical section to disclose a small compartment. There, hidden inside, was a tiny scroll. "What's written there is the Shema, the Jewish confession of faith, the most sacred Jewish prayer."

Marcelo's voice quivered as he began his story. "When my father was a young boy in Spain, the King and Queen, with the Church's approval, demanded that everyone living in Spain had to be Christians, members of the Catholic Church." Marcelo explained that both his parents had joined the Church, pretended to be good Catholics, but in their hearts and minds, were still Jews. Together, they continued many Jewish practices that were important for them.

"But my father wasn't careful enough hiding his family's beliefs and practices." He told Dancing Bull how they were summoned and brought before a group of Catholic priests for judgment. The priests were responsible for ridding the country of those who disagreed with their teachings.

"Dancing Bull, from the day I was born, my parents raised and educated me as a Catholic. I knew nothing of their Jewish customs until the day they received that dreadful summons. Before they were taken away, my father found a way to hide me from their fate. Then, I was secretly put on board a ship and sent to find my uncle in Mexico City. That's when I met Padre Sanchez, the priest who came to bless the farm." Marcelo continued with his painful story until he had told it all.

"My parents were found guilty of idolatry." He described how they were humiliated, tied to a stake and then burned to death. Then, he breathed a deep sigh; relieved he had finally revealed his secret to someone other than Juan Carlos.

Marcelo, staring blindly at the floor, spoke softly, "Dancing Bull, that's exactly what's happening to your people!"

That night Marcelo wept. He wept for both their dilemmas.

• • • •

Later that autumn of 1600, Don Juan de Oñate summoned Marcelo to San Gabriel. He was to provide an armed escort for the tribute collectors going from Pueblo to Pueblo demanding the required tribute.

Marcelo knew the plight of the Indians. Their food stores had been depleted by the drought. Right from the start, he thought it was cruel to demand what remained of their food, blankets and hides.

But, Oñate's orders were clear: If the Indians refused payment, collectors must enter their homes, take what food, blankets or hides they could. If the Indians fought back, soldiers were ordered to beat them with clubs or kill them.

When collectors entered their homes, many Indians were silent and offered no resistance. Some Indians begged the collectors to leave just what they needed for themselves. Everywhere they went, Marcelo saw intense looks of hatred; hate permeated the air.

Ten days later, Marcelo asked Oñate to relieve him from the task of collecting tribute. Reluctantly Oñate agreed and reassigned Marcelo to the San Gabriel troop, protecting the fort from attack. This meant Marcelo was away from his farm for longer periods of time. But Dancing Bull and his Indian helpers managed in his absence.

• • • •

When spring came, Oñate decided to hunt buffalo to alleviate the famine. In June of 1601 he led eighty soldiers and officers to the same far eastern plains that they had explored earlier. Marcelo, along with two priests, went with him.

They set out on the long journey with enough animals for food and two carts loaded with supplies. The animals were used to barter with Indians on the way. They first went to the Pecos Pueblo, then east to the Great Plains, following the trail they had used earlier. No buffalo were to be found; Oñate wondered if this journey was made in vain.

It was Oñate's good fortune when they came upon a small group of Indian hunters who offered their help. They realized the soldiers had difficulties. One of the Indians named Jusepe spoke some Spanish. He had come to the area in 1593 with an illegal expedition led by Captain Bonilla and Captain Humana. Eventually, those two leaders had disagreed and killed each other in a duel. Jusepe, an Aztec born near Mexico City, had been employed by Humana long enough to learn Spanish. He had escaped from that failed expedition and stayed on living with the Apache Indians.

Jusepe agreed to be their guide and interpreter and showed Oñate the route Coronado had taken on an earlier expedition. This route would take them farther to the east and deeper into the Great Plains. In just four days travel, Jusepe led them to a huge buffalo herd grazing on the plains. The expedition hunted there for a month, secured meat for sun drying and a prepared a generous number of buffalo hides.

Finally, they loaded their wagons for the journey back to San Gabriel.

Chapter 21
Scattering the Settlement

As the hunters rode into San Gabriel, Vicente Zaldivar hurried to speak with Don Juan de Oñate. "Don Juan! Many settlers, soldiers, and priests have fled the colony, gone back to New Spain." Zaldivar reported that some two-thirds of the Franciscan missionaries had left the colony saying they no longer had protection from the Indians in New Mexico.

Oñate, his face dark with anger, shouted so all could hear: "Each deserter is hereby declared guilty of high treason for abandoning the colony. When found they will be executed immediately!"

Turning to Zaldivar, in a confidential tone, "I am concerned some will go directly to the Viceroy in Mexico City. Their account of the Acoma conflict could mark me as cruel and unjust, label the colony as a failure." Oñate knew that if those reports reached the King in Spain, the King might well close down the colony. "Vicente, we haven't found any significant mineral deposits or sources of income. We could be stranded here with no hope of survival for the colony."

Zaldivar saw Marcelo and drew near, "Captain Espinosa, your friend that traitor priest Sanchez, abandoned his mission at Jemez. He better find a good hiding place! When we find him, he will be put to death immediately. Should he find his way to Mexico City and turn the Church against us, the colony will be in peril."

Marcelo was miserable, abandoned by Padre Sanchez and all those who had fled to New Spain. Now, there were only twenty-five colonists and some hundred soldiers to protect them all from the Indians.

Oñate spoke so all could hear, "Zaldivar, go now! Find and arrest each of these deserters. If they surrender, bring them back for punishment. I will forgive those who return without a struggle. But should they resist arrest, execute them immediately!"

However, the deserters had a two-month head start on Zaldivar. He couldn't find any of them before they had crossed the border into the safety of New Spain. Now, they were under the jurisdiction of the Viceroy in Mexico City. It was the same viceroy who had given Oñate so much trouble before the expedition left Santa Barbara.

So, Zaldivar returned empty handed to San Gabriel.

Oñate, anticipating the Viceroy's anger and response, ordered Zaldivar to take leave for Spain and plead his case directly with the King. Oñate was desperate; closing the colony would keep him from fulfilling his mission.

In his parting conversation, Oñate reasoned with Zaldivar, "Vicente, despite Acoma, several missionaries have had some success converting Indians to Christianity. I don't want to abandon either the Indians or the missionaries. I am confident, with time, I can make this colony a success."

Later on, Oñate learned, as he suspected, the missionaries had met with the Viceroy. They described Oñate's drastic retaliatory punishment of the Indians at Acoma. The hate created by the Acoma slaughter had destroyed any progress achieved in converting the Indians to Christianity.

Colonists reported even more, condemning Oñate. They were not allowed to use Indians as farm slaves but had to do most of the work themselves. A combination of poor land and harsh weather made profitable farming impossible. No mineral deposits or anything else of trading value had been found. Oñate knew full well the danger of living surrounded by resentful Indians, but had failed to provide adequate security.

The Viceroy was furious! He would ask for the King to relieve Oñate of his post.

• • • •

It was 1604 when Vicente Zaldivar returned from Spain. He reported to Oñate, "Don Juan, the Spanish Crown will not provide our colony with any new troops, supplies or support."

Don Juan de Oñate recognized his only hope for the financial future of the colony was to find minerals or pearls, something with a commercial value. At least, he could establish a port that would provide easier access to the newly colonized area. This was the objective he was pursuing when his nephew, Juan Zaldivar, was killed at Acoma.

Without a shred of doubt, Oñate started this new expedition purely out of desperation. He selected Marcelo and thirty soldiers. They set out on horseback taking only those supplies they could carry. Soon after passing the Zuni Pueblo, they lost their way. They had to ask the Indians for directions and supplies. Marcelo recognized hatred in the Indians' faces and was very uneasy. Word of mouth had spread reports of Acoma, the deeds of the Spaniards were widely known.

As they traveled further to the west, they no longer came upon Indians living in pueblos but rather in widely scattered mud huts. The farther they went from San Gabriel, the friendlier were the Indians. It was apparent these Indians knew nothing of Oñate's harsh methods at Acoma. They willingly offered guidance and helped them find their way.

Eventually, they came upon the Colorado River and followed its course to the Gulf of California. The waters there seemed too shallow for big sailing ships to navigate and safely find an anchorage. Nor had they found any indications of silver or gold or pearls. Oñate knew full well this place was much too far from San Gabriel to serve as a trading port.

Oñate's last expedition was a complete failure. They were exhausted, food had run out; they had to turn back. On their return, they depended on the Indians they encountered and took what food and supplies they needed. There were heavy rains that year so most villages had plenty food and were willing to share.

When Oñate rode into San Gabriel, everyone soon learned the expedition was a failure. Those remaining colonists were disheartened; their investment of time and money had not been profitable. All were troubled; support for the new colony was vanishing quickly. Oñate finally confirmed the Spanish Crown had withdrawn its support.

• • • •

Marcelo was glad to be back; he rode off to find Juan Carlos. He wanted the comfort of seeing his old friend. As he approached the stables, he saw the corral's gate was wide open; there were no horses.

Marcelo felt a sharp twinge of fear. Juan Carlos, Where are you?

Riding quickly through the roofed stable area, he saw several horses in their stalls. But no Juan Carlos. Marcelo jumped down from his horse, ran around to the back of the stables shouting, "Juan Carlos! Juan Carlos! Where— ARE— You?"

Marcelo heard a groan coming from behind a bale of dried grass. He found Juan Carlos' helper lying there in a pool of blood, a knife sticking out of his neck. He was barely conscious. Marcelo was stunned!

"My God, *hijo*, what happened? Where is Juan Carlos?" No reply, just a blank stare. The boy might die in a few minutes. Marcelo had to find out what happened to Juan Carlos. He kneeled, his ear close to the boy's mouth and asked again, "Where is Juan Carlos?"

"Four Apaches… stole horses… Juan followed them alone."

Those were his last eight words.

Within minutes, Marcelo and four soldiers galloped out of the compound. They tracked the Indians and Juan Carlos to the south along the east side of the mountain range. Soon, they found Juan Carlos' body; signs of a fierce battle, blood everywhere. Deep stab wounds pierced Juan Carlos' body, a long slash from forehead to chin, split his face to the bone.

Juan Carlos had fought bravely and with skill: three dead Apaches. One, throat slit from ear to ear. Another: gunshot to the head. The third: a broken neck. But, the fourth Apache took Juan Carlos' life, his prized pistol, horse and saddle along with the five prized horses.

Marcelo was stunned, consumed by rage; feeling acid bile surge to his throat, he vomited. When his senses returned, Marcelo wanted to ride on, track and kill that lone Apache, but his soldiers convinced him of its futility. Two soldiers carefully wrapped Juan Carlos' torn body in a blanket and draped it over the withers of Marcelo's horse. Still, numb from the shock of his dear friend's murder, Marcelo mounted his horse and began the sad procession back to San Gabriel.

Marcelo and his four soldiers rode slowly into the San Gabriel's square. Oñate was there, recognized Juan Carlos' body lying across Marcelo's horse. Oñate extended his hand to Marcelo, his face creased with sadness, "I am sorry for your loss. I, too, will miss Juan Carlos. He was a very special person. There is no way to seek revenge. Apaches roam the land, strike and disappear."

Marcelo, grief-stricken, could not stop his tears. He felt depression's weight returning: "This is my fault! I brought Juan Carlos here. Now, he is gone, murdered. This wilderness has taken the two people I cared most about."

Juan Carlos was buried the next day. Marcelo's solders tried to comfort him but it was to no avail. Marcelo returned to his farm, tried to heal his pain and loneliness. He knew hard work with his Indian friends would help.

• • • •

Several months later, a messenger delivered a brief note from Oñate. He would resign his post and could no longer provide protection. Marcelo immediately returned to San Gabriel. He needed one important favor. He walked from his lodgings to Oñate's office, asked to see him quickly. Oñate greeted Marcelo, thanked him for his service, "You have been a loyal, brave officer. You stood by my side through so many ordeals, both good and bad times." Marcelo was shocked by Oñate's appearance; he was so disheartened.

"As you surely heard, I will officially resign my post as Governor and Captain General in several weeks on August 24, 1607. Although I have invested heavily over nine years building this New Mexico Province, aid needed for our survival will not be forthcoming from the Crown."

"*Adelantado*, before you leave, please release me from my military duties. I'm now twenty-eight and want to dedicate all my time to my farm. I want you to know I believe you did your best."

"But of course, Marcelo, I will release you now without any hesitation. You have been a fine officer. I was fortunate to have you by my side throughout our long struggle."

Oñate sat down at his desk, took his long quill pen in hand and wrote, signed and sealed the official paper releasing Marcelo from all his military duties. He placed the document in an envelope, sealed it carefully and handed it to Marcelo. Oñate embraced Marcelo, tears glistening in his eyes, turned and quickly left the room, not wanting Marcelo to see his emotions.

Finally, Marcelo was free! His loyalty to Oñate had been rewarded.

• • • •

Marcelo again was insecure; where could he hide from the Inquisition? Was his destiny here? His mind was a blur as he considered leaving his farm. He knew that Don Juan de Oñate, agent of the greatest empire on earth, had explored the unknown, probed its mysteries but had little to show for his efforts.

They had raised Spain's flag in these new lands with the hope of finding wealth. But, they failed just as they failed to bring Christianity to the Indians. There were no rewards or riches for their efforts as there had been for Hernán Cortez and Francisco Pizarro before them.

Marcelo was relieved they hadn't found signs of either gold or silver deposits. If they had, the Indians surely would have been exploited, extracting and processing the treasure. However, they had established "El Camino Real de Tierra Adentro," the Royal Inland Road. It started at Mexico City, lead to Santa Barbara in Nuevo Vizcaya, then reached north to Santa Fe and San Gabriel. It provided a safer route for future trades and colonization in the New World.

Of the original Oñate volunteer colonists, Marcelo knew that only a few, perhaps forty, were still there. Many had been killed or had died of illness; the others had deserted.

Later, Marcelo learned that Oñate, humiliated and disconsolate, returned to Mexico City in 1609. He was put on trial for failure to support the Indian conversion to Christianity and mismanagement of the New Mexico colony. It was alleged that his actions and rulings caused extensive hostility among the Indians, making it difficult, if not impossible, for the missionaries to convert the

Indians. The Franciscan priests reported that, at most, four hundred Indians had been converted after ten years missionary work. Many colonists, disgruntled and critical, said Oñate's harsh rules were the cause of the colony's failure.

The Viceroy personally placed his own *estocada*, the final sword thrust by the matador. He accused Oñate of being interested only in finding riches rather than converting Indians to the Catholic Church.

In some ways, Marcelo felt sorry for Oñate. But, he had no doubts; the colony had failed because of Oñate's poor decisions. With Oñate's presence and influence gone, Marcelo felt alone, more vulnerable. Fear and loneliness haunted him with each passing day. Those few colonists and missionaries remaining were stranded.

Seeds of discontent had been sown effectively; fear of an Indian uprising was now growing rapidly.

Chapter 22
Vulnerable Again

Now, the few remaining Franciscan priests puffed up their conversion numbers. In new reports to the Crown, they claimed to have baptized some ten thousand Indians into the Catholic Church.

Because of this spurious report, in 1609, the Spanish Crown decided that the missions must not be abandoned. Instead they made New Mexico a royal colony. It was to be controlled by the missionaries and a new governor who was yet to be appointed.

Also, they wanted to ensure control of the land that Oñate had claimed for Spain. The expenses for colonizing the area would be paid by Spain's Royal Treasury if the remaining colonists promised New Mexico would remain a small colony; no new land added to its territories. Arrangements were made to send the newly appointed governor with fifty soldiers, six priests, and two lay missionaries. The search for gold and glory had come to its end.

The new Royal Governor, Don Pedro de Peralta, arrived in 1610. Shortly thereafter he moved the capital of New Mexico from San Gabriel to Santa Fe. It seemed to him this area was more strategically positioned among the Indian pueblos. They were far enough away so there would be no argument about land ownership. This beautiful location was at the base of the newly named Sangre de Christo mountain range. A rambling stream ran through the center of the town.

Marcelo had hoped the new governor would provide some much-needed stability to the area. But this wasn't to be the case. The missionaries were more and more punitive in their efforts to convert Indians to Christianity. They acted as if they owned the Indians, imposing their views of right or wrong. They firmly believed Spain's laws provided for these actions since the expedition's mission was to convert the Indians, not to colonize.

Without a clear definition of who was in control, church or government, deep resentment and confusion divided them all. Marcelo was sick at heart hearing these heated arguments. He knew the Indians were close to their limit; they would not endure more of the missionaries' abuse.

Now, a new Franciscan priest took over leadership of the mission. He issued edicts from his office at the Santo Domingo Pueblo just a short distance to the south of Santa Fe. Bitter conflict over ecclesiastical jurisdiction came into the open between the missionaries and the governor in Santa Fe.

This priest was not only arrogant but also claimed to be an agent of the Inquisition. He used this power indiscriminately, attempting to strike fear into all those who opposed him, even the governor. He claimed authority to excommunicate anyone who dared disagree with him in matters of faith.

Marcelo began to seriously consider leaving, exasperated by the constant bickering between government people and the missionaries. It wasn't an easy decision. He had to find a place where he could live, safe from the Inquisition.

He was no longer safe nor was there a future here. But, the thought of leaving was saddening and filled him with fear. Marcelo had come to love God, but the anger he held for the Catholic Church surfaced again, obliging him to question his faith.

• • • •

Again, drought had produced another year of hardship. Tension mounted between the Indians and the colonists. Marcelo heard the Indians grumbling. They hated the Spaniards; some spoke openly of killing them all. The Indians refused to pay the Spaniards their expected tribute. Skirmishes occurred when the soldiers demanded grain and pelts.

As the situation worsened, several Indians came to him; Dancing Bull was their spokesman. "Friend, we fear for your life. My people are angry; we may not be able to protect you. You must leave!"

Marcelo now recognized he was in real danger; his farm was too far from San Gabriel or Santa Fe. Indians wanted the Spanish out of their territory.

Marcelo was a lone Spaniard among the Indians! He had to find a safe haven.

Chapter 23
Time to Move On

The caravan had brought the usual letter from his uncle, but this time with amazing news. His eyes widened, and he gasped as he read. "Marcelo, I've found a Jewish woman as a possible wife for you. Her name is Rosita Benavidez Garcia. She comes from Portugal and speaks both Portuguese and Spanish."

Marcelo's eyes raced over the page. "Not only is she lovely of face, but I have found her to be well spoken, intelligent and longing for a family."

Marcelo was stunned! This is too good to be true! Thoughts of partnering with a woman, one who would share his life, were exciting. It filled him with hope of having a family. He longed for a woman who spoke his language, understood his way of thinking. A person with whom he could share his secrets; love him for whom he really is. So he read the letter a second time, slowly.

Finding a safe place was even more important now. Marcelo made arrangements with his Indian helpers to tend the farm until he could safely return. He loved this farm and its natural beauty. He would miss his Indian friends. They had grown close, sharing respect and understanding.

They were quiet as they said their goodbyes. Marcelo turned to Little Evergreen, she was standing alone, waiting, not understanding why he was leaving. Loving Little Evergreen was not like his love for Ana. Nor was it like his thoughts of learning to love Rosita, the Jewish woman his uncle had found.

His love for Little Evergreen was different. It was warm but free from passion. He was a brother to her brother, Dancing Bull. She was the sister he'd never had. Such a good and loyal woman, he was grateful for her love. His heart ached for the pain he was causing her.

Marcelo walked to her, lifted her sad face. Hoping she might understand, Marcelo spoke in his limited Tiwa, "Little Evergreen, thank you for the love and care you have given me. I would take you with me if I had any idea of how my future will unfold." Then, he gave Little Evergreen all the farm animals.

Marcelo and Dancing Bull dug a deep pit not far from the kitchen garden. They buried the farming and household tools they had used building the farm. Should Marcelo return, he would need them.

Last of all, Marcelo gave Dancing Bull his favorite horse and asked him to take care of his other ten horses. Dancing Bull placed a hand on Marcelo's shoulder. Together, they walked to a rise overlooking the farm. There, Dancing Bull placed a new prayer stick into the ground. Then, he blew corn meal in Marcelo's path, and chanted a prayer that his friend would someday return.

Marcelo's burro was loaded with a few small tools, clothing, his weapons and armor, along with good supply of corn, nuts, dried meat and beans. Marcelo left his farm, riding Juan Carlos horse, to join the caravan heading south to Mexico City.

Marcelo wept with sadness; everything that had given meaning to his life was again left behind. Taking count, Marcelo realized he had lived twelve years here in the New Mexico territory. Looking back, he was confident their colonization had given the Indians some valuable benefits, changing their lives. They had learned about new medicines. New tools improved their agricultural efficiency: new strains and different crop seeds were planted; oxen pulled plows, horses the wagons. And, some hunted with rifles replacing the bow and arrow.

Marcelo also knew they had given the Indians good reasons for conflict: humiliation, enslavement, and disease. By compelling the Indians to accept Spanish culture as better than their own, both government and religion, they created intense anger, and hatred. Marcelo was sure their hatred was so deeply imbedded it would last for generations.

Now, as he left the farm, where would he live? For several months, as he went about his work, Marcelo had given that question careful thought. Surely not in Mexico City though his uncle was there; the Inquisition was too powerful. Zacatecas was too close to Mexico City. He remembered Santa Barbara, the small village where Oñate had first organized his expedition.

Would Santa Barbara be the right place? Surely, it's beyond the Inquisition's clutch. Once there, he could find a way to start a new life. And, it's not that far from the farm.

One question remained: *Will Rosita Benavidez Garcia be my wife?*

Chapter 24
Santa Barbara, Mexico

January 12, 1612: A cold, clear day in Santa Fe. The caravan was formed, ready for the journey back to Mexico City. Marcelo took his place. The caravan was well supplied. The tribute tax soldiers had collected from the Indians assured they had plenty food, clothing, and water. Several colonists and priests who had joined the caravan worked with Marcelo to load salt, piñon nuts, and hides. Time was working against them. They knew they had to cross the Rio Grande del Norte before snow, thawing up in the mountains, flooded the river.

Marcelo's Indian friends, loyal to the end, rode near the caravan until they saw he was safely on his way. Then, the Indians reined in their horses, raised their arms in salute and turned back. Marcelo returned their salute with sadness. But, wisps of curiosity crossed his mind. What's coming my way now?

As the caravan traveled on south, Marcelo remembered *La Jornada del Muerto*, that hundred mile treacherous stretch he crossed years ago. The route had been clearly marked since Marcelo's journey north with Don Juan de Oñate's expedition. Now, the return trip was easier and safer. But, there was always a possibility of Indian raids.

The caravan's goal was to travel twenty-five miles each day. With no serious hardships, they planned arriving at Santa Barbara, 750 miles south of Santa Fe, in thirty days. Once there, the caravan would stay in Santa Barbara for a week, unloading and reloading supplies. So, Marcelo knew he would have time to study the town, its people and make his decision. He might go further with the caravan, even as far as Zacatecas.

• • • •

Santa Barbara was little more than a mining village. But, Marcelo learned that caravans frequently came to Santa Barbara, stopping to trade and replenish supplies. This could create opportunities. There was a rustic church and some forty-five houses. Most of Santa Barbara's population was scattered, they worked and lived near the neighboring silver mines without much social interaction. There were small Indian villages nearby that were said to be friendly.

Marcelo found no trace of Jewish persecution or any sign of the Inquisition's presence. Santa Barbara could be just the place to settle, safely raise a family. Then, other worries came to mind. Would Rosita come here from Mexico City? Once here, would she want to stay? Could he dare imagine a life here with Rosita? Would he ever stop thinking of Ana?

Santa Barbara seemed to be the perfect place for Marcelo to hide and make a new life. So when the caravan left Santa Barbara, headed back to Mexico City, Marcelo stayed behind and found temporary lodgings.

Marcelo had written a letter to his uncle and charged one of the soldiers in the caravan to make its delivery. He told Tio Tobias of his decision to make Santa Barbara his home. Marcelo carefully wrote a long letter to Rosita, enclosing it with his uncle's letter. He had struggled with words, invited her to make the difficult journey to join him in Santa Barbara. He assured her Santa Barbara was a small town. She would join with him to live on his farm. There, they could begin a family living in safety. Marcelo knew that if Rosita did accept his proposal, it would be at least a month before she arrived. So he did have time to prepare for her.

Marcelo made several inquiries. Riding his horse, Marcelo found an abandoned farm a short distance from the village. It had a small mud hut facing the river. The Indians in San Gabriel had taught him a lot about farming. He was confident this farmland could support his family.

Marcelo made notes. He could turn the mud hut into a Pueblo house. Larger, it would be sufficient for two. If Rosita decided to stay, when they had children, it could easily be expanded. Now, he began working feverishly, turning the hut into a house. Marcelo found several Indians willing to help. All the while, he knew, if she chooses not to come, he would be alone again in this small village.

Marcelo was plagued by uncertainty…

Why would any woman want to marry a stranger?

She might come and decide not to stay.

Maybe I won't like her!

Maybe she won't like me!

If she doesn't come, what will I do?

Even so he worked hard to get everything ready for Rosita's arrival. He tried not to dwell too much on his hopes: a warm woman beside him in his cold bed, the joy of conversation over a simple evening meal. Marcelo realized he didn't have much to offer. But, if Rosita did join him, this isolated village would be a much safer place to hide from the Inquisition.

More than a month had passed since Marcelo sent his letter to Tio Tobias. When would the caravan arrive? It had to be soon, so his anticipation grew. Only now would he allow himself to dream. Could I fall in love again, marry, and have a family of my own?

Then, word came! The caravan was but a day's distance from Santa Barbara. Next morning, Marcelo dressed in his best clothes. He wanted to look as presentable as possible. But, he was much too excited to complete even the smallest task. His anxiety grew with each passing hour.

Could Rosita be enduring this same uncertainty?

Is she afraid?

Or, is she filled with hope? That same sense of hope that I feel?

Chapter 25
Welcoming Rosita

Mounted astride his horse, Marcelo looked south and saw a long plume of dust rising on the horizon. *It must be the caravan!* He was anxious. *Was this really happening? Would Rosita put an end to so many lonely years?* He wished Dancing Bull were there. *He'd help calm my fears. How will I find her? What should I say?*

Marcelo held his horse in place until he couldn't wait any longer. Spurring his horse forward, he galloped out to meet the caravan. As he met the first wagon, he pulled up beside the trail, called out as each wagon passed, "Do you know Rosita Benavidez Garcia?"

And then, at last, "Yes, she's here with us! Are you Marcelo?"

The wagon pulled to the side; a woman jumped down as Marcelo dismounted.

"Yes, I'm Marcelo and you must be Rosita!"

They looked at each other guardedly, both wanting, more than anything, to like the other. Marcelo gathered in Rosita's appearance; unusually beautiful, curly black hair, bright green eyes, and slender figure. Rosita saw a handsome young man standing tall, curly dark blond hair, a neat beard, and mustache.

Marcelo hesitantly embraced her but spoke clearly "Welcome to Santa Barbara!"

Rosita introduced Marcelo to the family she had accompanied. Marcelo thanked them for their kindness. As Rosita said goodbye to each of the family, Marcelo was impressed with her gentleness and sincerity.

Then, as they collected Rosita's belongings, Marcelo's thoughts raced... *Maybe I can love this woman.* A slight smile crept on to his lips, he felt tingles of happiness again; it had been so long. He hadn't felt like this since Ana.

• • • •

Rosita and Marcelo talked constantly while getting to know each other. At the farm, days were filled with life stories each taking turn to reveal their past, their hopes for the future. Their lives had many parallels. Soon, they discovered both carried a burden of pain that needed confession. They became closer as they shared each episode.

Rosita wept as she spoke of her family. Her parents were wealthy Jews who fled from Spain's Inquisition by moving to Portugal. There, they were persuaded to convert to the Catholic Church but had difficulty adapting to Christian society. As with Marcelo's parents, they didn't abandon their traditional Jewish customs but kept them in secret.

Two politicians who disliked her father, a high-ranking diplomat, denounced the family to the Inquisition. When summoned, her parents knew they couldn't face the complications of escape again— they were too old, tired of running.

During her family's trial, Rosita insisted she was a devout Christian. Nuns who were her teachers testified in her favor. They testified Rosita was the only one of three daughters enrolled in a Catholic girls' school. With the school's Monsignor, they confirmed Rosita to be a perfect Christian student.

She was released and taken in by her father's closest friend.

Rosita's parents and two older sisters were tortured, and then burned at the stake. They had admitted to practicing Jewish traditions but refused to reveal names of other Jews in hiding. Later, when Rosita learned what the Inquisition had done to her family, her heart, and soul were ripped apart, just as had happened to Marcelo.

Rosita was fortunate her father had influential connections. Before he was killed, he had arranged with his friends to help Rosita escape to Mexico City, find a new life. Fortunately, once there, another family friend had taken her in and introduced her to Marcelo's uncle.

It was Tio Tobias who decided Rosita and Marcelo must meet. With a bit of luck, he imagined they would be attracted to each other, marry and settle down far from Mexico City's dangers. Tobias knew it was just a matter of time before the Inquisition would focus upon all the Jews living in Mexico City. Rosita was so afraid of the Inquisition that she, like Marcelo, wanted to be as far from them as she could.

"Marcelo, I didn't come to you blindly, I already knew you. Your uncle let me read all your letters. As I read each one, I felt an attraction growing within me. When your letter to me arrived, my feelings grew stronger; the future you hoped to create for us, wanting a family. I am so grateful God has led me to you."

Marcelo knew he had found someone he could trust and respect.

• • • •

As they shared more episodes, they began to share warm and loving embraces. As Marcelo's fondness grew, so did his passion. He had trouble keeping his hands away from her. Kissing her full and yielding lips was wonderful. As their feelings for each other grew stronger, they knew they were well matched. They had fallen in love.

It wasn't long before they decided to be married in the local Catholic Church. After receiving the priest's blessings they hurried back to the farm and celebrated the age-old ritual of lovemaking.

The very next day they carried out, in secret, a Jewish wedding ceremony as Rosita remembered from her childhood. In the shade of a tree by the river, they stood alone and imagined a rabbi standing before them.

Marcelo knew that the man always gives his bride something of value. So he placed an old gold coin in Rosita's hand. Then, he slowly removed the crucifix from around his neck and told her the story of how his mother gave it to him. That last time Marcelo saw his mother alive was many years ago.

Marcelo showed her how to open the cross, removed the small parchment, and handed it to her. Rosita wept with emotion and slowly recited the Shema aloud, "Hear, O Israel, the Lord is our God; the Lord is one." Marcelo then pledged his love and protection to Rosita. The couple shared in drinking a cup of wine, followed by Marcelo breaking the cup by stamping on it.

Marcelo felt his mother's presence and knew she was pleased. A loving ceremony, it meant more to them than their Catholic wedding. Now, they felt blessed to go forth and multiply. So they spent most of the next week trying to do just that. It was a good feeling; they had honored both their parents with their Jewish wedding traditions. They both felt a sense of exhilaration and liberation.

• • • •

Between their lovemaking episodes, they worked side-by-side developing their farm. It wasn't long before they had to hire several helpers. They had six cows, three horses, a flock of chickens, and a herd of sheep. They grew most of their vegetables as well as feed for the animals.

A year had passed when one day, over their noon meal of beans, lamb and potatoes, Rosita reached across the table and took Marcelo's calloused hand in hers.

"Marcelo, my darling, have you noticed anything different about my body these past few weeks?"

"Only that thoughts of your body call out to me when I'm working. I have to concentrate very hard, or I'll stop what I'm doing, come find you and make love to you!"

"No, no, no, Marcelo! That's not what I mean. See how round I've become… Marcelo, listen to me, I am with child!"

Marcelo stood up so quickly his empty cup clattered to the floor. He ran around the table, drew Rosita to her feet, wrapped her in his arms. "I am so blessed!" He couldn't stop his tears of joy. "What thrilling news," he shouted. "You are so wonderful!" Kissing her, he twirled her round and round.

Damian was born without difficulty— much to their relief— with the help of Maria, the wife of their leading farmhand. He was a fat, happy little boy with big brown eyes and reddish brown fuzz on his well-rounded head.

"What joy! At last, life is good!" Marcelo wept with joy.

Eighteen months later, Dámian was joined by a baby brother they named Gabriel. He was the very opposite of Dámian. Gabriel was small, wiry, and strong, and complained often with loud bouts of crying. Marcelo and Rosita now felt twice blessed; they loved their little family.

As the boys grew into childhood, Marcelo and Rosita began teaching them what they had learned about farming. On frequent hunting trips, Marcelo taught both boys how to survive in the wilderness: make a shelter; decide which roots or berries were safe to eat and how to shoot game for food.

One day, they hoped, both boys would manage the farm, build their own houses, marry and live nearby. They were extra careful to raise the boys as good, practicing Catholics. They were tutored by the local Franciscan priest and became good Christians. They had no knowledge of their Jewish heritage.

Rosita and Marcelo were careful so that no suspicion could be aroused. They never had pork in their home. A crucifix surrounded by images of saints was displayed on their kitchen wall. Rosaries demonstrated their constant devotion to Christ and the Church. They never shared any Jewish ritual with their sons. But, they did observe their Jewish ways unobtrusively never making these practices seem significant in any way.

Both Marcelo and Rosita felt a constant grating sense of guilt. Raised as devout Catholics, Church teachings were deeply engraved in their hearts and soul. But, there was deep jagged wound inside. The Catholic Inquisition had destroyed both their families. They wanted to be true to their Jewish heritage but could only do so in the privacy of their home, hidden from neighbors, lying to their children, far from civilization.

As time passed, many early settlers from New Mexico came to Santa Barbara. Many asked for Marcelo's advice, should they wait there until the Indian problem was resolved? Some stayed while many others returned to Mexico City.

Since both Rosita and Marcelo were raised as Catholics, they knew very little about Judaism. Books were not available and dangerous to own. They relied upon their memory to restore Jewish customs and rituals they had seen within their families. Together, as they grew closer to Judaism, their anger with the Inquisition gradually faded.

What friends they made were centered around the town's Catholic church. They made sure Damian, and Gabriel never socialized with neighbors they suspected of being hidden Jews. If ever summoned by the Inquisition, they knew they would be tortured to reveal the identity of other Jewish families.

It was common knowledge that children examined by the Inquisition had unwittingly incriminated others, including family members. Innocent though they were, children's testimony had caused torture and death for others.

When possible, their sons would go into town for their Catholic tutoring on Friday evenings. Rosita carefully organized her work. Before late Friday afternoon the house was clean, clothes and bedding were changed and cleaned linen was on the table.

When their sons were away, they would light Shabbat candles in the privacy of their farmhouse. At sunset Rosita and Marcelo would cover the windows and light candles, thanking God for Shabbat, the Jewish Sabbath. Marcelo gave another blessing, thanking God for the fruit of the earth and of the vine. Then, they dipped their bread in wine before eating it. No fire was kindled; no work was done until Shabbat ended at sundown, Saturday.

They loved these half-remembered, half-invented Jewish rituals, trying to keep Shabbat as their parents had done. They fasted on Yom Kippur and gave atonement as their parents had done. Whenever possible, Rosita prepared food in observance of the Judaic dietary laws learned from her family. As best they could, they made sure the meat they ate had been slaughtered according to Jewish law and avoided eating pork or eggs with specks of blood on the yolk. To avoid arousing suspicion they were never rigid in keeping these practices.

Living on an isolated farm made it easy for them to keep their secret. Their neighbors knew them as practical farm people working hard to provide for themselves. But in their hearts Rosita and Marcelo were honoring all their Jewish ancestors, especially their parents.

Indeed, the Inquisition had been idle in the New World. It had been years, since anyone had been summoned. But that was soon to change.

Chapter 26
The Spanish Bakery

Nomadic Indians had recently attacked and killed two nearby farmers. They destroyed and burned what was left after stealing everything they could carry. Marcelo decided it was time to leave the farm and move their home into Santa Barbara. He could tend his crops going to the farm on horseback with Damian and Gabriel.

Marcelo and Rosita felt secure that their Jewish heritage was well hidden. Townspeople had accepted them as good Catholics. But, they also knew moving into town would require much caution.

They found an old stone shelter built by Indians located on a large parcel of land near the village edge. Its four walls and roof provided a place to stay during the months needed to build their new house. Using skills the Indians had taught him, Marcelo designed an adobe Pueblo type house. There were two bedrooms, one for themselves, one for Damian and Gabriel, and a large main room and kitchen. Damian, Gabriel, and two Indians worked with Marcelo on construction.

"Rosita, I've noticed that Santa Barbara doesn't have a bakeshop. I learned baking skills from my father. I'm going to try my hand." There was enough room in the kitchen to set aside space for a small bakery shop. So, four *hornos de barro*— clay ovens— were built behind the house for baking bread.

Marcelo had brought both wheat and corn seeds from his farm in New Mexico and had already planted them here on his farm. When harvested, Marcelo baked several type breads popular in his father's shop in Madrid. Soon, the bakery had become a place where people would congregate. Baking made him a living and provided a needed service to the community.

In time, they realized that when the silver miners came for bread, they had nowhere to buy all their supplies. So Marcelo slowly responded to their requests, stocking clothing, tools and staples such as rice and beans. Caravans brought those items he ordered from Mexico City. Soon, he had created a small general store along side of the bakery.

Rosita involved herself with the Santa Barbara community. Marcelo noted that she was very outgoing, just like his mother. But, sometimes others were offended by Rosita's honest and sincere way of speaking. She always spoke what was in her heart believing she could help others find the solution to almost every problem.

• • • •

Now known as *el panadero*, Santa Barbara's baker, Marcelo was also respected as Captain Espinosa, a retired officer of the Spanish Crown and a twelve-year veteran, in good standing, of Oñate's colony in New Mexico. Frequently, people on their way to New Mexico would visit his bakery and ask for his advice. Marcelo would readily tell them what he had learned of farming, cooking, and survival in the wilderness.

Many said they were afraid of the Indians. He told them, "I have worked with many fine, trustworthy Indians. My best friend is Dancing Bull." Marcelo described how to trade with Indians without fear. He always advocated treating Indians with respect, honoring their customs and their way of life. Eventually, he learned that Santa Fe was becoming a safer place to settle because the Crown had provided more soldiers and the Indians were less threatening.

It was early morning; Marcelo had just placed the last bread loaves in the oven. A tall Franciscan priest came into the bakery and asked for him by name.

"*Sí*, Padre, I'm Marcelo Espinosa, how can I help you?"

The priest introduced himself boldly. "I am Padre Juan Torres. I was given your name in Mexico City. I understand you lived in New Mexico. I am on my way to Santa Fe."

The name 'Juan Torres' stood out in Marcelo's memory. Was this the same priest Juan de Oñate had rejected for the caravan? That 'Juan Torres' had been deeply involved with the Inquisition.

"Padre, I'd be happy to share what I remember, but surely much has changed since I was there. Tell me, what mission have you been assigned?"

"Señor Espinosa, I am not a *simple* missionary. I am the *representative* of the Grand Inquisitor in Spain: Defender of the Faith. I am charged with ensuring our colonies here are not *contaminated* with heretics!"

A violent wrench of fear sucked at Marcelo's soul. He recognized this priest's sanctimonious, official tone, sensed his rigid character. This priest is a threat to the life of any Indian, Jew, or nonbeliever he might come across. Marcelo wanted to alert those he had left behind but there was no way to warn them in time.

"I will be here in Santa Barbara for several weeks. I must orient your town's priest before I continue my journey. Surely you agree we must make an example of these Jews so that all know the Church and the King's Laws are sacred."

Then, the priest instructed Marcelo, "It is our duty to identify these insincere Catholics. When you bring your family to Mass tomorrow, my sermon will explain how to expose these Jews." Padre Torres turned and briskly left the bakery. Marcelo was speechless, terrified, in a cold sweat.

Marcelo closed the bakery immediately so he could tell Rosita about the priest's visit. As he repeated Padre Juan Torres words, Rosita began to tremble.

"Marcelo, I am far too frightened to go to Mass. Please, take the boys to church without me." Rosita moaned, "Will this never end?" Memories of her parents' death made her physically ill.

• • • •

On Sunday, Marcelo and his sons went to church and listened to the sermon. Padre Juan Torres instructed from the pulpit, "As a Catholic you must report any of your neighbor's behavior that might indicate the insincerity of a converted Jew."

One by one he listed the ways to identify those people who might be secretly practicing Jewish ceremonies and customs.

"Maybe you've noticed your neighbor never eats pork. Or maybe she always removes sinew before cooking a piece of meat. Do they always have a hearty hot midday meal on Saturday, meat and vegetable stew? Saturday is the Jewish Sabbath.

They always wear freshly cleaned clothes and rest from any work."

"There are other Jewish secret signs: When a family member dies, Jews will eat raw eggs. Some times during the year, they insist on eating only unleavened bread. That's required by their holidays. Maybe you will notice they do not cross themselves or kneel in church appropriately."

The priest closed by telling the congregation that most of the relevant evidence used to incriminate Jews had come from good Catholic's observing and reporting on their neighbors.

• • • •

Damian asked his father, "How can all those things listed by the priest be so bad? We do some of them here in our house…and we are good Catholics!"

"Why does he tell us to report people who clean their house on Friday? Maybe, many people clean their house on Friday, or Saturday, or Sunday, or any day— what difference does it make? We would look like Jews, and we're not. I don't understand!"

Marcelo searched his heart for a reasonable answer. The best he could offer…

"Sometimes, Damian, priests say things that don't make good sense to me either. I will speak privately with the Padre Juan Torres and learn more about it."

"Father, I fear some people will begin to look suspiciously at their friends and neighbors. The priest must know many things listed as Jewish are also practiced by Catholics. Surely, not only Jews have a hot midday meal on Saturdays. Shouldn't we be interested in helping our neighbors?"

This conversation made Marcelo very nervous. He knew both his sons would bring it up again. He had no choice other than reassure them that was good.

Late the following Friday afternoon, Damian and Gabriel were working at the farm. Despite the questions raised by their son and the terror struck into their hearts by Padre Juan Torres, they decided to respect the Shabbat. Together, Marcelo and Rosita lighted two candles and recited the Shema: "Hear, O Israel, the Lord is our God; the Lord is one."

• • • •

Mariela, Rosita's trusted housekeeper, also worked in the bakery. Sometimes she brought Olivia, her teenage daughter, to help with the chores. Late one Friday afternoon, Rosita and her two helpers started to clean the house while Marcelo closed the bakery. Damian and Gabriel had already left to meet their friends.

Rosita had asked for Olivia to sweep the floor from the corners into the center of the room where it would be picked up. This was the custom Rosita learned in her parent's home. Again, Olivia ignored her request and swept the dust and dirt out the front door.

Immediately, Rosita corrected the girl with sharp, angry words. Olivia, smarting from the tongue lashing, turned to Rosita and yelled, "Why can't you sweep the dirt out the front door as everybody does? Why do we do the house cleaning only on Fridays? Padre Juan Torres warned us to look for these things!"

Rosita lost her patience, berated the girl for asking so many questions. Then, she stopped, realizing too much of their secret lifestyle had been revealed. She could never explain why dirt in her house was never swept out the front door. Doing so would be disrespectful to the mezuzah hidden beneath the doorframe.

Rosita quickly regained her composure, apologized to Olivia and Mariela for losing her temper. But, Olivia was angry and resentful. She began crying, yelling at her mother, "You are a fool to work for these people!" And she ran out of the house.

Later, as evening came, Rosita and Marcelo began their Shabbat; Rosita lighted two candles; both said their prayers. Now, waiting the boys to return, they heard a clatter in the storage room. They both froze in horror!

Running to the door, they discovered Olivia, a menacing grin on her face. She had seen and heard everything. Before either could say a word, Olivia bolted for the door and ran into the night. Later, when Damian and Gabriel arrived, they didn't tell them anything. But, both Rosita and Marcelo were terrified. It was a sleepless night. What would happen to their family?

Early the next morning, Marcelo went to find Mariela. He hoped her daughter was no longer angry with Rosita; that she would not tell the priest what she had seen in their home. Mariela told him Olivia had gone to church for Confession. His heart sank. Would she reveal their secret to the local priest, Padre Leonardo?

Marcelo knew that after receiving instruction from Padre Juan Torres, Padre Leonardo was supportive of the Inquisition. Marcelo also knew the Inquisition in Mexico City had recently executed thirteen Jews; one was strangled, twelve burned to death.

Marcelo was paralyzed with fear; his family's future was now in danger.

Chapter 27
This Dreaded Summons

Eight days later a messenger delivered the Inquisition's dreaded summons. Marcelo and Rosita were stunned; fear and uncertainty crushed their hearts.

They had hoped Padre Leonardo might have ignored Olivia's statement, had seen them as good Catholics, members of his parish for many years. He had taught their children in all matters of religion. But, on matters of the Inquisition, they knew Padre Juan Torres had carefully given Padre Leonardo his detailed instructions.

They met with Padre Leonardo the next day. He seemed sympathetic and explained, "I am only following instructions of the Church. You were seen performing what appeared to be a Jewish ritual. Don't worry it's probably nothing."

Then, Padre Leonardo directed them to prepare, within a month's time, a full written confession. He assured them he would do his best to resolve this in their favor. If their confession were sincere and complete, surely they would be pardoned. But, if there were any problems, they could be arrested and taken to Mexico City for a more thorough investigation.

Padre Leonardo's words again struck fear into their hearts. They knew they could lose everything they had to the Inquisition. They left the church shaken, walked home slowly without speaking.

Neither Marcelo nor Rosita was sure they could survive the scrutiny of an investigation. Despite everything they might declare, they were Jews fleeing the Inquisition. They knew both the Crown, and the Catholic Church kept records that might easily incriminate them.

Marcelo still had the forged documents that Abbot Valdez had arranged for him. Those documents would prove that he and his parents are Catholic. Surely, Rosita's records would lead back to her parents, killed by the Inquisition. They would discover that Rosita was spared only because she was believed to be a sincere Catholic.

Both were terrified! Padre Leonardo might create sufficient doubt about their past to have them sent to Mexico City. There, they would suffer what he called a "more complete" investigation. Surely, they both would end up as had their parents; tortured, then burned to death.

At once it was agreed: Damian and Gabriel must leave home immediately. There was no other alternative. If their sons were called before the Inquisition, surely they would be forced to confess. Now, both Marcelo and Rosita understood the terror, the difficult decisions their parents faced when summoned by the Inquisition. Like many Jewish families before, all that mattered was survival of their children.

"Dios Mío! Rosita, our sons will have to understand and endure our own nightmare!"

• • • •

That evening they sat at the dinner table with Damian and Gabriel. Rosita knew both sons, now in their teens, would be hard pressed to understand their secret and their fears. Marcelo reached across the table with both hands. He spoke in a calm measured voice, "Damian, Gabriel... please take my hand. Your mother and I have a secret to reveal."

"You remember Padre Juan Torres preached about how some people claim to be Catholic but are really Jews secretly practicing their own faith. Well, both your mother and I have concealed our Jewish heritage from you. We live our daily lives as converted Christians but we are Jews. Both our parents, and their parents before them, were Jews living in Spain."

Marcelo explained that Queen Isabella and King Ferdinand decided they wanted only Catholics living in the Spanish Empire and the Church agreed. Both Jews and Moors had to decide whether to move on to another country or convert to Christianity.

"Your mother's family moved to Portugal and continued practicing Judaism. My family decided to convert, but secretly practiced their Jewish lifestyle and beliefs. Both your mother and I were raised as a Catholic just like both of you."

Marcelo described his memories of a *Quemadero*, how Jews, Muslims and heretics were persecuted, burned alive at the stake. Damian and Gabriel sat open-mouthed in disbelief, shocked by the horror as their father told how both their parents and families had been arrested, investigated and then killed. How they both had fled to the New World to escape the Inquisition.

Rosita broke in, "*Hijos mios*, please try to understand why we kept this secret from you. We raised you as Catholics to protect you from the Inquisition." Tears flowed as she cried out, "But now we face reality, everything can be taken from us."

Marcelo explained how Mariela's daughter, Olivia, had hidden in their house and observed them light two Shabbat candles, recite their Jewish prayers. Olivia reported this to Padre Leonardo who summoned them for an explanation.

Rosita exclaimed, *"Diablos!* They will do the same thing to us they did to my parents! Confiscate our possessions, jail us for investigation and trial. You both know this can end in death. Since we are...guilty."

"Hijos, Your mother and I have decided you both must leave tomorrow at daybreak. You will go north to my farm near Santa Fe, find my friend Dancing Bull and stay there. If we are released, we will find you there."

"Guilty, guilty of what?" Damian stood, shouted in a quivering voice. "Just saying a few prayers, lighting candles, Padre Leonardo can't ruin our lives just for that!"

Marcelo got up, went to both sons, took Damian firmly by his shoulders, "Damian, please listen carefully. Once the Inquisition has you in their clutches, they will torture you until you tell them whatever they want to hear. That's too dangerous a risk."

Gabriel broke in, "I would rather die than leave home."

"Gabriel, I cannot change what you want to do. Nevertheless, you will leave at daybreak tomorrow!"

Marcelo placed two maps on the table he had saved from Don Juan de Oñate's expedition. The first map described the route north to Santa Fe. He showed them how   to find and follow trail markers they laid down during the expedition.

The second map showed where his farm was located near Santa Fe. They were told to go there first and find Dancing Bull. If he wasn't at the farm, go to the Picuris Indian Pueblo— find him there. Marcelo trusted Dancing Bull to keep their secret and help them get settled on his farm. He warned both sons to avoid any contact with Padre Juan Torres, the priest whom they had heard at church.

Then Marcelo told them a caravan had passed through just a week before, headed north to New Mexico. He told them to ride fast, catch up with them. Tell the caravan's leaders you are joining your parents at Santa Fe. Offer your help to any settlers who might need assistance.

Rosita, trying to hold back her tears, removed the crucifix Marcelo had given her when they were married. Showing it to the boys, she explained, "This crucifix was given to your father by his mother as he was sent away to escape the Inquisition."

Quickly Rosita showed them where the crucifix contained a small hiding place. She explained the small scroll inside contained the Shema, the Jewish proclamation of faith. *"Sh'ma Yisrael,"* she chanted, sobbing, *"Adonai eloheinu Adonai echad."* Hear, O Israel, the Lord is our God, the Lord is one. *"Baruh shem kvod malkhuto l'olam vaed."* Blessed be the name of His glorious kingdom, forever and ever.

Rosita placed the crucifix around Damian's neck. *"Hijos míos,* no matter what may happen to us, never forget your Jewish heritage."

Marcelo gave each son a gold coin. One of those few remaining from what his father had given him when the Inquisition had summoned them. He was thankful he had taught his sons the skills they would need to make their way in the wilderness. He told Damian to show Dancing Bull the crucifix. When Dancing Bull saw the crucifix, he would know it came from Marcelo. He was confident Dancing Bull would understand his sons' plight and help them settle. Outside of Tio Tobias, and Rosita, Dancing Bull was the only living person who knew Marcelo's Jewish heritage.

Marcelo urged both sons to continue worshiping God as Catholics, never revealing their Jewish heritage. He knew the full strength of the Inquisition had already reached New Mexico with Padre Juan Torres.

Gabriel and Damian were ready to depart at daybreak. As Rosita and Marcelo embraced each son for the last time, Marcelo remembered how he felt when leaving his parents. Memories of his parents and their parting came flooding back.

As they watched both boys mount their horses, their hearts were breaking, tears spilling down their cheeks. They watched them quietly ride off, a third horse trailing behind loaded with their supplies. Marcelo was confident they would survive this journey.

• • • •

Rosita and Marcelo continued to live their lives as if nothing had happened. They told friends that their sons had left to find work in Mexico City.

Mariela was shocked, deeply saddened, when Olivia admitted she had reported Rosita and Marcelo to Padre Leonardo during Confession.

Olivia now regretted what she had done. She pleaded with her mother, "All I did was what the priests told us to do."

With tears in her eyes, she offered to change her story, say that the Espinosa's were perfect Catholics. They both knew the Inquisitor would tear her testimony to shreds.

A few days later Padre Leonardo summoned Marcelo and Rosita to his small office next to the church. He was obviously uncomfortable in this situation but made it clear that Padre Torres had carefully instructed him on how to conduct a hearing. With a cold, detached expression, he read them their instructions, what they must do to prepare for their hearing.

"As the accused, you must confess your sins. You will provide a written statement recognizing your sins in full detail. It is only through sincere repentance that you will avoid punishment. The test of true repentance will be your sincerity."

Padre Leonardo explained that the best way to prove sincerity would be to name others they knew to be secret Jews. He reminded them, if they were found guilty, their children would suffer disgrace and poverty for their sins. If there were any doubt as to the truth or sincerity of the accused, he had been instructed to refer the case to the Office of the Inquisition in Mexico City.

"Since we have no lawyers here, I have appointed a parishioner to serve as your advocate helping you prepare for a preliminary hearing."

Marcelo and Rosita left his office in a state of shock knowing full well their peril. Regardless of the church, they were, in truth, guilty. If only they could convince Padre Leonardo that, in their hearts, they had done nothing wrong.

• • • •

With the advocate's help, Marcelo and Rosita prepared documents stating their full confession, itemizing every detail of their transgressions and clearly expressing their repentance. They begged forgiveness for observing the Jewish Sabbath: avoiding work on that day, lighting Shabbat candles at sunset on Fridays, reciting Jewish prayers and observing Jewish holidays. They agreed to do penance, promised never to stray again from the path of Jesus Christ and the Holy Catholic Church.

By confessing each of their transgressions and expressing penitence, they hoped for a harsh but just punishment from Padre Leonardo. They would avoid further investigation in Mexico City where the Inquisition would be merciless.

Their advocate argued their case well. Several witnesses who worked for Marcelo at the bakery confirmed their way of life was different from most others in the community. They confirmed that Marcelo always closed the store early on Fridays; a helper managed the bakery on Saturdays.

There were no witnesses who would attest to Marcelo being a true Catholic. Nor were there witnesses to support Rosita's case. One member of the Oñate expedition was summoned. He verified that Marcelo, while in the new colony, was a dedicated soldier and lived an exemplary Catholic life.

Their home had been searched for anything that might prove they were observant Jews. Nothing was found other than a makeshift, questionable Menorah that supposedly held their Chanukah candles.

As the hearing ended, Padre Leonardo knew the advocate had failed to meet all the requirements stipulated so clearly by Padre Torres. They should have come forth with names of others who were also secret Jews. Furthermore, he did not believe the story of their sons leaving to find work in Mexico City. They must disclose where their children could be found.

• • • •

Several days later their advocate came to the bakery to confirm that Padre Leonardo had judged their repentance as lacking sincerity. They returned to his office immediately.

"Marcelo, Rosita," Padre Leonardo demanded, "You must identify other Jews hiding from the Inquisition. Do you not realize your lives are at stake?"

The advocate also insisted on the whereabouts of their sons. He hoped he could convince Padre Leonardo to change his mind. "Please tell him. You'll be treated less harshly if you tell him about your sons."

Then, Padre Leonardo threatened to send them to Mexico City for further investigation. Both would have died there and then rather than reveal their sons' true whereabouts.

Rosita insisted time and time again. "Our sons went to Mexico City to find work." She was dangerously close to losing her temper. Why won't he believe me?

Padre Leonardo declared, "You are not telling the truth!"

Rosita could never forgive the Inquisition. They murdered my sister and my parents. Now they want to destroy my family!

She broke down and screamed…

"I— will— never— accept— the— Catholic— Church…Never! No one so cruel could ever have my loyalty."

She raised her fist, pointed a finger to the heavens in accusation and released her rage; blasphemies spewed forth from her lips.

Marcelo felt defenseless; Rosita had destroyed any question of repentance.

Padre Leonardo, inexperienced as he was with affairs of the Inquisition, was frantic; he had to gain control. Grasping the crucifix on his desk, he raised it high, facing them. He pounded his gavel three times to silence Rosita. "I declare you both guilty of blasphemy! You will be jailed until taken to Mexico City for judgment."

Marcelo and Rosita were placed in separate cells so that they couldn't see or talk to each other. As Marcelo glanced around his filthy cell, the stench of human waste was overpowering. He cursed himself. What have I done to deserve this?

• • • •

Padre Leonardo issued orders for their immediate transfer to the Office of the Inquisition in Mexico City. Marcelo and Rosita knew their dreams and hopes for life were lost forever. They were penniless; the Inquisition would confiscate all their possessions.

Rosita and Marcelo were briefly reunited when armed soldiers took them to their house. The soldiers had been ordered to search for any incriminating evidence that might have been missed when previously examined. As the soldiers searched, they destroyed the family's furniture and personal belongings. Everything was thrown into a pile on the kitchen floor.

Looking on was devastating for Marcelo and Rosita. As the soldiers nailed their front door closed, both were sobbing. Rosita, overwhelmed, gave up all hope. Their once happy home was destroyed forever. They were returned to jail, again separated and alone.

Rosita, stared blankly, refused to speak. Deeply traumatized, she could no longer cope with her emotions.

Chapter 28
Mexico City – The Inquisition

Without warning, three soldiers dragged Marcelo and Rosita out of their jail cells. Their hands were tied securely behind their backs. Then, they were shoved to a caged, horse-drawn *carreta* holding three other prisoners.

As the soldiers shoved them into the cart, the jailer shouted, "*Rápido, Adelante* move quickly, wretched creatures. You're going to Mexico City with the caravan."

Slamming the cart's door shut, the jailer hollered, "You'll surely be wanting these papers but I doubt they'll do you any good!" He threw Marcelo's worn leather pouch into the *carreta*. Marcelo opened the pouch and was relieved to see the forged documents Abbot Valdez had prepared.

Marcelo had not seen Rosita since they were returned to the jail. He could hardly believe how she had deteriorated. Her face was a blank, her speech jumbled and confused. She had lost so much weight she looked like a skeleton. As Marcelo held her arms, he looked deeply into her eyes. The woman he loved so dearly was no longer there. Rosita had given up!

Marcelo peered out through the bars of the cart. He was humiliated to see the crowd; many had been the bakery's customers, their friends. As the cart passed them by, they pointed, laughed and jeered, "Heretics!— Jews!— Heathens!— Burn in Hell!"

The caravan waited for them at the edge of town. Marcelo, Rosita and the other three prisoners were chained together and led to a larger wagon enclosed with wooden bars. Struggling up into the wagon they sat together on a long, hard bench. Later that afternoon their chains were removed as the caravan rolled forward on its journey to Mexico City.

They sat crouched as the wagon rumbled over potholes and bumps in the roadway. As days passed, their clothes became more frayed and dirty. There wasn't enough room in the wagon for five prisoners to stretch out, sleep or rest. Soon, their bodies were racked with pain, cramps or spasms.

Men relieved themselves by urinating through the wagon's wooden bars. For Rosita, there was no delicate way. Eventually, she had to squat while Marcelo tried to hide her from view. When the caravan stopped for the evening, prisoners were escorted to a private place to relieve themselves. There was no end to the indignities; they began to feel even less human.

The three prisoners shared their stories of how they came to this miserable journey. One had killed a rancher while trying to steal his horse. Another killed his wife when he caught her with another man. The third was a convicted thief who had escaped from the town jail and was caught stealing again. Rosita and Marcelo were the only prisoners summoned by the Inquisition.

Their journey would last four weeks. As the prisoners bonded with each other through their pain and suffering, they tried to make Rosita as comfortable as possible. When they arrived in Mexico City they were sick, malnourished, weak and in constant pain. They had survived eating only bread and beans washed down with murky water.

The wagon's first stop was the Mexico City prison where the three male prisoners were taken from the *carreta*. Then, the wagon continued on to the Palace of the Inquisition on the Plaza de Santo Domingo. There, four priests dressed in dark brown hooded robes, took Marcelo and Rosita from the wagon. They were separated, stripped, washed, and then dressed with the *sanbenito*, the penitential garment and cap that identified them as Jews or heretics. They were placed in separate cells, distant one from the other.

• • • •

Marcelo soon found a way to send word to his uncle, Tio Tobias— he and Rosita were imprisoned in the Palace of the Inquisition. Marcelo worried that his uncle might be placed in danger by involving him in their predicament. But there was no other alternative.

Upon receiving Marcelo's plea for help, Tobias immediately went to the palace, used his influence to gain permission to see Marcelo. Tobias was anxious; how could Marcelo have become involved with the Inquisition?

A guard led Tobias to Marcelo's cell. As they hurried down the prison's dark corridors, Tobias knew that by helping Marcelo, his own secret might be revealed. He was also a hidden Jew, Marcelo was his family: He had to help.

The guard inserted a large key and swung open the heavy cell door. Tobias looked in, saw Marcelo and spoke in disbelief: "Marcelo…What have they done to you? Where is Rosita? And the children?"

Tobias entered the cell, sat down next to Marcelo on the dank floor and embraced his nephew. He had convinced the Captain of the

Guards that Marcelo's imprisonment must be a mistake. "My nephew cannot be a Jew."

Fearful they might be overheard, Tobias whispered, "Tell me what happened. What led to all this?" Marcelo, tears in his eyes, haltingly told Tobias how a servant had betrayed them. Betrayal led to a trial and imprisonment. Marcelo's sadness twisted to fury as the whole story unfolded. His uncle was stunned, banged his fist against the cell wall in disbelief. He feared for them all.

"Please Tio, I'm not concerned about myself; we must find a way to save Rosita. I'm afraid she has lost her mind."

"Marcelo, I'll help Rosita but I have to protect you too. Do you still have your documents? I'll need them to convince the tribunal you aren't a Jew."

"Yes, my documents are here in this leather pouch. Take them now; keep them safe."

"Tio, there is one person who might help us. I knew her as Ana Aldones before she married Juan Benavidez the Alcalde of Mexico City."

"Díos me libre! Ana Aldones de Benavidez is a very powerful woman. How did you get to know her? "

Marcelo explained he had met Ana aboard the ship coming from Cadiz. They became friends then lovers. Ana's family in Spain had arranged her marriage to the Alcalde. She dreaded her future as his wife. As lovers, they took advantage of their time together. They knew they could never have a life together.

"Tio, I believe Ana will help us. Let her know I'm here, she'll find a way to use her husband's power."

"Does Ana know the truth of your Jewish heritage?" Tobias asked.

"No, Tio, she doesn't. I'm sure it wouldn't matter. I know she'll do everything she can to get us out of this horrible prison."

"Padre Sanchez is another person who might help." Marcelo explained they had become good friends on the ship coming from Spain. They were together in New Mexico. Sanchez was troubled by the way Indians were being mistreated, so he had returned to Mexico City. "I'm sure he'll be a loyal and convincing witness."

"Marcelo, before anything else, I've got to find you a lawyer."

Two close friends helped Tobias convince *Abogado* Sergio Acosta to act in Marcelo's defense. Acosta, a lawyer well versed in ecclesiastic affairs, reluctantly agreed to take his case.

"Tobias, I swore I'd never take a case like this again."

Acosta explained that making a case with the Inquisition's tribunal is a very humbling experience. It means reasoning with priests who have already decided upon a conclusion. Before any hearing is granted, they make sure the prisoner confirms whatever they want said, regardless of its truth.

"That's just one of the many frustrations!" he said.

Acosta asked two priests involved with the Inquisition to review Marcelo's documents. He had worked with them before and respected their good sense. They reported that little could be done to release Marcelo prior to his hearing.

• • • •

Tobias and *Abogado* Sergio Acosta came back to meet with Marcelo in his cell. Marcelo was shaken when Tobias reported they had failed in their quest to have him released from prison.

"I don't understand, my documents prove I was born and baptized a Catholic in Spain. Both Rosita and I have received the Holy Sacraments of the Church. Sadly, Rosita doesn't have proof of her Catholic upbringing."

Acosta questioned Marcelo, "Have you ever prepared and signed a freely given confession of guilt?"

"Yes, I did."

Marcelo explained that when they were summoned, the town's priest counseled them to make a full written confession. He led them to believe that, by doing so, they would receive a simple penance and absolution. So, they wrote and delivered a confession.

Later, the priest demanded they prove their sincerity by giving names of other secret Jewish families and the whereabouts of their sons. When Marcelo refused, the priest brusquely turned against them, ordered them arrested and jailed.

"Is it possible," Marcelo asked Acosta, "that you know the wife of the Alcalde, Juan Benavides? Her name is Ana Aldones de Benavides."

"Yes, I've met her several times. Tobias has already mentioned her name. Do you really think she might be willing to help on your behalf?"

"Yes, I'm sure she will. Years ago, we became good friends as we made our passage to Mexico."

"Marcelo, I'll make sure she knows of your dilemma before the day ends."

The lawyer cautioned Marcelo that, in an attempt to draw out the truth, he and Rosita might be subjected to torture. Both Marcelo and Rosita had been weakened and distraught by the four-week journey. Marcelo doubted he could tolerate torture. He knew Rosita must still be traumatized. Torture could kill either one of them.

Abruptly, the guard banged on the door, announced their visiting time was up. As they left, Sergio told Marcelo, "We'll see Rosita now. We'll try to reassure her this mayhem will go away; soon, she will be with her family again."

· · · ·

As he entered Rosita's cell, Tobias could not believe his eyes. This couldn't be the same beautiful woman he had found for Marcelo. She was curled up on the floor in a fetal position, her face a blank stare.

Fearfully she looked up at Tobias and screamed, "Don't— touch— me! Don't— touch— me! *Don't— touch— me!*"

Sergio and Tobias took her arms, lifted her gently to a chair. Calming down slightly, she shouted. "Demons surround me! Blasphemy they say! Demons are everywhere!"

Rosita lowered her chin until it touched her chest; she hardly moved, her eyes were tightly closed. Then, sobbing, she quietly chanted the Shema, the Jewish proclamation of faith.

"Sh'ma Yisrael, Adonai eloheinu Adonai echad...Baruh shem kvod malkhuto l'olam vaed..."

Rosita took a quick breath, then, in a whisper, she chanted the Shema again...and again...and over again: "...Sh'ma Yisrael, Adonai eloheinu Adonai echad...Baruh shem kvod malkhuto l'olam vaed..."

Tobias tried to reason with Rosita, but she didn't hear. He realized there was no way they could help or comfort her. She was truly traumatized; she could no longer cope with her emotions. Rosita was no longer there...

• • • •

Marcelo's cell was located just off the main passageway leading to a large, domed chamber. It was there that torture was given those prisoners who refused to reveal the truth. Many prisoners passed by on their way to the dreaded torture room.

Marcelo could see through a crack in his door. Prisoner's feet were chained one to the other, hands closely tied to each ankle; they shuffled along like a crab, bowed over their feet. Each step had to cause agonizing pain; Marcelo heard them moan. Terror sliced into his heart as he visualized what this would do to Rosita and to himself.

Marcelo's day for questioning arrived, his dreaded visit to the domed chamber. Two young friars entered his cell. He was quickly blindfolded; hands bound to his ankles. Doubled over, with a rope around his neck, he was pulled like a donkey into the passageway and led to the domed chamber.

It seemed impossible that "Men of God" could be doing this to him. These were priests of the same order that had taught him, when a boy, of a loving and forgiving God.

Marcelo felt hands loosening his bonds. Slowly, he stood tall; his blindfold was removed. The room was dark, damp and musty. He faced a long wooden table, two large candles burned at either end. Behind, an enormous wooden crucifix was mounted against a white wall made of stones. The two candles illuminated three older, hooded Inquisitor priests. Marcelo looked directly at each priest.

The priest seated in the center spoke softly. "Please tell us your name and where you were born. Are you a baptized Catholic?"

Marcelo answered calmly, and then asked if his attorney had presented documents verifying he was a Catholic.

"For now, just answer my questions. We will ask for your attorney's presence in due time."

The priest on the left questioned, "Do you believe in Jesus Christ as your Savior, and his Holy Catholic Church?"

"Yes, I do." Marcelo declared clearly.

"Have you ever practiced Jewish rituals in your home?"

"No," he responded. "I am Capitan Marcelo Espinosa, a baptized, confirmed Catholic and a retired officer in the Crown's military."

"Is your wife a Jew?"

"No."

The third priest spoke harshly, "Perhaps I can help you remember the truth."

Marcelo glanced further to his right; saw the rack.

"Come! Lie down on that wooden bed. Perhaps a little pain will improve your memory."

The three friars took him to the rack, tightly tied his hands and feet so its levers stretched his body.

The priest repeated, "Is your wife a Jew?"

Marcelo was silent. He heard two clicks.

He screamed as the first turn of the rack seared his body with pain.

"Do you know any Jews?"

"No!" he gasped, "I do not."

A nod from the priest, another two clicks.

Marcelo twisted violently, his shriek echoed through the prison.

"Where are your sons?"

"I don't know!"

Another two clicks dislocated Marcelo's shoulder and silenced his excruciating pain with the bliss of oblivion. Marcelo awoke in his cell, his body throbbing with pain.

The friars came for him three days in a row. He was tied, led to the chamber and placed on the rack. Marcelo did not give them the answers they sought. Each day he managed to resist until unconscious. He asked himself, "How long can I last?"

On the fourth day another younger priest came to his cell. He sat on a stool beside Marcelo's straw mat. "Captain Espinosa, I arranged for you to be spared the rack today. I'd like to be your friend. If you'll just tell me the truth, I can make sure there will be no more torture."

Marcelo looked at him, "Padre all my answers have been the truth. How can I change them? Do you want me to lie?"

The priest was furious, rose quickly and hissed, "You will burn in Hell."

• • • •

Marcelo knew when Rosita was taken to the chamber. He recognized her voice as she cried out his name: "Maarrrcelllo!" Marcelo knew Rosita would have been stripped, placed on the rack. Her hands and feet tied to the device just as he had been tied.

The inquisitor stated the question: "Are you a Jew?"

Rosita was fully withdrawn, traumatized.

Two clicks. Silence.

"Are— you— a— Jew?"

Three more clicks. Rosita screamed.

Her scream turned into the first words of the Shema.

"Sh'ma Yisrael, Adonai…"

Then, silence.

Marcelo knew Rosita could no longer feel pain; she was dead.

He wept uncontrollably.

• • • •

Two guards burst into Marcelo's cell. He was blindfolded, hands tied together, then pulled hurriedly along the long corridor. Within a few minutes, he knew they were no longer inside the jail; no foul odors or screams, the air smelled clean. He heard a door open. Then, the guards forced him to sit in a chair. He felt them untie his hands, then remove his blindfold.

Marcelo blinked rapidly. Am I dreaming? Ana is standing here in front of me!

Speechless, both smiled, stared at each other for a few fully charged seconds.

Ana turned to the guards, with a commanding voice, "Please leave the room now." The guards left reluctantly; if needed they would be just outside the door. When the door had closed behind them, Ana went to Marcelo, knelt before him, reached up, and touched his cheek. He looks so helpless, dirty, emaciated.

"My dearest Marcelo, what have they done to you? I know why you're being held. My husband will help me get you released. Everything will be all right."

Marcelo's eyes were fixed firmly upon Ana's face. Memories, sealed shut, began to unravel. In a voice broken with emotion, he said, "Ana, I'm so grateful you're here. I'm sorry you have to see me like this."

Marcelo confessed both his body and spirit had been broken; his life ruined. Should he survive, his life would have little meaning; his family had been destroyed. "My wife was tortured until she died, my children are gone." Marcelo wept. Ana held him close until his tears were no more.

"Marcelo, please listen. We don't have much time; let's not waste a minute. Your attorney gave me all the facts. My husband is seriously ill, but he has enough strength to help save you. It's going to take time so you must stay strong and sane."

"I will… I promise…" Marcelo broke into tears, bowed his head in shame. Ana held him; they said no more.

Then, Marcelo looked up, "Ana, please tell me something about your life."

"Living with the Alcalde has been as I feared, horrible. I could never have learned to love him. I yearned for the joy of love we had shared. I'm envious you found someone else…I never lost my love for you."

"Marcelo, do you remember what that fortuneteller in Havana told me? She said, 'One day your lover will be in serious trouble; your fate is to save his life.' She was right!"

The guard was knocking at the door, rattling his keys. He opened the door, "Señora, your time is up! You must go now."

"Marcelo, I leave you with my love, please be strong."

• • • •

Marcelo's torture stopped. Either the Inquisitors believed he wouldn't reveal any more information. Or, influence was playing its proper role.

Several days later, Sergio Acosta began meeting with Marcelo daily, preparing him for his imminent trial. Acosta believed his case stood a good chance of release because of his fully documented papers. Marcelo had never revealed he was Jewish.

Sitting alone in his cell, Marcelo had resigned himself to Rosita's death— and, maybe, to his own. But, when he thought of his two sons, Damian and Gabriel, his spirit rallied and soared.

Marcelo knew he had to live: "I promised my sons I'd find them!"

Chapter 29
Marcelo's Trial

The day of Marcelo's trial was now upon them. Two friars dressed Marcelo in the traditional *sanbenito* attire. They led him, manacled, to the Inquisition's principal chamber located in the Dominican monastery, part of the Church of Santo Domingo. The chamber was illuminated by two sets of three large candles bound together. The Grand Inquisitor sat behind the center of a long wooden table, two hooded Dominican priests at each side. A large ceiling high crucifix stood behind them, at its side, the banner of the Inquisition.

Marcelo stood before the inquisitors, his manacles removed. The priest seated to the right of the Grand Inquisitor rose, took documents from the table, pushed back his hood, and read aloud the charges.

"Marcelo Espinosa you are hereby charged with three violations of the Inquisition."

"One: You freely confessed in writing to observance of the Jewish Law of Moses in your daily life. Witnesses bore the fact that you recited Jewish prayers on Friday evenings and avoided work on Saturdays. You practiced rules set by Jewish Law regarding personal habits, clothing and cleaning your house."

"Two: In due time and with careful examination, your repentance was determined to be to be insincere."

"Three: You pretend to be a Catholic but are, in fact, a Jew."

The Grand Inquisitor spoke, "How say you to these charges?"

Marcelo said clearly, "*Exelencia*, I am innocent of each charge."

The priest scoffed, "Do you claim to have proof?"

Marcelo turned to the Grand Inquisitor, "*Exelencia*, with your permission, I request that my advocate, *Abogado* Sergio Acosta, present my defense against these three charges."

Each priest looked contemptuous as Acosta stood, prepared to begin Marcelo's defense with *el discurso de la vida*, his Christian life story.

Acosta was able to prove, beyond a doubt, that both Marcelo's parents, and his family over generations, were Catholic. They had all been honorable Christians, defenders of the Holy Faith. Acosta's detailed explanation was supported by documents, those prepared by Abbot Valdez in Madrid.

Acosta proceeded to describe Marcelo's dedication to the Catholic Church and the Seven Holy Sacraments. As an infant he was duly baptized. Then, as a youth, he received Confirmation and Eucharist. Later, he regularly confessed his sins and received a priest's absolution. The very priest who had denounced them had married Marcelo and his wife. Documents, including his birth certificate, proved that Marcelo had been brought up in Abbot Valdez' parish and was educated there by Franciscan monks in his monastery.

Then, Acosta confirmed that Marcelo, living the life of a true Catholic, had become a novice to the Franciscan order. He was duly prepared by Abbott

Martinez of the Order of Cistercians of the Strict Observance at his Trappist monastery in Spain.

Marcelo had come to New Spain voluntarily as a Franciscan missionary. When he arrived in Mexico City, he sought religious counsel and decided to leave the religious order to attend military school. He thought he could better serve God in the Crown's military. Commissioned a captain, he had served a long and distinguished career as a Christian officer.

Acosta, before calling Tobias Espinosa, qualified his testimony as that of a devoted Catholic and decorated officer in the service of the Crown, a long-standing and highly respected member of Mexico City's community.

Tobias confirmed he had known Marcelo since birth. He described his nephew as a sincere Catholic and a devoted military officer who had volunteered to join Don Juan de Oñate on his expedition to New Mexico.

Two soldiers who had served under Marcelo's command on the expedition to New Mexico also testified to his integrity as an officer and sincerity as a Catholic.

Fernando Trujillo was the leader of a caravan that, over many years, had regularly traded with New Mexico. Trujillo had met with Marcelo many times as his caravan passed through Santa Barbara. Trujillo testified that Marcelo's business had been very successful, and that he was a valuable member of the community. He had frequently helped the town's miners and aided travelers who were heading north.

Acosta then called a medical doctor. He instructed the doctor to examine Marcelo's private parts. Acosta then stated, "The Jewish Law of Moses requires circumcision. Is Marcelo Espinosa circumcised?" The doctor confirmed, "No, he is not."

The Grand Inquisitor nodded, used his gavel and prayer to adjourn proceedings until the following day.

• • • •

Testimony in Marcelo's defense continued the next morning. Marcelo was exhausted, he hadn't been able to eat or sleep. He watched as two Dominican priests, with a certain degree of respect, escorted Ana into the Inquisition's chamber. She looked so thin, elegant in a long, flowing black silk dress. Yet, her voice was clear and determined. Ana glanced to Marcelo; as their eyes met, Marcelo saw the fire of determination she would bring to her testimony.

The two Dominican priests guided Ana to a chair facing the Inquisition's table.

The Grand Inquisitor showed his surprise, "Please, tell me why our esteemed Alcalde's wife, Doña Ana de Benavides, is here today? Why do we have the privilege of your presence? Do you know this man, Espinosa?"

"*Exelencia, muchas gracias...*Excellency, may I thank you for your kindness. I regret my husband is unable to be here. As you know, his health has been failing. He entrusted me to speak for him, tell you what I know, in his name."

Ana stated that she met Marcelo when crossing from Spain. He was a novice friar and had saved her life during a dreadful storm at sea. She knew that Marcelo had learned and practiced Catholic rites and prayers. He used his knowledge throughout the voyage to help pacify nervous passengers and to sanctify those who had died at sea. She told how Marcelo had given her Catholic religious instruction. And Ana testified she had never observed any sign of Jewish behavior.

"*Exelencia*, I pray your deliberations will find it possible to set free Marcelo Espinosa. He is an exemplary Catholic, the friar who saved my life."

As Ana rose and turned to leave the chamber, she glanced at Marcelo, sent him a message of encouragement and strength. Within that glance, Marcelo read a clear message of love.

As the two Dominican priests accompanied Ana from the chamber, she discreetly took three deep breaths to steady herself. Her heart had skipped and fluttered; she fought the tightness growing in her breast. Ana knew she would always love Marcelo. Somehow she must keep him from harm.

The chamber door opened again. Padre Sanchez, Franciscan priest and Marcelo's devoted friend, boldly entered the chamber. His sandals thumped loudly on the stone floor as he walked swiftly across the chamber to the awaiting chair. Sanchez turned to look at Marcelo and gave him a confident smile.

The Grand Inquisitor broke the silence, "Padre, state your name and credentials, tell us what you know of the accused, Marcelo Espinosa."

Padre Sanchez confirmed his own Franciscan assignment. Then, he stated that Marcelo had received religious training to become a Franciscan monk at a Trappist monastery near Madrid, Spain. He and another Franciscan missionary priest met Marcelo in Cadiz. Marcelo had accompanied them when they left Cadiz sailing to Vera Cruz. Sanchez expressed approval of how Marcelo, on the sea journey, had performed his duties as a novice monk.

Later, Padre Sanchez said he worked with Marcelo in New Mexico. Marcelo was a Captain serving with Don Juan de Oñate. In this later role, Sanchez pointed out, Marcelo was deeply involved in providing vital support to the Franciscan missionaries' evangelizing the Indians to Christianity.

The hearing had now lasted for two full days. Acosta had carefully observed and noted the reactions of the Grand Inquisitor and each priest seated besides him. He was confident their initial, contemptuous reactions had been modified. The several witnesses' testimony had been well received; no significant objections had been brought forth. Chances were strong that Marcelo could be acquitted.

It was then that Acosta asked for the Grand Inquisitor's consent to close his argument. Acosta rose, took time to look squarely at each priest. He spoke clearly in a slow measured cadence:

"*Excelencia*…Padres. Yes, Captain Marcelo Espinosa did sign a confession of guilt. He signed that confession only when his parish priest had promised a simple penance and absolution. And…he did so only to protect his wife!"

"You may be sure that Captain Marcelo Espinosa is fully repentant and begs your forgiveness for his involvement with his wife's Jewish practices. Gracias."

Acosta was sure the only way Marcelo could be spared was to place blame upon Rosita. Time would prove him right.

Marcelo was dismayed. Acosta had portrayed him as a perfect Catholic deluded by his wife to venture into Judaism. But he kept his silence. The trial was over.

• • • •

Two days later, Marcelo was brought before the Grand Inquisitor; his chains were removed. As he stood there, head bowed, the priest seated to the right of the Grand Inquisitor rose to speak.

"Captain Espinosa, This court has decided you are innocent of those charges brought against you. You are free to go."

The Grand Inquisitor interrupted.

"Captain Espinosa, we know you lied when you made a confession of guilt to your parochial priest. We recognized you had acted recklessly; you should have been more prudent. So, you will have to share part of the blame for your wife's mistakes. Your sentence of penance will be read at the next auto de fé…"

"Now you are free to go."

• • • •

Tio Tobias was there for Marcelo as he left the Inquisition's chamber. "Come Marcelo, a bath and fresh clothes are waiting for you at home." He had been in this prison for more than two months.

"Tio, I cannot leave Rosita's remains behind."

"Marcelo, I have already made arrangements for her funeral. It's a miracle they found you innocent! At least one of you survived this insanity. Nothing can be done until you publically receive the sentence for your penance at the *auto de fé*, the *Quemadero*."

There was no choice. Marcelo had to stay at his uncle's home until his sentence was read publicly. All his money had been spent on the trial. The final amount wouldn't have been paid without his uncle's help.

In spite of his acquittal it had been ordered that, for the next few months, he must wear the *sanbenito* robe whenever he left the house. The *sanbenito* robe was made of coarse yellow material with a large "X" stamped on both the front and back. It was draped over the shoulders and extended to the knees.

Marcelo stayed at his uncle's home as much as possible. He was humiliated wearing that hideous robe in public. Once his penance was completed, he knew this humiliation would last forever. This *sanbenito* robe, labeled with his name, would be placed on display in Mexico City's Cathedral.

Soon after Marcelo's release, Acosta confirmed that the Inquisition court had found Rosita guilty. Had she not died from her torture on the rack, she would have been burned at the stake.

Acosta quoted the Inquisitor: "The crime she committed is heresy and heresy is evil incarnate. Therefore, the punishment must emulate the fires of hell."

Marcelo shuddered, "These priests are the evil ones! God could not condone such torture. Surely, they will be the ones damned to burn in hell!"

Marcelo's anger melted into grief, and he wept, "She did not deserve to die!" He realized that Rosita's downfall was her honesty. She had clung tenaciously to her Jewish faith. She refused to defend herself from the people she hated most.

Marcelo was haunted by nightmares and sleepless nights; his waking hours were filled with pain and despair. Rosita was dead.

Marcelo was consoled by a recurring vision of their two sons, Damian and Gabriel. He struggled to remember each wonderful year he had shared with Rosita. They had raised a family; a dream neither had dared hope for. A sword had pierced his heart; the pain would remain forever.

Marcelo took comfort that, together, they had deceived the Inquisition and kept their children far from their grasp.

• • • •

Marcelo had received permission to collect and bury Rosita's remains with one stipulation: burial must be in the Jewish cemetery located on the city's outskirts. He received a small rectangular coffin from the jailers at the Inquisition's palace.

Tobias' servants opened a grave in the cemetery. Marcelo, sobbing, promised Rosita he would find their children, be part their lives. Uncle Tobias stood by Marcelo's side, embraced him. He too was moved to tears.

Dark days followed. Marcelo was filled with anger and guilt. He blamed himself for Rosita's death. Both their parents had met the same fate. The Inquisition's judgment was right in one aspect: He had acted recklessly; he should have been more prudent. They both had become comfortable, careless in their Jewish practices.

How could he have allowed himself be lulled into that false sense of security? He prodded himself; "I learned nothing from my father! His carelessness destroyed our family." Marcelo fell into a bottomless abyss of depression.

Sergio Acosta brought the news: "The *auto de fé*— the *Quemadero* is next Sunday!"

As was the custom, those who attend— men, women and children— were promised special treatment in heaven.

Marcelo mumbled, "How can these people believe this madness?"

. . . .

Sunday morning Marcelo knew he had to be at the *Quemadero*. Acosta had negotiated his release from marching with the prisoners. He decided to wear his normal clothes fearing the crowd might turn against him. He would tuck his *sanbenito* robe under his arm just in case he was ordered to wear it. Should he be ordered to wear the *sanbenito*, before putting it on, he would wander away from the crowd.

Marcelo and Tio Tobias arrived early at the city square. They were astonished! The setting for the *auto de fé*— the *Quemadero*— had all the appearances of a circus. People were coming in droves, a festive atmosphere, all smiles and laughter. A big grandstand had been built for spectators. Vendors were at every corner selling food and religious souvenirs. The altar was there next to the stakes awaiting their victims.

Marcelo was jolted into reality. He heard the somber drumbeat that proclaimed the processions arrival. Twelve Dominican priests led the parade holding high the Inquisition's flag, their faces hidden by black and white cowls.

The Church hicrarchy followed, archbishop, bishops and priests. Then came a strutting group of city magistrates, each wearing the symbol of their office. The military drummers followed striking the slow sonorous cadence of impending death. An officer and four soldiers in full military regalia, mounted on horses, escorted the prisoner's wagon. Then, three horse-drawn carts, each loaded with stacks of wood for the Quemadero fires.

A Dominican priest took his place on the altar, turned to face the crowd, made the sign of the cross and shouted out, "En nombre del Padre, Hijo y Espirito Santo."

When Mass was completed, a hooded priest climbed the stairs to the altar. Turning to the crowd, he called out the name of each prisoner, their verdict, and punishment. Marcelo listened carefully, heard his name at the very end of the list.

"Marcelo Espinosa...Not Guilty...Wear *sanbenito* for two months." Marcelo Espinosa was the only name not condemned to burn at the stake.

The prisoners, all wearing the *sanbenito*, were led to their stake and tied in place. They were motionless as the priest walked to each one, extended the crucifix, begged each prisoner to repent, kiss the cross, and ask for God's forgiveness.

Then, the priest read the proclamation, "Having been tried by the Tribunal of the Holy Office of the Inquisition, found to be guilty of disobeying God's laws, practicing heresy and refusing repentance, you are hereby sentenced to die in Hell's fire."

The crowd shouted angrily, "Burn the Jews! Death to the heretics!"

Several friars put torches to the wood stacked beneath each prisoner. Flames quickly rose to surround each one. They screamed wildly with pain as the flames devoured them. When their screams ended, only the sound of crackling flesh could be heard. Smoke, spiraling skyward carried their ashes. The crowd was silent; they drifted away slowly, one by one.

Marcelo had seen his own parents' horrendous death within the flames.

• • • •

Tio Tobias insisted that Marcelo remain at his home until fully recovered from his sadness and depression. Marcelo's soul ached. What would he do? Where would he go? He knew he could never return to his home and the bakery in Santa Barbara.

With time, Marcelo began to recover his health, in spite of his bleak outlook on life. Gradually he grew stronger, began to feel frustrated by the time it took for his body to heal. Eventually, he recognized that life not death is important. Damian and Gabriel had to be the center of his life. Death is mourned and slowly but surely fades into the past.

Marcelo stayed with his Tio Tobias for several months recuperating, slowly strengthening his body. As the Inquisition ordered, he took the *sanbenito* robe to the Cathedral. It would be displayed with the other robes of those who had suffered examination.

Marcelo had learned his lesson the hard way. Survival demands the surrender of his Jewish heritage— forever. The Crown, the Inquisition, the Catholic Church had won.

Now, Marcelo felt an urgency to find Damian and Gabriel.

Were they alive? Did they find their way to his farm? Had they met Dancing Bull? He had to know!

Chapter 30
Reencounter with Love

"You must give up this idea of going back to New Mexico!" As he spoke, Tobias' hand was firmly placed on Marcelo's shoulder. Marcelo was busy making preparations to leave within the month joining Fernando Trujillo on his next caravan going north.

"Marcelo, you've suffered enough. You endured a long, painful ordeal with the Inquisition and you were acquitted. Now, you're free to make your home here just as I have. There's no need for you to go back into the wilderness."

"Tio, I know you're concerned with my health and happiness. But, I must search for Damian and Gabriel. Rosita and I wanted them to know they were born with great love and pride. There hasn't been a day that I haven't longed for them. I promised Rosita I'd find them. Tio, please try to understand. I don't have a choice."

"Marcelo, I knew that would be your answer. It's surely not the answer I'd prefer, but you do have my admiration and respect. So, go find your boys with my blessing!"

"Tio, I do need another favor. Before I leave, please invite the Alcalde's wife, Doña Ana, to lunch. I want to thank her formally for her help at the trial. She has been a valuable friend."

"An excellent idea, Marcelo. I'll send her an invitation before midday."

Tobias, over the years, knew Ana Benevidez Aldones to be a remarkable woman, one deserving admiration. He had seen from afar how she managed, with grace and ability, the Alcalde's social as well as behind-the-scenes political affairs. He remembered when Ana first arrived; she was so young and inexperienced.

"Marcelo, Doña Ana has survived quite nicely."

Marcelo's conscience reacted with a razor-sharp twinge. If only… If only things had been different!

• • • •

Marcelo heard the clatter of horses' hoofs at noon on Thursday. A carriage had entered the front gate. He walked quickly to the door. There was Ana walking up the path to him, her red hair flowing, radiant with the sun's reflection.

Marcelo's heart leaped, stunned by her beauty. His mouth was so dry he couldn't speak. Instead, he kissed her hand. Then, gallantly led her to the library mumbling those trite, traditional greetings.

Marcelo closed the door, turned to face Ana. He knew this moment had to last him a lifetime. Ana looked at him, gave a tender smile. He looked at Ana but couldn't move. They both felt their emotions mount. Marcelo stepped forward, gently took her in his arms. Without a word, they held each other for a very long time and wept. Then, as tears were wiped, Marcelo led Ana to a comfortable nook where they sat to talk.

"Marcelo, my dearest, I am so sorry about Rosita's death. I know you loved her very much." Ana explained she too had suffered a loss. Her husband's health had taken a sudden turn for the worse and, within a few weeks, he had succumbed.

"Didn't your uncle tell you the *Alcalde* had died?"

"No, Ana, I'm sorry, I didn't know. Most likely Tio Tobias didn't want to upset me with news of another death. I don't think he knows how deeply we care for each other."

While he spoke, Marcelo realized what the *Alcalde's* death could mean for their future. They could be together…

"Marcelo, your uncle told me you are planning to join the next caravan going north. Is that correct?"

"Yes, Ana it is…"

"I came here today to beg you not to go. I want you to stay here. I want you stay here with me. Marcelo, perhaps we can rekindle the love we had so long ago. Perhaps we can find a life together. Tears welled in her eyes, spilled down her cheeks.

Marcelo smiled then stood, took her hands in his, pulled her up and to him.

"Oh, Ana, my precious one, I never thought this would be possible. But Ana, I must go, please understand. Rosita and I had two wonderful sons. Both are hiding somewhere in the wilderness to escape the Inquisition. They have no way of knowing if their parents are dead or alive. I have to find them!"

Ana smiled, "You said you have two sons. My love, I'm sorry but you have three sons!" Ana paused seeing surprise in Marcelo's face, "Yes, Marcelo, you do have another son, one you never knew. He was conceived before we reached Mexico City. He is our son, yours and mine!"

Marcelo sat down— astonished— then he blinked. Could this really be true?

Ana explained it was only because of the son Marcelo had given her that she was able to endure those long horrible years living with the *Alcalde*. Without the boy, she never could have withstood the abuse she received from the *Alcalde* and his mother. She loved her son, not only for his own spirit, but because he was clearly a part of Marcelo.

"Our son brought me close to you, even though you were far away. As he grew I could see you in so many ways. Now, at last, I can share him with you."

Ana took Marcelo's hand in hers, "Our son's name is Martín. You'll be proud of him, he has grown into a wonderful young man. Martín manages the *Alcalde's* stables and is considered the best Andalusian horse breeder in Mexico City."

"Ana, why didn't you tell me before? Can this really be true?"

"Marcelo! Yes, this really is the truth. Be still and you'll hear the whole story."

Ana sat down facing Marcelo and began her tale. "I realized I was with child soon after we had parted. I had no way to tell you. I knew I couldn't. The *Alcalde* had to believe Martín was his own child. Had there been any doubt, he would have banished me to the poor house."

Ana told how her husband considered himself to be her master. She suffered both his and his mother's abuse without end. There was no escape. The *Alcalde's* people would have found her and her punishment would have been severe. Ana was given freedom to spend as much time as she wanted with her child. Martín became her escape. She taught Martín, nurtured the behavior and skills she valued.

A curious and alert boy, he grew into a strong and caring young man. Martín stayed close to his mother and together they dedicated themselves to the care, breeding and training of the *Alcalde's* Andalusian horses.

"Marcelo, when you see Martín, any doubt will disappear."

Marcelo had leaned forward while listening. He was examining Ana carefully, trying to decide if what she was saying could be true. He wanted it to be true. Closing his eyes, excitement charged his body but he quickly stopped himself. Is this story meant to keep me here in Mexico City?

Ana recognized Marcelo's doubt. Disappointed, she stood up, let her arms fall to her side, tears flowed, and her chin fell to her chest. Why? Why does he doubt me?

Silently, Ana counted to twenty— took two deep breaths and flexed her fingers until they were fists. Then she lifted her face— no more tears— her chin jutted out, her eyes flashed and she spoke with grim resolve.

"No! Marcelo, you will never leave me again! I have no life without you! I will go wherever you go!"

Marcelo sat back, astonished. Can I be dreaming?

Ana took a moment, breathed deeply and said, "My love, please understand. I want to be with you. I want to help find your sons. I want to wake up every morning in your arms. I want to live the rest of my life at your side."

Ana struggled for breath, brought the back of her hand to her mouth. "Marcelo, we must put death aside and live our lives together."

Marcelo grasped Ana's trembling hands in his.

"Ana! Yes! Come with me! This is more than I could ever have hoped!"

Hesitating, Marcelo bowed his head, "Ana, I must share a secret with you now. It may take you from me." Marcelo confessed he was, in truth, a Jew. His parents were Jewish as were their parents. The Inquisition had murdered his parents in Madrid. He was fleeing the Inquisition when they had met in Cadiz.

"You are one of very few who know my secret. Tio Tobias is also a secret Jew. He may not be comfortable that I've told our secret."

"Marcelo that could never turn me away from you."

Ana explained she had often wondered if she had Jewish blood. Could her family's business arrangement have had more to do with their secret revealed? Did her parents, fearing the Inquisition, send her here for her own protection?

"I'll never know the truth, but this I know: I love you. I want to be with you. Let the others worry about how to worship God. Let's just find a way to live in peace."

Marcelo quickly got to his feet, swept Ana into his arms. Singing out with joy, he lifted her up, spun her around. Then, his hands found her face; he kissed her longingly. Marcelo laughed, clapped his hands resoundingly— shouted for all to hear, "Ana, please marry me! Be my wife forever."

Ana, beaming with happiness, cried out, "Yes, Yes! Marcelo I will marry you!"

• • • •

Tobias was about to announce lunch when he heard Marcelo's shouts. Tobias hurried to the library, opened the door, "What happened?"

"Tio…" Marcelo embraced his uncle, "We have amazing news! Ana and I are going to be married!"

Marcelo reminded Tobias they had they had fallen in love on the voyage from Spain. Ana had told him her love had survived all these years. He had just learned the result of their love was Ana's son, Martín who had been recognized as the *Alcalde's* own.

"Tio, Ana is going north with me as my wife. We'll make a life together in New Mexico."

Tobias was stunned.

Marcelo and Ana looked at each other lovingly.

Tobias gathered his wits, smiled. "Dios Mio! This is a miracle!

"Tio, forgive me, I told Ana our secret, I trust her with our lives."

"Ana, is there any question your son might side with the Inquisition? Has he ever expressed hate for Jews or Muslims? Could he be trusted to keep our secret?"

"Tobias, I trust Martín with my life, he would never betray us."

Ana explained that, following tradition, Martín had been raised as a Catholic, attended Catholic schools. He had never been devout or cared much for the church. She was confident that once he understood, he would keep the secret safe.

"After all, your secret will be his secret, too." Ana added, "Martín doesn't know his true father is a Jew or that his mother might Jewish. Once I've told him, I'll bring him here. You can judge for yourselves."

• • • •

There was very little time before the Caravan would leave for New Mexico. Tobias began planning in his systematic way. "You must find a way to have a private wedding in the Catholic Church. Your marriage must protect us from any suspicion."

Marcelo agreed to ask his friend, Padre Sanchez, to perform the marriage ceremony. Then, Tobias set about getting several more *carretas*, wagons Ana would need to pack those important things she would take. Marcelo suggested Ana would need sturdy clothes and shoes.

"You both have my blessings." Tobias added, "Protect yourselves from those who would do us harm. Marcelo has already suffered the penalty of being careless with our Jewish heritage."

Ana excused herself to return home, promising to return for lunch the next day. Ana was deeply concerned about how she could best present all this to her son, Martín.

• • • •

Later on that evening, Marcelo shared his worries with Tobias. "Maybe Damian and Gabriel will not accept Ana and her son Martín." He wondered how Ana would adjust to the hard life in the wilderness, so few luxuries and the ever-present danger of Indians.

Tobias counseled, "Follow your heart, Marcelo. Live every day as if it were your last; be loving, supportive and have compassion. Damian and Gabriel will be saddened by their mother's death. But, they know you are a devoted father. You'll have to decide what you want to tell them about how Rosita died. It may be best if they didn't hear the entire story."

• • • •

"How shall I tell Martín about Marcelo? That we will be married! Will he believe me? " In her present state of mind, most likely Ana would just blurt out everything.

Ana changed her clothes, tried to be calm before joining Martín for dinner. Later, entering the dining room, she found Martín gazing out the windows, looking out to the garden. His hand was on his hip. How handsome he is…how much he looks like his father.

Hearing footsteps, Martín turned to her with a smile, went to take his mother's hands, started to embrace her— but stopped.

"Madre, why the tears?"

"*Mi hijo querido*, these are tears of joy! Since your birth, I've hidden a secret deep within my heart. Now, I can share it with you."

They went to the dining table. Martín held his mother's chair and then poured wine for them both. Ana bowed her head, "Please God, help us find understanding, Amen."

Ana looked up, hastily blurted out, "Martín, the *Alcalde* was not your real father."

Confused, Martín countered, "What do you mean, he wasn't my real father?" Stunned, Martín was silent for a moment and then exclaimed, "Madre, if the *Alcalde* wasn't my father, then who was?

"Martín, your real father was Capitan Marcelo Espinosa."

Now less tense, Ana explained how she had met Marcelo on the voyage coming from Spain. During a violent storm, he had saved her life. Both young and frightened, they found great solace together. Soon, they had fallen deeply in love.

"Martín, I would not have survived that voyage without Marcelo's care."

Ana made it clear that she had come to Mexico promised in marriage to the *Alcalde*. Her father had sold her to the *Alcalde* to save the rest of their family from financial ruin.

"There was no way we could have stayed together. It was only after we had both gone our separate ways that I discovered I was with child."

Ana explained she had married the *Alcalde* soon after she arrived in Mexico City. So, the Alcalde always believed she was pregnant with his child. Neither the Alcalde nor his mother ever had a reason to suspect otherwise. When Martín was six years old, the Alcalde's mother died and Ana's abuse became even more severe. Ana had sought refuge guiding her child's education and training.

As his mother's story unfolded, Martín rose, began pacing angrily, back and forth.

"*Hijo mio, calma...* I was determined to spare you from my husband's evil character: his alcoholism, his blind political ambition, and, above all, his cruel disdain for me. Truly, his death was a welcome release."

With his mother's last word, Martín grabbed the wine bottle, threw it violently across the room, shattering the large mirror that hung on the wall.

Martín was enraged. "That drunken, rotten bastard!"

Hands to her face Ana cried out, "No Martín! No... please!"

Madre, I knew he was cruel. I knew you weren't happy living with him. But, now I realize how unhappy you must have been. I'm so sorry..."

"Your real father is here in Mexico City. I've arranged for you to meet him tomorrow."

"Where has he been all these years?" Ana explained Marcelo had been trained and commissioned an officer of the Crown. He had gone north with Oñate's expedition, married and was living in New Mexico. Several months ago he and his wife were summoned by the Inquisition, accused of being Jews. His wife died from the Inquisition's torture, but Marcelo was eventually acquitted.

"Your father's uncle, Captain Tobias Espinosa, is a well-respected officer in the military. He has invited us to lunch. You'll meet Marcelo tomorrow."

"*Hijo*, please understand, you must keep this secret: Both Marcelo and his uncle are hidden Jews. I suspect I may also be Jewish. Our lives depend on absolute secrecy"

"*Dios mio!* I'm to meet my real father tomorrow. You say he is a Jew, and it's possible that you too may be Jewish— Madre, that means I'm a Jew!"

How much does she expect me to absorb all at once!

"Martín, there's more. Marcelo and I, after all these years, still have deep feelings for each other...we will be married soon."

"*Madre*! Please stop— This is beginning to be unbelievable!"

Ana paused, smiled lovingly at her son, and continued her story. To save his sons from the Inquisition, Marcelo had sent them to New Mexico. Now, he must go north to find them.

"Martín, please understand, I love Marcelo. I had two choices. Either loose him again or go with him to find his sons.

"Madre! This is incredible!"

"Martín, I want your support, your understanding. I need the joy of being with the man I've always loved."

Ana paused looked closely into her son's eyes, "Can we say adios to each other for a while... tell me whether you think I've made the right decision."

Martín slowly drew close to his mother and then embraced her tenderly. He looked into her eyes, nodded in approval.

"Yes, Madre, I want you to find happiness, do what's in your heart. I love you more than anything in this world."

Now, they talked for hours about the future, what it might hold. Martín would seek his own love, a woman to be the mother of Ana's grandchildren. He would lead the Andalusian stables to even greater importance and value. Eventuallyi, he would come find them in New Mexico. They agreed the future would be a new, exciting adventure.

"Madre, I want to meet my half-brothers, know more about life in the north."

"Hijo mio, Gracias! Thank you my son, you are my reward for everything I've endured here. Bless you!"

• • • •

Tobias and Marcelo waited impatiently. Ana and Martín would be there within the hour. Tobias fidgeted with his lists while Marcelo paced the floor. There was a melancholy mix of nervous energy, uneasiness, and curiosity that was spread among all four.

Martín was seated in the carriage beside his mother. He blotted perspiration from his forehead though the day was mild. Ana nervously flicked open her black lace fan— fanned a bit— snapped it shut, once, twice then again.

A servant welcomed Ana and her son at the door and led them to the living room. Marcelo and Tobias were waiting. Tobias stepped forward, touched his lips to Ana's cheek, and then quickly turned to face Martín. Marcelo went to Ana's side, gently took her trembling hand. Martín took her other hand and held it tightly. Silence.

Ana moved each of their hands, gently turning them to the other, and with a frivolous voice, "Martín...Meet your real father, Marcelo Espinosa!"

"I couldn't believe my eyes," blurted Marcelo, looking up at his son, somewhat taller but with coloring that matched his own. "You look as I did when I was your age. You have your mother's beautiful eyes."

Bowing slightly, Martín extended his hand. Marcelo took a half step forward, his hand also extended. Both paused, looked into each other's eyes. Then both swiftly moved to an embrace; tears flowed from all four.

Martín finally spoke. "Marcelo— or should I say Father— mother has told me how you met, saved her life, fell in love, and why you had to part. Now, she is determined to marry you quickly so she can go with you to find your two sons. With a smile, he added, "They are my half-brothers and I'd like to meet them, too."

"It's all true. I've always loved your mother and now you, another fine son. I'm overwhelmed! Once I know my other sons are alive and well, my life will be complete." They embraced again; tears of joy were shed in silence.

"Padre, Mother has told me your secret. I am honored to learn I have Jewish blood. I gave her my word to carry this secret to my grave." Tobias was greatly relieved and all agreed this topic would never be spoken of again.

• • • •

Soon, those inhibited tensions passed; tears turned to laughter. Lunch was served. Marcelo and Ana talked about their wedding. It was to be secret and with few attending. Martín agreed to give Ana away. Tobias would be Marcelo's best man and Teresa, Ana's faithful servant, the matron of honor.

Ana changed the subject, "Martín has agreed to take charge of the Alcalde's estate including our Andalusian horse farm. Tobias, please give him your counsel if he should have problems. I've also suggested he start looking for a wife of his own, start a family."

Martín blushed, kissed Ana's cheek and whispered, "Madre, I love you."

Marcelo looked at Martín, "I have a farm near Santa Fe with a house my Indian friends helped me build. I'm sure Dancing Bull has kept it safe. He is a Picuris Indian who is like a brother to me. I pray that he will know where to find my sons."

After lunch, Marcelo and Martín took a long walk. They spoke about those many things one had to know about the other. They agreed how fortunate they were, father and son, to find a new beginning. Ana and Tobias, still sitting at the table, agreed that life's turns and twists are, at times, quite unbelievable.

• • • •

Frenzied preparations for their departure began early the next morning. Tobias offered Marcelo money sufficient to buy additional supplies for the trip north. But, Ana had already provided the monies needed. She had included some horses from her stables, eighteen mares and two stallions with four goats, four sheep and two cows.

As Tobias watched over their preparations, he muttered to himself, "It's unlikely his sons have survived, surely this will lead to nil!"

Ana and Marcelo began to reconnect slowly, then in more important ways. Their physical attraction reasserted itself pulling them together whenever they were close. A touch on the arm, any slight contact generated a thrill, that sensation they had known before. They had agreed to wait until after their marriage ceremony before seeking its consummation. Purposely, they worked long hours.

Ana and Martín worked together to settle many countless details concerned with the Alcalde's estate. Teresa helped Ana sort through those personal things she would need to take north.

Marcelo and Ana quickly gave their approval when Teresa and her husband, Patricio, asked to go with them on their journey.

Marcelo purchased two *carretas*, each wagon pulled by two oxen. Experience told him what they would need as he prepared a long shopping list. He included tools for the farm, bedding, soaps, wine, sewing materials, water jugs, medicines, dried food, salt, and as many types of seeds as he could collect and package. Marcelo arranged for weapons and ammunition. Patricio and Martín helped Marcelo pack everything into their two *carretas*. Ana and Teresa went to select gifts and items they could use to barter with the Indians.

Now, Marcelo had to find Father Sanchez.

• • • •

Tobias had gone to the Franciscan monastery to inquire about Padre Sanchez. He learned that Padre Sanchez had been assigned as pastor of a church located in a small village a few miles beyond Mexico City's outer edge. He assignment was punishment for leaving his post with Oñate.

Marcelo rode out to the village, found the village square, and entered the church. He found Padre Sanchez hard at work making repairs to the church windows.

"Padre, I came to thank you again for your testimony at the Inquisition. I was glad Oñate hadn't found you! He swore he'd chop off your head!"

Both laughed and shared a warm embrace.

"I heard news of your acquittal. How are you faring?"

"Padre, I've put all that dreadful experience behind me. It's an amazing turn of events that brought me here. I'd wanted to share it with you. Then, there's another favor I have to ask of you."

So the story of Ana spilled out in Marcelo's fast running rush of words. The priest's expression changed as he stitched the story together: from the sublime to the outrageous.

"Now, Padre, Ana and I ask...plead with you to marry us. We want you to perform the ceremony in secret. We need yours, and God's blessing so we begin our journey as good Catholics. Will you do this for us?"

Padre Sanchez smiled, threw his arms around Marcelo and gave a hearty laugh. "Now, it all makes sense! On the ship, I often wondered about you two. When you looked at her, your smile and your eyes lit up like a lantern. Marcelo, tell Ana it will be a great joy for me to perform your marriage ceremony."

"Marcelo, tell me why you are going back to New Mexico? That God-forsaken place! You have so much here in Mexico City!"

"Padre, Rosita and I had two sons, Damian and Gabriel. When the Inquisition summoned us, they fled to my farm in New Mexico. I hope they're alive, protected by my dear friend Dancing Bull. Now do you understand?"

Sanchez embraced Marcelo, tears in his eyes, "Yes, *mi hijo*, I do understand. May almighty God be with you and protect you on your journey. I will pray for you and your family every day."

"Padre, the caravan leaves in five days. Can the wedding take place with such short notice?"

"How could I say no? It will happen quietly with no announcements."

"There will only be four others present: Ana's devoted servant, Teresa and her husband, Patricio, Tio Tobias and my son, Martín. Surely you remember Teresa. She accompanied Ana from Havana to Mexico City."

"Yes I do remember her. It's remarkable she stayed with Ana all these years. She must very devoted to Ana to accompany you both to that insane place called New Mexico."

• • • •

The wedding took place two days later, late in the afternoon. Tobias had arranged for a four-in-hand carriage to take them all to the church. Ana sat between Martín and Marcelo; few words were spoken. Padre Sanchez greeted them at the church door. Once inside, he closed and locked the door to ensure privacy.

Padre Sanchez led them to the altar. Inside, the church was small, almost too small for its elaborate Spanish décor. Candles cast a dim glow. Ana and Marcelo stood reverently before Padre Sanchez. Tobias, Teresa and her husband stood behind them.

Marcelo couldn't take his gaze from Ana. She is so beautiful! Ana was dressed in a white Madrilenian gown, white lace and tiers of cascading ruffles. Her hair was swept upward, held in place by a delicate white pearl comb. A long lace veil descended from the comb. At her neck, a regal necklace of matching pearls, a wedding gift from Tobias, and a small gold crucifix. Candlelight made Ana's red hair seem to sparkle.

Ana couldn't take her eyes from Marcelo. He looks so happy, healthy and at peace with himself.

Marcelo wore a dark suit taken from his uncle's wardrobe and a traditionally ruffled Spanish dress shirt. His clothes were slightly oversized; he hadn't regained the weight lost in prison. Ana could only see how handsome he was.

Ana had waited so long for this dream to come true; her eyes brimmed with tears of joy, spilled down her cheeks. Marcelo took her hands, leaned close and gently kissed away each tear. Ana responded with the most beautiful smile Marcelo had ever seen.

They stood facing each other, together in their own time and space. Padre Sanchez asked for them to kneel and declare their love for each other before God. Then, Marcelo took her ring from his pocket, placed it gently on her finger. In turn, Ana did the same for Marcelo. Padre Sanchez gave them God's blessing.

As they stood, Marcelo lovingly brushed Ana's veil back from her face; his two hands cradled her cheeks as he kissed her, long and lingeringly.

Ana whispered, "Marcelo, I love you, only you, and will love you throughout all eternity."

Marcelo sighed, "I love you forever."

Her hands rose, touched his silvering temples. Marcelo felt she was looking so deeply into his eyes that surely she must see his very soul. He was filled with desire.

Tobias thanked Padre Sanchez who bid them all farewell. *"Dios los bendiga!* God bless you all. I pray He will care for you and your families. *Adios amigitos lindos."*

As they walked to the carriage, Marcelo spoke with Tobias. "Tio, I owe you my life. Thank you for all you have done. My parents would have been so grateful."

Tobias turned to Ana and Martín. He took their right hands, placed them with Marcelo's then covered them with his hands, top and bottom.

"I am honored to have each of you as part of my family. God has been kind allowing me to share in your lives. Martín, after your parents leave, I hope you will honor me by considering yourself as family in my home."

· · · ·

The four-in-hand carriage left Tobias and Martín at his house then went on to Ana's home. Tobias had invited Martín to stay, leaving the newly weds to themselves.

Both were filled with excitement and anticipation of what would be their first really unhurried and luxurious time together. Now married, they were free to enjoy each other endlessly. Ana eagerly awaited the whole night in his arms. For years, she had longed to wake with Marcelo next to her.

Teresa supervised the serving of a sumptuous dinner at a beautifully arranged table. Patricio served them a very special wine. They toasted each other silently. When the meal was finished, Teresa and her husband disappeared, retreating to their quarters. Marcelo and Ana were alone, bathed in soft candlelight.

Ana leaned forward, a flirtatious look in her eyes. Coyly, she came around the table untying the sash at her waist and stood before Marcelo. He began unbuttoning her dress with clumsy fingers. Then, Ana with a quick shake of her shoulders, allowed the dress to fall to the floor. Ana stepped closer to Marcelo. With a toss of her head she unpinned her hair. It fell from her shoulders, tumbling down over her breasts to her waist.

Marcelo sighed releasing the breath he had held all this time. "Ana, you are so beautiful…Ana, my wife, *mi esposa.*" As he looked down upon her sensuous body there in the candlelight, he felt more intoxicated than wine could ever make him feel.

Ana unbuttoned her lace *pantaletas* and they fell at her feet. She stood shyly in her nakedness, almost as she had done their first time. She wanted him. She needed him. "Now my love, take me to our bed."

Marcelo swept her into his arms, ran up the stairs leading to the master bedroom. He placed her gently on the oversized bed.

Ana murmured, "Now, Marcelo, I want to see you undress."

Marcelo backed away, stood tall. His shirt came off quickly. With one hand, he pulled off each boot; one after the other fell to the floor. Then, he loosened his wide leather belt. Finally, his trousers fell. Ana was delighted with the man standing before her.

He moved to her slowly. Anticipation could be contained no longer. He fell to the bed. They wrapped their bodies around each other and held each other tightly. Touching became frantic, and at last, he entered her. He began a slow rhythmic thrust. His heavy breathing and her groans of pleasure increased only the passion they both were feeling.

"I love you," Marcelo sighed.

Ana whispered "Yes, now! – Oh yes!"

They were locked in a euphoric embrace, closer now than either had ever dreamt possible.

Chapter 31
Caravan Heads North

Mexico City, 1623 – Would this be their last farewell? Marcelo remembered that day, some twenty-five years ago, when he left his uncle to join Don Juan de Oñate's expedition. Now fifty-five, he realized he was saying farewell to his uncle a second, maybe the last time.

Everything was in order; everyone was ready to leave. Tobias had organized loading both wagons with the help of several soldiers and servants. Before departure, families traveling with the caravan had met with the leaders for their instructions. Marcelo was thankful nobody recognized Ana as the wife of the Alcade. They were known as Marcelo Espinosa and his wife returning to their farm in northern New Mexico. But he wondered, "Will we ever be free from the Inquisition?"

Finally, the caravan started to move. Marcelo helped Ana climb aboard their *carreta*. Then he took his place with reins securely in hand. Teresa and her husband were on the wagon right behind them. Marcelo glanced at Ana, perhaps with a sense of anxiety, "Ana, we're off on a new chapter of our life!" She turned, gave him a quick kiss.

The caravan rolled out of Mexico City, headed north to Zacatecas and Santa Barbara. Both seemed lost in thought as they sat side by side. Marcelo's thoughts turned to his two sons, Damian and Gabriel. Please God let them be alive and well.

Marcelo debated, Should I tell them the whole truth about the Inquisition? How they had killed Rosita. Then, they would carry hatred in their soul; pass it on to their children. In order to survive, they must be sincere Catholics. Maybe he would tell them their mother died of an illness during the Inquisition... nothing more.

As the weeks passed and the caravan moved north into the wilderness, Marcelo reassured Ana. She had grown accustomed to a life of luxury and wasn't used to the life of a caravan. But Ana kept smiling, always in good humor. But in reality she was hiding her fears.

"Marcelo, this journey reminds me of when we crossed the ocean. We didn't know where we were going or if we'd get to our destination alive. What kept us going was our love for each other."

Marcelo was frequently plunged into deep depressions; sleep was elusive. When he closed his eyes, he saw his parents screaming in pain as they burned. He struggled mightily to shake loose from those flaming images. Then, he would hear Rosita's last scream, *"Sh'ma Yisrael, Adonai eloheinu Adonai echad..."*

Many nights, Ana tried to hold him, comfort him. But his trembling and his screams were persistent. Gradually he improved, learned to cope with his memories, bury his guilt. He had survived.

"Ana, I'm coping with Rosita's death imagining she is here with us. If we're happy, she is happy. I'm trying to have only good days. Most likely Rosita will help us find Damian and Gabriel."

"Marcelo I feel the same way. I'll do all I can to give you good days, good for us and for Rosita."

When the caravan entered the southern limits of Santa Barbara, Marcelo and Ana camped on the outskirts of town. He still harbored hatred for those people who had betrayed his family and did not want to be recognized. Marcelo remembered his neighbors screaming insults as they were carted off to their trial in Mexico City. Nothing remained of the bakery and farm. Marcelo wanted no part of Santa Barbara. Nothing.

Patricio with Ana and Teresa went in to town for the supplies they needed.

Two days later the caravan moved on. Marcelo pointed out trail markers that Don Juan de Oñate had insisted they construct to guide future travelers. Ana could not imagine how they had traveled with thousands of animals.

"Ana, I've often wondered if Oñate made us build those markers so others could find our dead bodies." As they passed through each portion of the Camino Real, Marcelo gathered his memories of the journey with Oñate, their fears, trials, and adventures. He would tell his stories every evening as they lay together under the stars, resting for the next day.

The Indians along the way meant them no harm and seemed satisfied with the small gifts they received in trade for food. Twenty-eight well-armed soldiers traveling with the caravan provided their protection.

Marcelo felt more secure returning to Santa Fe knowing that the Crown had decided not to let the colony die and was now giving support. He had worried that after Oñate's failure, the colony could have been abandoned.

The colonists in the caravan seemed to be a hardy group. Marcelo saw they were hard workers, people who would thrive developing the land parcels they had been promised. Five Franciscan missionary priests also traveled with the caravan, sent by the government of Mexico. The Catholic Church was still seeking conversion of the Indians. Marcelo knew this meant trouble.

When Marcelo saw the first Indian Pueblo, he was relieved because he knew that the most difficult part of the journey was over. The Pueblo Indians traded goods for the food and water that the caravan needed so desperately, but he could see the look of anger and mistrust in their eyes. The priests must have closed their kivas, as there were no signs anywhere of the religious objects that he had seen there before. The priest stationed at the Pueblo appeared relieved to see them. But, he was especially pleased to see the new soldiers who would protect them. With the help of the Indians along the way, they managed to restock the caravan as they continued north.

The caravan arrived in Santa Fe, New Mexico in April 1623. It was an eerie feeling for Marcelo as he walked with Ana around the town square. It had been nineteen years. Many thoughts came to his mind, the struggles he had lived through while here with Oñate.

"Ana that hut and stables, is where my dear friend Juan Carlos lived and worked before he was killed by the Indians. Juan Carlos was a wonderful soul that loved horses just as much as you. You would have loved him. His death was one of the saddest moments of my life."

Marcelo felt like a stranger as they walked around the town square. The only people they recognized were from the caravan. Ana was silent trying to imagine how she would adjust to life here. She was attracted by the rustic surroundings, especially the Indians in their native clothing.

At the town hall Marcelo found the names of the original colonists, soldiers, and missionaries listed in the government files. There was no record of either Damian or Gabriel Espinosa nor did anyone know of their whereabouts. But, Marcelo did find that the tract of land Oñate had assigned to him was still listed under his name.

"Ana, we will start our search going to my farm. If they are not there, we will find Dancing Bull at the Picuris Indian Pueblo."

They previsioned both wagons and arranged for help taking everything to Marcelo's farm. The journey took two days and was filled with keen anticipation; surely the boys would be there. When they drew near, Marcelo's heart sank, in the distance he could see the fields had been abandoned.

Arriving at the house, Marcelo saw there were no signs that anyone had been there recently. But, when he went to the vegetable garden, there was one small consolation. He dug up the tools he and Dancing Bull had buried so many years before. Now, Marcelo was desperate to find Dancing Bull.

Once Marcelo was satisfied that Ana, Patricio and Teresa would be safe and well provided for, he left for the Picuris Pueblo to search for Dancing Bull. The two-day ride seemed to take forever. As he arrived, two Indians recognized Marcelo and called out, "You'll find Dancing Bull at his place."

When Dancing Bull caught sight of Marcelo he shouted, "Your sons are here! Viejo, where did you find all that gray hair? I hardly recognized you!" Marcelo was so relieved and filled with emotion that he began to cry uncontrollably.

Dancing Bull embraced him and held him tightly. "I didn't think you'd ever come back. But, when your boys arrived, I knew you'd eventually find your way home. And here you are, the best friend I ever had."

Marcelo placed his hands on Dancing Bull's shoulders, "It's good to see you amigo. The signs of age have fallen on you, too. That long braid of yours is almost white. Your smile and gentle eyes haven't changed over the years."

"Gabriel is living at the San Juan Pueblo, and Damian is farming nearby. I'll send a messenger to bring your sons. It may take two days for them both to get here." Then, seeing Marcelo was both physically and emotionally exhausted, Dancing Bull persuaded Marcelo to stay in his home, get some rest. Marcelo tried to take a nap but couldn't close his eyes. There was too much excitement.

After dinner, he and Dancing Bull took a long walk. Marcelo poured out his story to his dear friend, a flood of pain and agony from the Inquisition.

At first, his words came slowly, a trickle. He told how his uncle had found Rosita, how they had met, fallen in love and married. She was Jewish and, like him, her family had been killed by the Inquisition. Marcelo told of their life, raising their sons, first on the farm and later at their bakery in Santa Barbara. They both felt safe.

Now, Marcelo's words came in torrents, white sheets of pain. Their betrayal as Jews; both sons fled to save their lives. Arrest by the Inquisition: trial, torture and judgment. Rosita had died at the hands of the Inquisition, tortured to death. He had been exonerated. The blame was placed upon Rosita.

Dancing Bull held Marcelo while he wept.

Through his tears Marcelo saw a familiar figure coming to him, Little Evergreen, Dancing Bull's sister. Without a word, she took him from Dancing Bull's embrace, put his arms around her and placed her hands gently on Marcelo's face.

The three sat on the ground facing each other. Dancing Bull asked Marcelo if he could tell Little Evergreen his story. Then, as Dancing Bull translated the story, Little Evergreen wiped tears from her face.

· · · ·

"Now, Marcelo, here's happy news! Little Evergreen has a tall man and a fat baby boy. They have made our tribe very proud." Marcelo was thrilled to hear this. He offered his left hand to Dancing Bull, his right to Little Evergreen. He held their hands high, smiling his approval. "I want to see that fat one soon!"

Dancing Bull and Little Evergreen took turns describing their surprise and joy when Gabriel and Damian had arrived at their Pueblo a little over a year and a half ago.

"They were almost dead from exhaustion, terrified they would never see you again. They found refuge in our Pueblo with the priest. The priest couldn't understand why they kept asking for Dancing Bull."

At first, nobody believed they were your sons. But, they were persistent saying they had to find Dancing Bull who was reluctant to see the boys. Then, Little Evergreen gave him no choice; she took him to the priest's house. When he saw the boys, Dancing Bull saw no resemblance to Marcelo, he didn't believe a word they said. However, when Damian showed him the crucifix with the hidden compartment, Dancing Bull knew everything was true.

Finally, the priest allowed Dancing Bull to take the boys to his home. Little Evergreen took care of them, brought them back to health. Dancing Bull didn't understand why Marcelo wasn't with them but he knew there had to be a good reason.

When the boys began to trust him, they told him the truth. The Inquisition had arrested their parents. They said they had no choice. Marcelo insisted they flee to safety and find Dancing Bull. Now, he understood because Marcelo had once told him why the Inquisition had burnt his parents to death.

Dancing Bull explained why he had told the boys not to live at their father's farm. "They might have been recognized and arrested that close to Santa Fe. So far, no one has asked questions, both are safe in their new lives."

Marcelo put his arms around Dancing Bull and Little Evergreen, thanked them for all they had done. "My sons would not be alive if it weren't for you both. I have another happy story, but it will have to wait until my sons are here."

• • • •

Dancing Bull told Marcelo that his sons had lived together until Gabriel moved in with his bride, Morning Cloud. She was a wonderful Indian woman from the San Juan Pueblo where they had set up their home. Dancing Bull had heard that she was with child. Damian was living not too far from the Picuris Pueblo. The Indians knew they were Marcelo's sons and, out of respect for Dancing Bull, watched over them carefully.

There was little sleep for Marcelo that night. The expectation, the emotions of seeing his sons again were almost too much. Around midday, still half dozing, Marcelo heard hoof-beats, galloping horses approaching from a distance. He jumped out of bed, threw on his clothes and ran to the front door. His heart was pounding in anticipation of seeing his sons.

Three horses came to a halt in front of Dancing Bull's house. Damian, Gabriel and Morning Cloud jumped down from their horses. Both boys, shouting their greetings, threw their arms around their father and danced with joy.

Damian looked around and asked, "Where's Mother, is she inside?"

Marcelo's face clouded; he looked down.

Gabriel exclaimed, "Then Mother's at the farm?"

Marcelo nodded his head no.

"Padre...where is she? What's happened?"

Both boys saw sadness cloud Marcelo's face as he choked back his tears. In an instant, both Damian and Gabriel realized their mother had died. Not a word was spoken until they were seated inside the house.

Marcelo told them that Rosita's resistance had been worn down by the Inquisition's incessant questionings. She had developed pneumonia, died in prison and was buried in a Jewish cemetery near Mexico City. He said as little as he could to avoid revealing the real horror of Rosita's death.

Both boys remembered Rosita as a strong vibrant woman. It was hard for them to realize she was really gone. When their tears subsided, they sat quietly and talked, trying to catch up on what had happened since they were last together. Dancing Bull watched them silently content they were reunited.

All this time, Gabriel's wife, Morning Cloud— four months with child— sat quietly by his side. Gabriel realized her Spanish was limited and, with everyone speaking so rapidly, most likely she hadn't understood a word. He had seen her eyes search the room for Rosita. Now, as Gabriel explained his mother had died, her happiness from meeting Marcelo turned to sorrow. They held each other in silence.

Talk was difficult for everyone. Marcelo suggested they go outside, sit together at an old table under a large cottonwood tree. It was always cool there even with the heat of midday sun.

Marcelo spoke first. "Your mother and I knew you had to leave home and risk your lives. We knew in our hearts there was no alternative. Your survival was our constant worry. I wish your mother had lived to see you here, safe and happy."

Damian began telling their story. "When we left home we were frightened beyond belief. During four days, we pushed our horses to the limit until we found the caravan."

The leaders of the caravan had found it difficult to believe that two young boys wanted to join them going into the wilderness. Damian convinced them that Indians had killed their parents; they had barely escaped with their lives. They claimed to be going north to find their uncle who had settled near Santa Fe.

Fortunately, an older couple asked them to join with them provided they helped along the way. It was a perfect arrangement. They needed help keeping their animals alive and surviving in the wilderness. They had no children of their own so they "adopted" both boys. Damian and Gabriel had used many things their father had taught them about surviving in the wilderness.

Gabriel added, "Once we arrived in Santa Fe, we made sure our guardians were settled in. Then, we set out to find the farm and Dancing Bull. We found the abandoned farmhouse thanks to the map you made. Nobody had been there for years."

Both boys were determined to find Dancing Bull so they kept going. Now, they had to find the Picuris Pueblo, but they lost their way. Ten days later they straggled into the Pueblo disheveled, hungry and thirsty. They found the Franciscan priest, asked him to help find Dancing Bull. They convinced the priest their father had been Dancing Bull's good friend.

"Finally the priest arranged for Dancing Bull to meet us." Damian added, "Padre, you should have seen his face when I showed him your crucifix."

Both boys agreed, "Thank God, Dancing Bull and Little Evergreen took us in."

Dancing Bull had found a plot of ground where they could settle and grow their own crops. It wasn't long after that Gabriel met Morning Cloud and they fell in love. Gabriel had moved to the San

Juan Pueblo where he had been accepted and they married.

Damian added, "I stayed near Dancing Bull, farmed the land and soon made friends with the Indians."

Gabriel said, "When I married Morning Cloud, Dancing Bull and Little Evergreen came to the wedding as part of our family." First they were married in the Catholic Church at the Pueblo. Then, next day, they were married with the sacred Indian ceremony. Dancing Bull had made it clear they had to keep their Catholic ways. Otherwise, the Inquisition might suspect Gabriel's Jewish heritage.

Marcelo put his arms around Dancing Bull and Little Evergreen, thanked them for all that they had done for his sons. Then, silence. Only the rustle of the wind in the cottonwood's leaves could be heard.

• • • •

"Gabriel, Damian, I've never told you about my parents, Antonio and Josefina. They, like your mother and I, acted in every way like good Catholics but in secret, practiced their Jewish faith. They were decent, loving and honorable people. I love them dearly and miss them every day of my life."

"Gabriel, I was about your age growing up in Madrid."

Marcelo explained his father had owned a very successful bakery where he had learned the trade. Antonio had hired a young ambitious apprentice who managed the bakery on Saturdays. Ultimately, the apprentice wanted to take over the bakery so he had betrayed them to the Inquisition.

"When summoned by the Inquisition, I was sent away just as I sent you. I was hidden in a Trappist monastery as a Franciscan novice. Later, my parents were found guilty and burned at the stake."

Marcelo's voice broke, as he fought to continue. "My beloved mother and father died in order to keep me alive. I was so lost and scared and depressed, I just wanted to die."

Then he regained his composure, "I was put on a ship sailing for the New World. I was told to find my uncle, Tobias, who lived in Mexico City. He was my only living relative."

Leaning forward, Marcelo took the crucifix Damian was wearing between his fingers. "This crucifix and that gold coin I gave you both... that's all I had left from my parents."

Marcelo paused— he couldn't find the right words— so many dreadful memories came to mind that sorrow overwhelmed him. Both sons' eyes were riveted on his face. They clung to each word and expression.

"Soon after leaving Cadiz, I met a young woman on board the ship. She was my age and we became best friends. Her name was Ana, Ana Aldones. I learned from her that kindness, caring and love were still very much alive. We fell in love, deeply in love, although we knew we could never be together. Ana's father had made a business arrangement for her to become the bride of Don Juan Benavidez, the Alcalde of Mexico City."

Marcelo looked at each son pensively, "I've learned since then that God works in many mysterious ways. When we parted, we thought we'd never see each other again. But, it was the Alcalde and Ana who helped your mother and me during our trial. They helped me gain my freedom. Not too long after your mother lost her life, Ana's husband died."

"I was preparing to come find you when Ana and I found our love was reawakened. We wanted to spend our lives together. I'm so fortunate to be loved by two wonderful women; your mother, whom I adored, and now Ana, with whom I'll share my later years."

Silence. Marcelo took a deep breath, "There's more— Ana has a son, Martín. He is our son and your half-brother. I think you will like him. Hopefully, you will meet him eventually. We love him very much. He has been a wonderful son for Ana. Now he is part of our family."

Marcelo stood, sensing his sons had understood his story. First Gabriel, then Damian, rose, came to embrace Marcelo. Then the three hugged each other, wiping away their tears with their shirtsleeves.

"Now, we must all go to the farm, Ana is waiting there to meet you."

Marcelo along with his two sons, Dancing Bull and Little Evergreen set out for the farm on horseback. Marcelo's excitement grew as they reached the last hill overlooking a lush, peaceful valley. His farm could be seen in the distance. Marcelo's heart began to pound as he wondered how his sons would respond to Ana.

• • • •

Ana was startled, then frightened by the sound of horses approaching at a fast pace. She quickly loaded her rifle and yelled for Patricio and Teresa to get inside the house. They were all relieved when they heard Marcelo's voice calling out not to be afraid. After tying up the horses they all met in front of the house. Marcelo gave Ana a hug and a kiss. She rested her head on his shoulder, relieved that he was back alive and that his sons were with him.

She had wondered, What if Marcelo's sons resent me? I am not their mother! What if they don't like me? Please, God, let them accept me as I am.

Marcelo introduced Ana very lovingly. He sensed she was anxious, although eager to meet the boys and Marcelo's two special Indian friends. When Marcelo saw she had calmed down, he took her aside. He explained he had told everybody what had happened to Rosita; that the boys had seemed to understand.

Ana was still concerned about her relationship with both boys. "Ana, They'll learn to love you as I do." She sighed doubting it would be so easy.

As they entered the farmhouse, Damian sensed Ana's insecurity and approached her. She saw in his face Marcelo's kind eyes, now filling with tears. He stepped closer, lifted his arms and timidly embraced her. Ana was afraid to speak.

Damian stepped aside and Gabriel came forward.

Gabriel was younger, but darker, had long braided hair, and dressed in Indian clothing. He raised his arms and embraced her. Gabriel looked deeply into her eyes. No tears. His hug was strong and welcoming. Marcelo came to Ana and they all embraced in silence.

Marcelo took Morning Cloud's hand, presented her saying, "Ana, this is Damian's wife, Morning Cloud." Then, he introduced Dancing Bull and Little Evergreen. This was a meeting filled with warmth and caring. Very soon they all found themselves laughing, talking, with one another. It was a joyous event.

After lunch, Ana invited Gabriel and Damian to the corral behind the house. "Marcelo and I want you both to have one of our Andalusian mares. It's our gift honoring your mother."

Both smiled, surprised, and gave Ana a grateful embrace.

Gabriel and Damian talked with Ana about the care and breeding of their young horses. Amazed with Ana's working knowledge of horses, they asked her question after question. As they returned to the house, Damian came close and spoke softly, "We both think mother would be happy you're here." Ana smiled, happy the ice was broken.

• • • •

"Ana, there's so much to be done! I've asked the boys to stay awhile." Dancing Bull and Little Evergreen also offered to help. "We'll have a full house!"

Within the month, the house was repaired, stables built for the horses, fields prepared for planting. Dancing Bull had brought several Indian friends to help turn the earth and plant their crops. Little Evergreen and Morning Cloud worked with Ana and Teresa to weave a large rug. Ana and Teresa learned how to make clay pots for the kitchen. Soon, the house was a more comfortable place to live.

As he saw them all working together, Marcelo began to feel at home again. Surely, he has found that sense of peace lost so long ago.

Marcelo knew the farm's isolation was hard for Ana; she missed her son. Ana, smiling, reassured

Marcelo, "We have more here than all the Alcalde's wealth." However, Ana did worry. She worried about their safety from marauding Indians, especially if she were alone.

When all the tasks were finished, Damian and Gabriel prepared to return to their homes. Marcelo took them aside. "Please honor the anniversary of your mother's death. Simply light a candle, silently remember your Jewish heritage."

Marcelo realized the Inquisition had won in their time. But, he was confident the Church would eventually be defeated in the battle for their hearts, souls and cultural identity.

· · · ·

As the months rolled by, Damian and Gabriel came frequently to help Marcelo make sure everything was peaceful on the farm. One day Damian asked Marcelo if he could move to the farm, help him with the work. Damian had heard of Apache raids and wanted to protect them. Ana and Marcelo both welcomed the idea, so move he did.

Late one night the peaceful silence enveloping their farm was disrupted. Marcelo and Ana had long gone to bed. Damian heard horses snorting, obviously disturbed. Fearing Apaches, he called Marcelo.

"Ana, stay here!" Marcelo ordered as they took up rifles.

Much to their surprise, four strange horses were in the corral, rearing, circling and snickering. "The gate is still locked; they must have jumped the fence!"

"Good Lord!" Marcelo called to Damian, "These four could be offspring from Juan Castro's horses! Their markings are almost identical."

He told Damian how, many years ago, Juan de Castro had lost his life fighting Apaches who had stolen several of his horses.

"Padre, most likely they're just looking for our mare! She's in heat."

"Well, let's see if Ana will let her mate. Maybe we'll have another foal in our stables."

Marcelo sighed, Juan Castro, true friend, I do sense your presence.

Marcelo took Ana back to bed, wondering. He told her stories of Juan Castro, his love for horses and their adventures on both sides of the ocean.

• • • •

At sundown, when day was done, Marcelo and Ana would often sit by the river under the giant cottonwood trees. Now, the great river was called Rio Grande. They could see the glorious white-capped beauty of their mountains. They felt fortunate to be alive. Marcelo had found peace even though always concerned about everyday matters. Soon, he would hold his first grandchild.

A messenger arrived from Gabriel's Pueblo with news. Marcelo's grandson, Sun Bird, had been born. Several days later, Gabriel and Morning Cloud arrived with the baby. Ana and Marcelo examined Sun Bird from head to toe, admiring his chubby brown body.

Marcelo gathered everyone together for the first celebration of Sun Bird's birth. What a happy reunion that was! After they finished their meal, Gabriel asked them all to attend two ceremonies.

Sun Bird would be baptized in San Juan Pueblo's Catholic Church with the Christian name Antonio, in honor of Marcelo's father. The second ceremony, initiation of Gabriel into the San Juan Tribe, would be held in a secret place in the wilderness.

Marcelo had ambivalent thoughts about these two ceremonies. He felt more comfortable with the Indian initiation than with the baptism. But since survival depended on keeping Catholic rites, he swallowed his pride and said nothing.

A month passed before they made their way to the pueblo's church for Sun Bird's baptism. The Franciscan priest had known Padre Sanchez and gone out of his way to be friendly. But, while inside the church, Marcelo felt an unbearable anxiety. Dark memories flooded his consciousness. Surprised, he thought they had been buried years ago. When Ana looked at him curiously, he decided to keep them to himself.

Summer was gone when Gabriel came to the farm to speak with his father. "I'll soon be initiated into the San Juan Tribe. I've learned to be comfortable with their values, their way of life. I'd like you to witness this sacred event."

Gabriel disagreed with the Catholic Church on many issues. He knew some of the old ways of Judaism but wasn't practicing them. He was comfortable living the Indian's life. So he chose to make the best of all three cultures. "I'll be Catholic for my son, a Jew for my parents and an Indian for my wife."

The time came for Gabriel to escort Marcelo, Damian and Ana to the ceremony. Marcelo explained to Ana they would dress as Indians traveling to the Pueblo. Disguise was necessary to avoid any conflict with the Franciscan priest— he was suspicious of everyone. So, Damian brought robes for both his father and Ana. Their skin was darkened with tree bark and Ana's hair was braided.

They met Dancing Bull and Little Evergreen to make the evening trek to San Juan Pueblo and rested there for the night. Dancing Bull carefully chose the best hours to travel. They had to avoid being seen by soldiers or the Catholic priest.

Marcelo was nervous taking this risk; it could endanger his whole family. But, he was determined to fulfill his son's wishes. They continued on towards the mountains; a secluded site had been selected for the initiation ceremony.

Dancing Bull knew a special escort was waiting for them not too far ahead.

Chapter 32
Saving their Secret

Overhead the sky was filled with glittering stars; the waning moon gave just enough light to see the way. They were met by an escort, nineteen San Juan Pueblo Indians all wearing their traditional clothes and headdress. Each face painted as their ancestors had done for centuries. As the walked, four Indians followed behind, carefully erasing any trace of footprints.

For centuries, this ritual was held within the pueblo's Kiva, a square-walled chamber built mostly underground. Kachinas, small-carved figures representing deified spirits, and ceremonial masks were part of the ceremony.

Now, all Pueblo beliefs, rituals and gathering places were branded as blasphemy, forbidden by the Catholic Church. Tension was high. Discovery by the soldiers or the Franciscan missionary would mean arrest, maybe death.

They found their way into a small valley— part of the Sangre de Christo Mountains— hidden from their Pueblo by its mountainous surroundings.

• • • •

Indians were already gathered around a carefully constructed ceremonial fire. Muffled drums gave a constant beat to the leader's chant. It was time for Gabriel's initiation into the San Juan tribe, become a member of his wife's family clan. The ceremony was planned to end some two hours before dawn. They'd have enough time to return to the Pueblo without their absence arousing suspicion.

Mesmerized by the drumbeat, the vibrant sound of the chant, Marcelo's thoughts wandered. The fire cast an eerie light as Marcelo gazed at both his sons. He pondered,

"Will my grandson, Sun Bird, ever learn of his Jewish heritage?"

No! It's much too dangerous!

"Should my sons know about Rosita's torture, her last words?"

Never!

"My questioning, torture and trial, the humiliation of the Sanbenito?"

It could harm them all…only survival is important.

"My sons have to keep their families safe, hidden within the Catholic Church. If they ever reveal their Jewish heritage to their children, that decision must be theirs, not mine."

The drums' increasing cadence, the Indians' chant caused Marcelo's memories to run rampant. He remembered scenes, one after another, of growing up in Madrid. His grandparents and those before them had lived in Spain for more than seven centuries.

Our Jewish traditions and rituals, they'll die here with me…maybe that's best.

• • • •

Dancing Bull led them back to the Pueblo. As they arrived, the sun was just starting to show itself in the east, behind the mountain range. A faint red glow enveloped the Pueblo. The Indians slipped silently away to their homes, they knew the priest would be awake, preparing for an early Mass.

Marcelo, Ana, Damian, Dancing Bull, and Little Evergreen quietly saddled their horses. Not a word was spoken until the Pueblo was far behind.

• • • •

It was a blistering hot, windless day at the farm. Ana had worked with Teresa to finish all the chores that mattered. Now, late in the afternoon, Marcelo came in from the fields, wiped his brow.

"Ana, there's a place Dancing Bull told me about. It's up in the mountains, not too far. There's a mountain river and a waterfall that drops into a good-sized pond. Interested?"

They saddled up their favorite horses, trotted a steady pace for more than hour. Then, guiding their horses carefully, climbed a steep trail into the mountains. By sunset, they still hadn't found the waterfalls.

"Ana, it's a good thing you brought food."

But, food wasn't on their minds. Soon, they heard the distant rumble of the waterfall, its cold water rushing to the pond. It had to be near.

Ana called out, "There it is!" Both dismounted quickly, tied their horses' reins to a tree. Marcelo wrestled off his boots, stripped down and ran to the pond plunging into its cooler depths. Ana, barefoot by now, removed her clothes and hurried, somewhat more cautiously, into the shallow water, sitting down in an attempt to be graceful.

First, each focused upon bathing, removing dust and dirt from the day. Then laughing they played joyously, rejuvenated, reveling together in the water.

Marcelo remembered that one special afternoon in Cuba.

"Ana, do you remember?" They were alone on an isolated beach at sunset. The lapping murmur of the ocean's waves, a sweet fragrance of wild flowers. Ana had lain seductively beneath the protective limbs of a blossoming tree, her eyes and lips smiling warmly, her arms outstretched for Marcelo.

The love they felt for each other now was just as overwhelming.

So on that night, alone besides a mountain pond, Marcelo and Ana made love again. First, gently and tenderly... then heated by passion, their spirits blended into one.

Entwined, Ana cradled him in her arms, his head resting upon her breasts. He looked up. They kissed. Ana lovingly stroked his face. Soon, they fell asleep in each other's arms. Later, when they woke, a full moon lighted their surroundings; the pond shimmered; stars twinkled brightly above.

They dressed and were ready to leave— one horse neighed, and the other stomped impatiently. A coyote howled in the distance. But, something curious compelled them to stay put. Here in the mountain woodlands, next to the waterfall and its pond, holding each other, they both felt really safe.

It was as if something— or someone— was protecting them from the dangers that lurked outside. The Church's Inquisition searching relentlessly for heresy; their intolerance rewarded by torture and death. Angry Indians each one waiting for a spark to inflame a violent uprising; death for all the Spaniards. An unforgiving environment: drought, torrential rain, blizzards, famine and disease.

Together, they realized their protective circle was their love of God, each other, their family and their beloved friends who shared their lives.

Ana took his face gently in her hands, "Dearest Marcelo, let's keep this moment safe, place it securely in our hearts. Let it be our guide no matter what our future brings."

He whispered, "That anger burdening me for so many years— it's gone. I'm grateful to God for bringing us together again, giving us happiness."

"Ana, I love you forever."

Epilogue

The future was not easy for Marcelo's offspring. On August 10, 1680, Indians laid siege to Santa Fe. Indian chiefs had vowed to destroy all vestiges of Christianity. The missionaries had caused the Indians to suffer too much humiliation. Colonists fled south to El Paso del Norte now Ciudad Juarez, Mexico where they remained in exile for twelve years.

Don Diego de Vargas, newly appointed governor, was successful in establishing and stabilizing a new colony in Santa Fe during 1692. A critical episode of New Mexico's restoration, Don Diego negotiated a remarkable peaceful reconciliation with Pueblo Indian Leaders.

But a year later, when he went to bring back a group of settlers, the Pueblo people broke their peace agreement and again captured Santa Fe. This time, Don Diego retook the city by force— hundreds of Pueblo fighters were killed or later executed. For the next several years, warfare continued between both sides. But by the end of the century the Spanish colonization was fully stabilized.

With time, the Spaniards began to understand what the Indian people had learned from their Pueblo gods. They lived with each other in peace with a spirit of mutual respect, cooperation and harmony. The re-conquest was more than the end of an Indian revolt; it was the beginning of the end of New Mexico's isolation at the edge of the Spanish empire.

The words of Sultan Bayezid II were prophetic. Sephardim have enriched the world in— and far beyond— the Mediterranean Basin. Here in the United States, it wasn't just those who came to the Spanish New World. Others fled to England, France and the Netherlands and then came to their colonies— Massachusetts, Rhode Island, New York and New Jersey, Virginia, Georgia and South Carolina.

This story would not be complete without the words of Pope John Paul II given during his visit to Israel in March 2000: "I assure the Jewish people the Catholic Church is deeply saddened by the hatred, acts of persecution and displays of anti-Semitism directed against the Jews by Christians at any time and in any place," he added that there were "no words strong enough to deplore the terrible tragedy of the Holocaust."

Many of those early crypto or secret Jews did hand down something of their Jewish traditions although it meant endangering the lives of their families. Their secret was so deep and their fear of discovery so strong, that they needed to find creative, clandestine methods to prevent their heritage from being destroyed.

So, small vestiges of these customs can still be found today within their descendants' family traditions. But, they are often subtle and hard to define because they have been carefully hidden for so many centuries.

George L. Vergara, July 2011

30817186R00205

Made in the USA
Middletown, DE
07 April 2016